THE FRENCH
FOUNDERS OF
NORTH AMERICA
AND THEIR
HERITAGE

THE FRENCH
FOUNDERS OF
NORTH AMERICA
AND THEIR
HERITAGE

Sabra Holbrook

ATHENEUM   1976   NEW YORK

Au Nid d'Aigle,
son hôte et sa hôtesse,
de leur "habitante,"
et en joyeux souvenir de notre "Feuille"

Library of Congress Cataloging in Publication Data
Holbrook, Sabra.
The French founders of North America
and their heritage.
SUMMARY: A history of the French in North America
from the earliest explorers to today's separatist
movement in Quebec. 1. America—Discovery and
exploration—French—Juvenile literature.
2. France—Colonies—America—Juvenile literature.
3. French-Canadians—Juvenile literature.
[1. America—Discovery and exploration—French.
2. French in North America—History. 3. French Canadians]
I. Title. E131.H64 970'.004'41 75–13574
ISBN 0–689–30490–0

Foreword

W hen we Americans in the United States think of the explorers and early founders of our continent, we tend to think English. Actually, it seems probable that the first explorer to set foot on the continent, or at least a continental island, was the Norse Leif Ericson, in the year 1001. There is evidence that he attempted, though unsuccessfully, to start a colony in Newfoundland. He was followed by John Cabot, who also landed in Newfoundland in 1497, but with no thought of colonizing.

Then came Verrazano, an Italian commissioned by the French king, Francis I. In 1524 he skirted the coast from North Carolina to Nova Scotia, landing when he needed water.

Ten years later exploration began in earnest with the

French explorer Jacques Cartier, the first European to pene-
trate beyond the shorelines. He also established the first North
American colony, at Cap Rouge on the Saint Lawrence River,
in 1541. However, it survived only a year.

From 1585 to 1587 Sir Walter Raleigh tried without success to colonize an island off the coast of what is now North
Carolina. In 1604, the French explorer Champlain established
a colony in Nova Scotia, which hung on for three years—
longer than any of the previous ones.

Then in 1607 the London Company, an English trading
group, founded the first permanent settlement in North
America, at Jamestown.

A year later Champlain founded Québec, which was to become the capital of the kingdom of New France. Champlain
was also the discoverer of the New York-Vermont lake that
bears his name. He explored much of the land that now
forms those states, as well as the Penobscot River and a good
deal of present-day Maine. He sailed and charted the North
American coast from the Saint Lawrence to Cape Cod.

By the time the Pilgrims landed at Plymouth, the French
had pushed as far west as the Great Lakes, and by the time
William Penn founded Pennsylvania, La Salle was entering
the Mississippi.

The purpose of this book is to acknowledge the North
American debt to French pioneers who opened up and civi-
lized a vast section of our continent. An equal part of the purpose is to show the impact that French New World history
has had on modern Canada.

Culturally speaking, there are two Canadas today—French
and English. We are accustomed to divided countries in our
world; Germany, Ireland, Vietnam, China, Korea, for example. But in none of these cases does culture or language divide.
The borders are purely political. The two Canadas—with two
official languages, two histories, and no national boundary between—are even more provocative. Among French Canadians
there are those—a minority, but a growing minority—who

believe that the addition of political division is necessary to safeguard their heritage and their future. That question, too, is the subject of this book.

For invaluable help in collecting the necessary background, I am indebted to: Léandre Bergeron, Professor of French, Sir George Williams University; Mlle Lyse Demers, Québec Ministry of Intergovernmental Affairs; Mme Madeleine Doyou Ferland, University of Laval; Marcel Gingras, Editor of *Le Droit;* Gérald Godin, of the *Québec Presse;* Claude Lavadour, Language Administration Branch, Canadian Federal Government; Michel Marois, teacher at L'École Saint Dominique, Québec; Ministry of Education officials in Québec —Mme Thérèsc Baron, Claude Bernard, Maurice Mercier, André Pardoen; Claude Morin, National School of Public Administration, Québec University; Mme Lorraine Parent, General Delegation of Québec in New York; Jacques Parizeau, School of Advanced Commercial Studies, University of Montréal; Madeleine Smith, Gaston and Louise Tremblay and their friends; Elinor Green, then Information Officer, U.S.I.S., Ottawa; U.S. State Department officials in Canada—W. M. Johnson, Consul General in Ottawa, Harrington E. Manville, U.S.I.S., Montréal, and his assistant, Mlle Loretta La Plante, Everett K. Melby, Consul General in Québec, John Topping, Consul General, Montréal; Jay Walz, *New York Times* Bureau, Ottawa; Paul Wyczynski, Research Center for French Canadian Civilization at the University of Ottawa, and Mme Wyczynski. My warm thanks to them all.

SABRA HOLBROOK

Some Important Dates in French Canadian History

1628	British lay siege to Québec, under command of Lewis Kirke. Champlain refuses to surrender. Kirke's fleet starves the colony.
1629	Québec surrenders to Kirke. Champlain is imprisoned in England.
1632	Québec returned to the French.
1633	Champlain returns to Québec.
1635	Champlain dies.
1640's & 50's	More colonists arrive. Farms established. Fur trade develops.
1666	La Salle arrives in New France.
1669	La Salle's first expedition to the west. He follows Ohio River to junction with the Mississippi.
1672	Frontenac appointed governor of Québec.
1673	Jolliet and Marquette reach Mississippi via Wisconsin River.
1679	La Salle sets out to build western forts and return to Mississippi.
1680	Father Hennepin, a member of La Salle's party, reaches Mississippi, via the Illinois.
1682	La Salle travels the Mississippi to the Gulf of Mexico. Frontenac is recalled. Radisson and Groseilliers reach Hudson Bay.
1684	La Salle sets out from France to search for Mississippi mouth by sea. He founds a Louisiana colony, later abandoned. Expedition fails.
1686	La Salle is assassinated. Indian wars peak.
1686–1697	Pierre Le Moyne d'Iberville commands five expeditions to the Hudson Bay area.
1689	Frontenac reinstated as governor.
1690	British admiral Phipps attacks Québec and is defeated.
1698	D'Iberville sets out to seek Mississippi from the sea. He founds the colony of Biloxi. Frontenac dies.
1699	D'Iberville ascends Mississippi from its mouth. Becomes governor of Louisiana.

1749	French-English rivalry over possession of Ohio River valley begins.
1755	English governor Charles Lawrence deports French from Acadia.
1756	Montcalm arrives in Canada.
1757	Montcalm takes Fort William Henry.
1758	Montcalm defends Fort Carillon (Ticonderoga) against the English.
1759	Battle of the Plains of Abraham. Québec falls to the English. Montcalm and the English general Wolfe die of battle wounds.
1760	Montréal is surrendered to the English.
1763	The Peace of Paris cedes all Canada to the English.
1775	Americans Benedict Arnold and Richard Montgomery are defeated by French Canadians in an effort to take Québec.
1812	Birth of Patriot party, led by Louis Joseph Papineau.
1832	French Canadians riot against the English.
1837	Lower (French) Canada rebellion begins, led by Patriots. Rebellion in Upper (English) Canada instigated by new settlers.
1838	The Durham report suggests ways to unite Canada.
1847	Under Louis Hippolyte La Fontaine as prime minister in Canada East (formerly Lower Canada) and Robert Baldwin as prime minister in Canada West (formerly Upper Canada), and the Earl of Elgin as governor, public offices are made elective—as recommended in the Durham report.
1867	After many conferences, a Confederation of Canada is established by the British North America Act.
Early Twentieth Century	English economic and cultural domination of Canada.
1950's	Seeds of the Quiet Revolution are planted.

1960's   The Quiet Revolution. Prime minister Lester
              Pearson aids its progress. Separatism is born. Rise
              of Pierre Elliott Trudeau.
1963   Hydroelectric power transferred from private to
              provincial ownership in Québec.
1967   De Gaulle visits Canada and calls for a free Qué-
              bec.
1968   Trudeau elected prime minister of Canada.
1969   Official Languages Act makes Canada bilingual
              in theory.
1970   Kidnapping of Cross and murder of Laporte by
              FLQ, violent wing of the revolution.
1972   Trudeau's government falls. He is reelected, but
              barely.
1973   Parti Québecois, the Separatist party, receives 31
              percent of the vote in Québec elections.
1974   Trudeau reelected by a vast majority. French de-
              clared the official language of Québec.

Contents

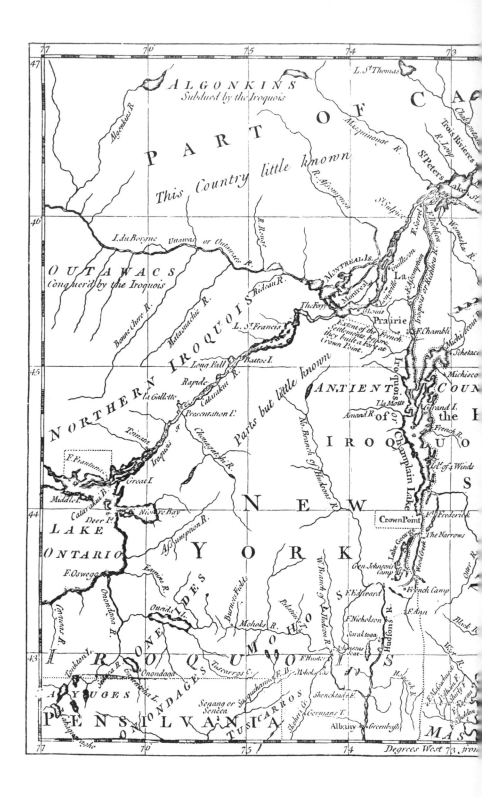

77   76   75   74   73

47

ALGONKINS
Subdued by the Iroquois

L. St Thomas

Algonkins R.

PART OF C A

Mesquinonae R.

Trois Rivieres
R. Loup
St Peters
Lake

R. Assomption

St Sulpice

R. Sorel
R. Richlieu
Womaske R.

46

I. du Borgue   Uttawas   or   Ontarico R.

R. Rouge

This Country little known

O U T A W A C S
Conquer'd by the Iroquois

MONTREAL Is.
La
Guilleon
Levaville
Montreal
Prairie

R. Assomption
Temps of Richlieu
F.Chambl

Bonne chere R.

Rideau R.

Matasuachic R.

L. St Francis

The Fort
St. Louis

Extent of the French
Settlements known
they built a Fort at
Crown Point.

Michigou

45

Long Fall
Rapide
la Gallette
Presentation I.
Toinate

Cataraki R.
Buttoe I.

Parts but little known

No. Branch of Hudsons R.

Ila Motte
Amand R.
of

Michisco
COUN
the F
G'rand I.
French R.

Schetace

N O R T H E R N   I R O Q U O I S

Chenegatche R.

A N T I E N T

I R O Q U O
S

Iroquois or Champlain Lake

I.of 4 Winds

F.Frantunac
Great I.

Middle I.
Deer F.
Cataraki B.
Niowre Bay

Assumption R.

N E W

CrownPoint

F' Frederic
The Narrows

44

L A K E

O N T A R I O

F.Oswego

Eamere R.

Onondona R.

Canaras R.

Oneida L.

Y O R K

Burnes Fields
Palatines
Mohoks R.

W. Branch of Hudson R.

Lake Geor.
Wootcreek

Gen. Johnsons
Camp
S.E.Edward
F.Nicholson
Swaktoga
Johnsons
Seat

French Camp
E.Ann

Otter R.
Black R.
War R.

Hudson R.

43

Lonton L.
Seneca R.
Cazenevia L.
Onondaga

Tuscarros C.

F.Hunter

H. Sock R.
E.Mahaskust
A.Ihan F.
Shrify
E.Kaenau

A Y U G E S

Senang or
Seneca

Susquehanna F.B.
Mohok. Ca.

Slober V.
Germans T.

Shencktad F.

Albany   Greenbush

MAS

P E N S I L V A N I A

TUSCARROS

Degrees West 73 fron

77   76   75   74

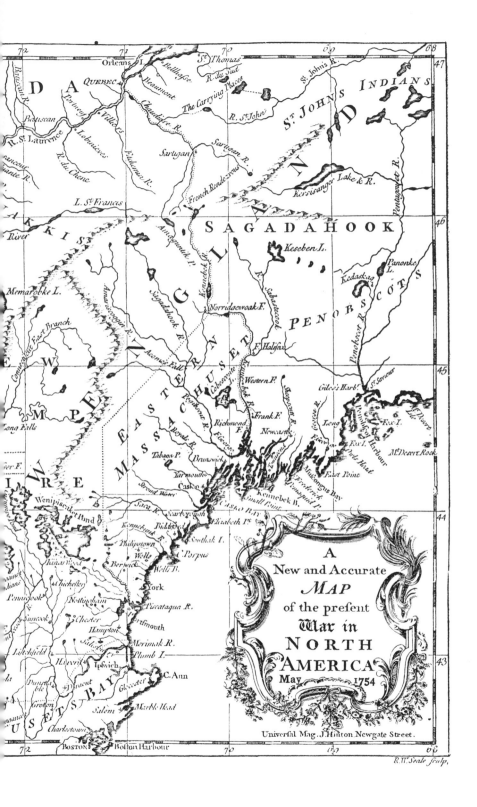

A
New and Accurate
MAP
of the present
War in
NORTH
AMERICA
May   1754

Universal Mag. J. Hinton, Newgate Street.

R. W. Seale sculp,

THE FRENCH
FOUNDERS OF
NORTH AMERICA
AND THEIR
HERITAGE

To the New World: Adventure and Mission

Twenty days on the open Atlantic had given the two square-rigged vessels a wet and windy beating. The sixty-one-man crew who had kept the prows pointed westward day and night despite the weather was overjoyed when land at last was dimly sighted. May 10, 1534. The captain noted the date in his log.

A few of the sailors had been this way before on fishing expeditions. They recognized the misty outline of icebound New-foundland toward which the filled sails flew, masts creaking with the strain. Reaching the coast, they pulled into a small indentation, later named Catalina Bay. There they weighed anchor to repair their damaged ships.

Ten days later they were heading northward, gaping at strange animals and birds on the shore. First they met polar bears swimming—"as great as any cow and white as a swan," according to their captain's log.

Then they passed a small island that he named Island of Birds because it was dense with nesting auks, black and white birds about the size of a goose, which are now extinct. The sailors shot enough of them to fill two rowboats and salted them down in six barrels against the day when food, in this unknown region, might be hard to come by.

They had need of their foresight. Continuing north and veering slightly west, they neared the mouth of a great river to which later explorers would give the name of Saint Lawrence. Their captain named only a small part of the entrance-way, *La Baye Sainct Laurins*. The weather favored them until they rounded the northernmost tip of Newfoundland. There the two vessels were lashed by storm and trapped by ice for ten days. The sailors were glad of those birds.

The name of their captain, a tough, seasoned mariner from the French fishing port of Saint Malo, was Jacques Cartier. He had been commissioned and outfitted by an angry and ambitious king of France, Francis I. Francis's anger was directed at Pope Alexander VI who let it be known that he believed the new land to the west, just beginning to be explored, should be divided between Spain and Portugal.

"I would like very much to know what clause in Adam's will," said King Francis, "excludes me from a part of the world." Whereupon he speedily dispatched Jacques Cartier on the first of three voyages to North America.

This first voyage, mainly a scouting trip, began a 225-year-long chapter of French exploration and settlement from the North Atlantic coast to the Mississippi River in the area the Indians called Kannata or Zandata. Moving through this stretch of time and out across the land was a motley band, drawn overseas by varied dreams and ambitions. Explorers were magnetized by rivers leading no one knew where. They hoped to discover one flowing straight through the continent to the Pacific, forming the fabled Northwest Passage that all

Europe sought as a shortcut to the riches of the Orient. Adventurers answered the call of the unknown, betting on finding it better than the known.

Patriots were fired with the desire to claim new territory for France. Soldiers were shipped over to guard the land acquired and to fight for more. Profiteers and slicksters sought quick fortunes. Politicians maneuvered for influence and prestige in the royal court back home, supplying it with embellished reports of their exploits.

Sturdy settlers battled bitter winters, bush and rocky soil to carve out farmland. Fur traders penetrated almost to the Arctic in search of beaver pelts. Priests canoed to outposts, seeking to convert Indians to Christianity.

Glory was the aim of Jacques Cartier. Twice during his first voyage his heart beat high with the hope that he might be the navigator with the good fortune to discover the Northwest Passage. Turning south from the ice of Newfoundland, he sailed for a month through the Gulf of Saint Lawrence, searching the coastlines of what are now Nova Scotia, New Brunswick and the Gaspé Peninsula. Without result. Then he came upon the Baie de Chaleur. Veering west, he plumbed on and on through this 125-mile-long inlet between New Brunswick and the Gaspé. Was it the Passage? The landlocked end told him no.

His disappointment was lightened when, again turning north, he reached Anticosti Island, which he called Assumption. Skirting the western tip, he saw that the Gulf of Saint Lawrence narrowed into a continuing passage beyond the island. He couldn't enter it—August, the month of Atlantic gales, had caught up with him. He had to beat the winds home. But he counted on his careful record keeping, his maps, his descriptions of the land and the people he had found to persuade King Francis to send him back. His log describes the island now called Prince Edward as a land of "many goodly and sweet-smelling trees . . . cedars, yews, pines, white elms, ash, willows and many others to us unknown. The grounds where no wood is are very fair and all full of peas, white and red gooseberries, strawberries, blackberries. . . ." Quite enough to make the king's mouth water.

Cartier writes of the Indians living on the shores of the Baie de Chaleur who came out in canoes by the hundreds, welcoming the expedition with gifts of cooked meat. Not understanding, the frightened French sailors fired shots over the Indians' heads; but undaunted the Indians returned with fur pelts, which, they indicated in sign language, they wanted to trade. In exchange for knives and beads, the French obtained a great quantity. Quite enough to waken avarice in the king's treasurer, the man who must dole out expedition finances. Fur was an extremely popular—and high priced—item in Europe.

At the entrance to the Gaspé Bay, Cartier laid claim to the area he had explored by planting a thirty-foot-high cross. At its center he hung a shield, engraved with three fleurs-de-lis, the symbol of French royalty. At the top he carved *Vive le Roy de France*—Long Live the King of France. The ships' crews knelt around the cross and raised their hands to heaven.

The meaning of this ceremony was not lost on Indians watching from the distance. The next morning they sent a protest delegation to the ships. With gestures they made clear that this land belonged to them. Cartier gestured back that the cross was only meant to mark the harbor entrance, not to signify ownership. The Indians accepted the explanation.

When Cartier set sail for home, two chieftains' sons accompanied him with the blessings of their fathers. Cartier wanted to bolster his reports by showing off the sons, Taignoagny and Domagaya, at Francis's court. He also wanted to reserve them for guides on his next voyage.

He had no trouble in persuading Francis to sponsor another voyage. His detailed report found immediate royal favor. And the Indians, after learning French, gave the king alluring accounts of Kannata, a great kingdom reached by the waterway that Cartier had sighted from Anticosti. Cartier spent the winter equipping three ships, the *Grande Hermine,* the *Petite Hermine* and the *Emerillon,* and recruiting sailors for them in Saint Malo. On May 19, 1535, he set out on his second expedition to North America.

The crossing was wild. Storms buffeted and separated the ships. Not until July did Cartier, in command of the *Grand Hermine,* sight Newfoundland. At the end of that month the other two ships caught up with him. After making repairs of the storm damages, the three set out along the north shore of the Gulf of Saint Lawrence. In mid-August they started up river. But it was a keenly disappointed Cartier who entered the river's mouth. The water was fresh! If this were truly a Northwest Passage, Cartier reasoned, the water would be salt. Having no idea that he was exploring a small section of a whole new continent, he envisioned it as assorted land masses separated by sea. Nevertheless he pushed on. Who knew what riches might be discovered in Kannata?

According to his Indian guides, that kingdom began near the present-day city of Québec. On the Île d'Orléans, mid-river just opposite the clifftop on which Québec would later be founded, a band of Indians waited for the explorer. Cartier, with his guides, landed among them. The guides explained that theirs was a peaceful mission, and the Indians followed the French back to their ships, bringing a great supply of corn and pumpkin.

As news of the French arrival spread, parades of loaded canoes paddled down river. The Indians circled the ships, gawking curiously. Finally their chief, Donnacona, appeared. His canoe glided to each of the three ships in turn, and at each he made a long ceremonial address in his native language. The guides translated it as a speech of welcome to his people's territory. Cartier acknowledged it with gifts of food and wine and, at the chief's request, shot off a cannon or two. The river swarmed with merrymakers.

But when Donnacona discovered that Cartier intended to push on to Hochelega, the Indian name for what is now the city of Montréal, the atmosphere changed. Cartier's guides refused to accompany him and went to live with the other Indians on shore. Donnacona offered the explorer a little girl, his own niece, if he would give up his plan. The gift of children was a common Indian custom.

When Cartier remained steadfast in his aim, the Indians tried a new tack. One day three of them, dressed as devils, "arrayed in black and white dogskins, with horns as long as one's arm, and faces colored black as charcoal"—according to Cartier's description—canoed swiftly past the ships to shore. There the three fell over as though dead. Other Indians carried them away. From the woods floated eerie sounds of mourning.

Shortly after, Donnacona and the two guides emerged from the woods. One guide called three times on Jesus. The other called on Jesus, Mary and Jacques Cartier. When Cartier asked what the matter was, they answered, "Ill news." Donnacona explained that the three canoers had been messengers from their god, Andouagny. The messengers said tremendous ice and snow would bury Cartier's expedition if he went to Hochelega.

Cartier replied that Andouagny didn't know what he was talking about. Jesus, he insisted, would protect the French from ice and snow. In his private opinion, Donnacona was not about to share with up-river Indians presents that would be distributed among his own people if Cartier stayed where he was. He departed hurriedly in the *Emerillon,* leaving crews in the other two ships to pacify Donnacona.

All the way up river he was greeted warmly by Indians and given much fish, in return for which he offered knives and beads. Sometimes he was also given children, whom he took along for the ride and returned on his way back. He describes the river banks in lush detail: "We discovered as fine a country . . . as one could wish, covered with the finest trees in the world, such as oaks, maples, elms, walnuts, pines, cedars, spruce, ash, boxwood, willows . . . and better than all a great quantity of grapevines, which were so loaded with grapes that the sailors came aboard with their arms full of them. There are likewise many cranes . . . geese, ducks, large pheasants, partridges, blackbirds, thrushes, turtledoves, goldfinches . . . nightingales, sparrows and other birds . . . in great numbers."

Nearing Hochelega, he landed three or four miles down river. On the way he had been warned of sandbars that obstructed direct passage to the settlement. Word of his coming had traveled ahead of him and an astounding welcome had been organized. As Cartier describes it: "There came to meet us more than a thousand persons . . . men, women and children who gave us as good a welcome as ever father gave to his son. . . . The men danced in one row, the women in another and the children also apart by themselves. After this they brought us great quantities of fish and of their bread, which is made of Indian corn, throwing so much of it into our longboats that it seemed to rain bread. . . . And the women brought their babies in their arms to have the captain and his companions touch them. . . . The captain had the women all sit down in a row and gave them . . . beads, and to . . . the men he gave knives. Then he returned on board the longboats to sup and pass the night, throughout which the Indians remained on the bank of the river as near the longboats as they could get, keeping many fires burning and calling out . . . *aguyase,* which is their term of salutation and joy."

The next morning, he and his men hiked into Hochelega. "As we drew near their village," Cartier records, "great numbers of the inhabitants came out to meet us. . . . We were led . . . into the middle of the village. . . . They signed to us that we should come to a halt. . . . And at once all the girls and women of the village crowded about us, rubbing our faces . . . and giving us the best welcome they could. . . . After this the

men made the women retire and themselves sat down upon
the ground around us. . . . Several of the women came back,
each with a four-cornered mat, woven like tapestry. These they
spread upon the ground and made us place ourselves upon
them. When this had been done, the ruler and chief of his
tribe was carried in, seated on a large deerskin."

It appeared that the chief had palsy, a disease that causes
uncontrollable shaking of the limbs. The Indians believed
Cartier could heal him. Like most French explorers of the
time, Cartier carried his Bible and prayer book with him
wherever he went. Now he took them both out. From the Bible he read the opening verses of Saint John's Gospel, "In the
beginning was the Word, and the Word was with God, and
the Word was God." He continued through the fourteenth
verse, "And the Word was made flesh, and dwelt among us
. . . full of grace and truth." Then from his prayer book he
read the story of Christ's crucifixion. Afterward he made the
sign of the cross. He doesn't tell us what the effect on the
chieftain was, but evidently the Indians were pleased with
his effort. The squaws lined up and tried to prevent him from
leaving.

Before he returned to his longboats, the Indian men took
Cartier to the mountain that reared behind their village. The
explorer named it Mont Royal, from which Montréal derives.
Standing on the summit, the Indians pointed out rushing rapids in the Saint Lawrence below. They touched a silver
chain that Cartier wore and the gold-colored dagger hilt of
one of the sailors to explain that those metals were to be
found beyond the rapids in a kingdom they called Saguenay.
Once more Cartier's hope of a Northwest Passage revived.
Could there be a network of navigable rivers across this land
mass, connecting sea with sea?

As the longboats made their way back to the *Emerillon* and
the *Emerillon* cruised down river to join the vessels left behind in Donnacona's territory, Cartier was already planning

another voyage. During his absence the men who had not accompanied him had built a fort on shore and moved into it. As a result of a courtesy visit to Donnacona, Cartier decided he had better strengthen the fort. The chief had shown him scalps of five Indians "stretched on hoops like parchment." Enemies, Donnacona had explained. Cartier got the hint.

He had a moat built around the fort. A small drawbridge across the moat provided the only entrance. Inside he kept fifty men on guard, night and day, divided into watches. When the watches changed, the Indians across the river could hear the French bugles blow, the notes lingering in the still, pine-scented air.

By the time Cartier had returned from Hochelega, it was mid-October. Crimson maple and golden oak leaves drifted in the river's current. Already the weather was chill. The winter that soon set in was fierce. The river ice was twelve feet deep, freezing the French ships at their moorings. Propelled by bitter winds, driven snows swirled into great drifts around the fort.

Within it, one man after another fell sick. Their legs swelled and turned black. Their sinews shrunk. Their arms hung useless at their sides. Their teeth fell out. Scurvy. This dread disease haunted all the early explorers. It results from a lack of vitamin C, which is found mainly in citrus fruits, and to a lesser extent in tomatoes, potatoes, cabbage, fresh green vegetables and some berries and also in the organs of some animals, such as the seal. All of the fruits and vegetables were impossible to procure in the Canadian winter wilderness, and no one knew the value of eating some animals completely, including the entrails.

By December all but three or four of Cartier's men had scurvy. Twenty-five lay dead of it, their bodies frozen beneath the snow. The three or four who had escaped the disease kept up a clatter of hammering whenever they sighted Indians on the opposite shore, the idea being to project an image of healthy men hard at work. One day Domagaya, one of Cartier's ex-guides, appeared at the fort. He looked well, although Cartier had heard that he too had been sick with the scurvy only ten days before. Pretending that a servant was ill, Cartier asked Domagaya what remedy had cured him. The Indian told Cartier to boil white spruce needles and bark, to give the servant a daily dose of the mixture and also to rub it on his swollen and blackened legs. Cartier took the advice. In eight days his men used up an entire tree.

In astonishment Cartier recorded: "[It] produced such a result that had all the doctors of Louvain and Montpellier[1] been there with all the drugs of Alexandria,[2] they could not have done so much in a year as this tree did in eight days; for it benefitted us so much that all who were willing to use it recovered health and strength, thanks be to God."

The winter passed. By mid-April, the ice was softening sufficiently to let the French ships float free. The *Emerillon* had been crushed by the ice but the other two vessels were seaworthy. Scurvy had so diminished the French ranks that the remaining two had plenty of room for the survivors. Events in Donnacona's camp continued to make Cartier uneasy. A large number of strange Indians were congregating in the tents. Donnacona himself refused to receive Cartier's messengers. Cartier determined to capture him and some high-ranking members of his council and take them home to the king.

On May 3, 1536, Cartier planted another cross on the river bank, this one thirty-five feet high. It was inscribed with fleurs-de-lis and a Latin text: Francis I, by the Grace of God, King of the French. A few days later Donnacona was captured. On May 6, the expedition set sail for home. When Donnacona was told that the king of France would make him fine presents, his objections to the kidnapping changed to anticipation of the visit. From shipboard he calmed down his people on the shore. In canoes and by foot they followed him to the river's mouth, calling their farewells.

At the royal court, the Indians did indeed receive fine presents, including rich raiment and housing. They were well cared for according to sixteenth-century French standards. But indoor life, far from their open skies, their boundless forests and catapulting streams proved too much for them. Within a few years they languished and died.

They had lived long enough, however, to whet Francis's appetite for the New World. He decided to colonize it.

Toeholds
That Slipped

As head of his colonizing expedition King Francis appointed a man-about-court, Jean François de la Roque, Sieur de Roberval, at the same time commissioning Cartier under Roberval as captain general and master pilot. Why Francis decided to split the leadership of this venture between a seasoned mariner and a man ten years his junior who had never been to sea, no one knows. It was an ill-fated decision.

At the direction of the king, Roberval recruited colonists from the jails of certain French cities: Paris, Toulouse, Bordeaux, Rouen and Dijon. He was prohibited from taking anyone charged with heresy, treason or counterfeit; otherwise he had a free hand. Cartier was directed to equip the ships.

On May 23, 1541, Cartier left ahead of Roberval with five

ships full of chained convicts of both sexes, teen-agers to forty-five-year-olds. Their offenses ranged from assault to murder. Among them was an eighteen-year-old girl, Manon Lescaut, unconvicted of anything, but insistent on accompanying her jailbird boyfriend. She chained herself to him in order to be taken aboard. Along with these candidates for colonization, Cartier carried supplies for two years, a great quantity of vegetable seeds and a Noah's ark assortment of farm animals.

The five ships were separated at sea by severe storm. During the long voyage, water became so scanty that cider was given to the animals. Eventually, however, all made the harbor at Newfoundland's northern tip where Cartier had put in on his first voyage. There they paused, repairing ships and waiting for Roberval. Roberval did not arrive.

In August, Cartier started up the Saint Lawrence without him. When he reached the Île d'Orléans, Indians met him clamoring for news of Donnacona. He replied that Donnacona had died, but that those who had accompanied him had married in France and become great lords. The chief who had taken Donnacona's place was far from disturbed by this news. Embracing Cartier, he gave him a leather crown and two bracelets made of wampum, shells of mollusks, which the Indians used as money.

Cartier left his ships at anchor, took two longboats and proceeded eight or nine miles up river to a bluff now called Cap Rouge. He had observed the spot on his previous voyage and had a mind to start his colony there. Inspection of the site confirmed his earlier judgment. He brought the ships in and landed the colonists.

Naming the settlement Charlesbourg-Royal, after Francis's son Charles, Cartier directed the building of two forts with a protective palisade around them. Within the palisade the colonists planted cabbage, lettuce and turnips. So fertile was the blufftop soil that within a week shoots poked green tips above ground. Outside the palisade men found shiny particles in the soil, which they thought were diamonds. At the bottom of the slope, along the river bank, they discovered what Cartier describes as "leaves of fine gold as thick as a man's nail."

Encouraged by these findings, Cartier set off to achieve the ambition he had cherished since the moment he had stood at the summit of Mont Royal and heard the Indians' tale of the Saguenay kingdom of precious metals, which lay beyond the rapids. Not only did the prospect of treasure intrigue him: the dream of a Northwest Passage still beckoned.

By portaging overland, he traveled as far as the north bank of the rapids. Here young men from a nearby Indian village made him a map with sticks to show that beyond these chutes, which drop forty-two feet in three miles, another great descent of water hindered passage to the Saguenay kingdom. Actually, either the Indians' geography was poor or they were deliberately misleading the explorer. The so-called "kingdom" lay some two hundred miles northeast of Mont Royal, around the shores of Lac Saint Jean, the source of the Saguenay River. Had Cartier been able to maneuver through the Saint Lawrence rapids, he would have been sailing in just the opposite direction—southwest. As it was, he gave up.

On returning to Charlesbourg, he found the colony fearful. The Huron Indians, who surrounded the settlers, no longer offered to sell them fish and game. They surveyed the colony constantly. It seemed as though they were planning an attack. And attack they did, in the winter of 1541–42, killing thirty-five people. Scurvy also attacked. The disease was defeated by white spruce, but the garrison was too small to ward off any new Indian attacks. No reinforcements were in sight, for there had been no news of Roberval.

So, in June of 1542, Cartier packed all the colonists aboard ships, along with nineteen barrels of what he believed to be gold and diamonds. Before the end of the month he entered the harbor of Saint John's, Newfoundland. There, rocking at anchor, were Roberval's ships.

Where had Roberval been for the past year? History's reports are conflicting. One has it that he had misspent royal funds given him for the trip and was pirating in the English Channel to recoup the debt. Another is that he reached Cape Breton, in Nova Scotia, in 1541, and not finding Cartier, returned home to prepare a new expedition for the following year.

When the two commanders met in Saint John's harbor, Roberval ordered Cartier to return to Charlesbourg. Instead Cartier departed under cover of night and sailed for France. Roberval, with around 150 colonists, reached Charlesbourg in July, 1542. Renaming the settlement France-Roy, he set about building houses. By fall, food had run short. Cartier's gardens, untended, quit producing. The biggest staples in the new settlers' diet were dried fish and dried beans. Scurvy set in. Crime rose. The ex-prisoners in Roberval's group must have been more hardened offenders than those in Cartier's, for the crime problem required erection of a gallows. By spring, a third of the colony had died or been hanged.

Nevertheless, Roberval persevered. Like Cartier, he had heard tales of the Saguenay kingdom and was possessed with the desire to explore it. In June, when the river current abated somewhat, he set out upstream with seventy men in eight boats. He was stopped by the rapids at Mont Royal, just as Cartier had been.

Meanwhile, his chief pilot Jean Alfonce, a sailor from Brittany in northern France, had traveled in the opposite direction, downstream. Reaching the three-mile-wide confluence of the Saguenay and Saint Lawrence Rivers, he describes the meeting of the waters as "a terrible *raz*," a Breton word for turbulent currents. He added that farther up the Saguenay, the river widens and "begins to take on the character of an arm of the sea, for which reason I estimate that this sea leads to the Pacific Ocean or even to the China Sea." Here his record stops. He could not have penetrated far upstream or he, too, would have been stopped by rapids.

The heavy, round-bottomed European longboats were no vessels for shooting rapids, and they were burdensome to portage. The sharply-keeled, lightweight birch-bark canoes of the Indians were far better suited to Canada's rushing waters. It wouldn't be long before the white man would learn this lesson and also take to canoes, penetrating deep into Indian land.

Meanwhile, however, both Cartier and Roberval failed to obtain their objectives. Their explorations were checked by geography; their settlements by the hardships of climate, fear of Indians and general unpreparedness for wilderness living.

What happened to the two explorers? Cartier returned to Saint Malo, where he was showered with honors. He became a consultant on seafaring for his local government and the town favorite as godfather for the children of fishermen and sailors.

As for Roberval, he returned to France, taking his colonists with him. Some say that Cartier was dispatched to bring him and what was left of the France-Roy colony home. Being a cousin of the king's mistress, Roberval slipped easily back into his former profession of man-about-court. He died in the civil wars between Protestants and Catholics, which tore France apart in the second half of the sixteenth century.

During those wars the nation was far too preoccupied with its own internal crises to give any further thought to external exploration. If Canada was mentioned, it was only with sneers. Cartier's diamonds had turned out to be pyrite, a mineral crystal containing iron. His gold was mica, mineral sheets embedded in rocks, which may have a bright yellow hue. "Canadian diamonds" and "Canadian gold" became synonyms for counterfeit in sixteenth-century French.

Although fishermen, fur traders, and a few adventurers, including one seagoing monk, continued to sail the North Atlantic coast, there were no notable attempts at colonization or exploration by the French until after the turn of the century. In 1598 a Breton marquis, Troïlus de Mesgouez, attempted to colonize a Nova Scotian sandbar called Sable Island. Only eleven of the colonists survived. These eleven, all men, were eventually rescued and transported home. Clad in shaggy pelts with beards reaching below their waists, "they looked like cavemen," commented an observer who witnessed their return.

Another attempt to found a settlement was made at Tadoussac, an Indian village on the northern bank of the Saguenay where it hurtles into the Saint Lawrence. There, in 1600, one Pierre Chauvin landed sixteen colonists. A year later he returned to find the men living with the Indians, as Indians.

All such missions were individually conceived and financed; they were not projects of the French state. In 1588 the king had granted a fur trade monopoly to two men, but their efforts were all at their own expense. Then in 1603, royal interest in North America revived. The king on the throne was Henry IV. He had managed to end France's religious civil war. His court geographer, son and grandson of a sailor, was Samuel de Champlain. With the King's blessing and encouragement, though without access to the king's treasury, Champlain set out with an expedition headed for the Saint Lawrence, the Saguenay and the Gaspé.

The lack of royal funds was due partly to an international plot, partly to the stubbornness and short-sightedness of the king's treasurer, the Duke de Sully. At that time the Dutch were belatedly beginning to look westward. Wanting time to catch up with the French head start, they paid Sully to withhold backing for French expeditions. The bribes reinforced Sully's own disposition not to spend money on faraway ventures. "Things which remain separated from our body by foreign lands or seas will be ours only at great expense and to little purpose," he insisted.

So the financing was private. It came from Aymer de Chastes, one of the first of many French merchants to recognize the profits to be gained from abundant Canadian furs. Strategic command was in the hands of François Dupont Gravé, a mariner from Cartier's Saint Malo. Champlain's interest was the old European itch: discovery of a Northwest

Passage. He hunted passageways while his companions hunted profits. The voyage added little to the maps Cartier had already made, but it fired Champlain, who had previously visited the West Indies and Mexico, with eagerness to return to the northern section of the New World.

His ambition was fulfilled within a year. He had a chance to sign on with a group pulled together by the Sieur de Monts. De Monts had now been granted by the king exclusive rights to whatever fur trade he could set up. With this monopoly he easily attracted financial investments from the French ports of Saint Malo, La Rochelle, Saint Jean de Luz and Rouen. The expedition, in which the top figures were de Monts, Champlain, Dupont Gravé and Jean, Seigneur de Poutrincourt, sailed from Le Havre on March 7, 1604. Their purpose was to explore the Atlantic Coast south of the Saint Lawrence until they found a suitable site for a permanent colony and then to found it. The colony was also to serve as a trading post for furs.

It was a quality expedition. No convicts. Instead there were 120 tradesmen and "a large number of gentlemen," as Champlain says. They were accompanied by a Protestant minister, de Monts being Protestant, and a Catholic priest. De Monts had chosen the minister, but one of the sponsoring towns, Rouen, had refused to accept a Protestant clergyman as competent to "convert heathen," and therefore both Churches were represented. It was the law of the day that no colonization could be undertaken without clergy along, not only for the benefit of the colonists, but as missionaries to the Indians.

On May 8, the ships anchored off the coast of New Brunswick. De Monts sent Champlain, as official geographer, on a trip to explore and map the coastline. On his return the French flag was raised on the tiny island of Saint Croix in the Bay of Fundy, where de Monts had decided to land. A mill and a community oven were built; gardens were planted.

Champlain was again sent south to explore. With twelve men and two Indian guides, he threaded the myriad islands that lie between Passamaquoddy Bay and the mouth of the Penobscot River. Entering the river, they traveled upstream almost to the site of the city of Bangor, Maine. Though Champlain itched to sail on, a dwindling food supply drove him back to Saint Croix.

The winter on that island was wretched. Snow arrived October 6. By December 3 the shoreline was bound by cakes of ice. In the dirt floor storehouse all liquid provisions froze except sherry, which was kept fluid by its alcoholic content. Cider was dispensed in blocks, by the pound. "For water," says Champlain, "we were forced to melt snow, as springs and brooks were frozen." Breakfast, lunch and dinner consisted of salt meat and/or salt vegetables. The inevitable result was scurvy. By spring, two-fifths of the colonists were dead. Half of the rest were on the point of death.

Champlain's comment on this wintry ordeal is typical of the man. By contrast with Cartier's bubbling-over descriptions of everything pertaining to his voyages, Champlain's diary is terse and understated. In referring to the winter's tribulations he says, merely: "All this produced discontent in Sieur de Monts and others of the settlement."

The preceding autumn, Dupont Gravé had sailed back to France for provisions. In June he returned with them. Then he, Champlain, de Monts and twenty sailors set out southwestwards, looking for a better place than Saint Croix to establish a settlement. They sailed as far as Cape Cod. There de Monts insisted on turning back. He had found no Indian trappers with furs to trade along the way, and he knew that fur was what his sponsors were after. Fur was his bread and butter. The life of the colony depended on it. His problem was to find a climate more livable than Saint Croix's without losing access to pelts. He decided to transport the colony across the Bay of Fundy to Port Royal (now Annapolis Royal), taking along as much as possible of what had been built up—even the framework of the houses.

Trying to make the new site homey, many of the colonists,

Champlain among them, planted not only vegetable but also flower gardens. Champlain even laid out a fishpond. His garden, he records with a rare burst of eloquence, "was surrounded with ditches full of water in which I placed some very fine trout, and into which flowed three brooks . . . from which the greater part of our settlement was supplied. I also made a little sluiceway toward the shore, in order to draw off the water when I wished. . . . I constructed a summer house with some fine trees, as a resort for enjoying the fresh air. I made there also a little reservoir for holding salt water fish, which we took out as we wanted them. . . . We often resorted to this place as a pastime; and it seemed as if the little birds around took pleasure in it too, for they gathered there in large numbers, warbling and chirping."

In October, before the work of resettling was completed, de Monts left for France, taking de Poutrincourt with him. Others were clamoring against the monopoly on the fur trade the king had granted de Monts. He needed to protect his interests. He told the colonists frankly that he was uncertain of the outcome. Anyone who wanted to go home with him was free to do so. In case he didn't return to Port Royal by July, the alternative would be for the colonists to make their way to the Gaspé as best they could, there to search for transport home. The Gaspé was used as a general stopping and re-supplying depot. Many were not willing to risk such a doubtful future and sailed for France with de Monts. Champlain remained, with forty-three others. He hoped for the chance to complete the southern voyage from which de Monts had turned back at Cape Cod.

The winter, luckily, was mild. Around March 1, Dupont Gravé, who had been left in charge of the colony, began fitting out a vessel to make the voyage of discovery Champlain urged. Their goal was Florida.

Mid-March, the two set out with their crew. Fog, which so often shrouds the Nova Scotia coast, followed by storm, drove them home soon after they had started. In April they set out again and again were foiled by storm and high seas. Their ship was driven onto rocks. As Champlain describes the experience: "At the first blow of our boat upon the rocks, the rudder broke, a part of the keel and three or four planks were smashed and some ribs stove in, which frightened us, for our barque filled immediately and all we could do was wait until the sea fell, so that we might get ashore. For otherwise we were in danger of our lives in consequence of the swell which was very high. The sea having fallen, we went on shore amid the storm."

Indians in canoes helped them rescue as many provisions as possible from the doomed vessel before it split into pieces. "We praised God for having rescued us from this shipwreck," says Champlain, "from which we had not expected to escape so easily."

July came and went. No sign of de Monts. The colonists packed up, according to his advice, and began their trek northward. Fortunately, they had not gone far before learning that de Poutrincourt had been appointed lieutenant governor of the colony and had arrived with a large ship full of provisions. They returned to Port Royal where they found de Poutrincourt and forty new colonists already disembarked.

The occasion called for celebration. De Poutrincourt ordered a cask of wine to be opened and invited all to drink freely as long as it lasted.

When the gaiety was over, he got down to the business of the colony. He set men to planting wheat, rye and hemp. He had a boat readied to make a new try at a Florida cruise. The vessel set sail early in September and by mid-October the exploring party anchored off Cape Cod. They could have made better time, but much to Champlain's annoyance, de Poutrincourt wanted to see for himself the ins and outs of the coastline, which Champlain had already mapped on his previous voyage with de Monts.

De Poutrincourt decided to disembark at the Cape and explore on foot. Several of the crew brought flour ashore and built a stone oven in which to bake bread. Near dusk, when the exploring party returned to the ship, the bakers were still at their task. A shallop was sent back for them, but all except one refused to return, saying they preferred to sleep on the shore for the night. At dawn they were attacked by Indians armed with bows and arrows. Only one escaped alive.

Champlain's journal gives no reason for the attack. But an observer who accompanied the expedition does. The observer was Marc Lescarbot, a lawyer who had successfully defended de Poutrincourt's interests in several cases in France. He had opted to come to Port Royal with his client because, in his words, he wanted "to examine the land with my own eyes and to flee a corrupt world." He spent a year in the colony. On his return to his law practice in France, he wrote three books in verse and prose about life in the New World. Explorers, colonists, Indians moved in swift pace through the narratives, which he embroidered with rich, factual detail. French readers were spellbound. His books became best sellers and did much to bolster the influence of those at court and in business who were urging expansion of French exploration and settlement in North America.

Lescarbot had said he wanted to see with his own eyes. Little escaped them. In the case of the Cape Cod Indian attack on the bakers, he tells us that two of the French had previously shot at the Indians. The attack was in revenge. Champlain and the others went ashore to bury the dead men, erecting a cross at the burial place. The Indians reappeared, tore down the cross and dug up the bodies—"which displeased us greatly," understates Champlain. The French reburied the bodies and re-erected the cross before sailing away, but they knew in their hearts the bodies would be dug up again.

Their ship's next anchorage was off the island now known as Martha's Vineyard. It was late October. They could go no farther, if they were to regain Port Royal before snow fell. For the third time Champlain's wish to sail south had been frustrated. Had it not, the French might have reached the Hud-

son River two years before the Dutch. The New France that
the explorers were carving out of the wilderness, almost inch
by inch, might have extended as far south as New York City,
which the Dutch claimed and christened New Amsterdam.

In mid-November, after several narrow escapes from shipwreck, Champlain, de Poutrincourt and their company sailed
into Port Royal. The winter lay ahead. To ward off doldrums
in the colony and to encourage proper diet as a preventive for
scurvy, the reticent, conservative Champlain took what was
for him a most uncharacteristic action. He founded a merry
eating and drinking society, *L'Ordre du Bon Temps,* the Order
of Good Cheer. He devotes only a few words to it in his journal, but again, the observant Lescarbot gives us a full and
lively account. "To this order each man was appointed Chief
Steward in his turn. . . . There was no one who, two days before his turn came, failed to go hunting or fishing and to bring
back some delicacy in addition to our ordinary fare. So well
was this carried out that never at breakfast did we lack some
savory meat of flesh or fish, and still less at our midday meal;
for that was our chief banquet at which the ruler of the feast,
or Chief Steward . . . having had everything prepared by the
cook, marched in, napkin on shoulder, wand of office in hand,
and around his neck the collar of the order . . . after him all
the members of the order, each carrying a dish."

Almost always among the tempting platters were cabbage
and potatoes, dressed up and seasoned according to a variety of
recipes. Though not as high in anti-scurvy vitamin C content
as fruits and more perishable vegetables, they had the advantage of being preservable. Underground pits, reached by
tunnels, had been dug for cold storage of such necessities.

Indians, invited to attend some of these meals, must have
been amazed at the pageantry. At the end of the Chief Steward's period of service he turned his collar of the order over to
his successor. Each toasted the other with wine; then the toasts
became general among the entire company.

The winter of *Le Bon Temps* was the last winter of the

Port Royal settlement. Just when it had begun to surmount the challenge of a new way of life in a new land, de Monts lost his battle to protect his monopoly. In Paris, would-be fur traders, blocked by his exclusive rights, made an alliance with the powerful hatters' guild, a trade association. The guild was interested because the best-selling hats of the day were made from beaver fur. De Monts's one-man control allowed him to set his own prices on pelts. The hatters wanted lower prices, also more pelts. Competition would lower the price; more traders would provide more pelts. Hence the alliance, which was aided and abetted under cover by the Dutch. Henry IV gave in to the pressure and canceled de Monts's charter. With the monopoly broken, de Monts's sponsors would no longer back him. There was no way to support the colony. De Monts sent word that it must be abandoned. Champlain and Lescarbot both reported the abandonment in characteristically different style. Wrote Champlain: "A young man from Saint Malo, named Chevalier, brought letters from the Sieur de Monts to Sieur de Poutrincourt, by which he directed him to bring his company back to France."

Lamented Lescarbot: "I fear he (de Monts) may be forced to give it all up, to the great scandal and reproach of the French name. . . . We find a set of men full of avarice and envy who would not draw a sword in the service of the king, nor suffer the slightest ill for the honor of God, but who yet put obstacles in the way of our drawing any profit from the province . . . men who would prefer to see the English and Dutch win possession of it rather than the French, and would fain have the name of God unknown in these quarters. And it is such people who are listened to, who are believed, and who win their suits."

On August 11, 1607, Port Royal was vacated. The good gardens would go to seed, as Cartier's had at Charlesbourg; the houses would tumble in. The third French effort at American colonization had failed. The failure this time was not through any lack of foresight or organization among the colonists. They were on their way to becoming winners in the struggle with the wilderness. It was greediness and skulduggery in the motherland that did them in.

The Port Royal experiment was the first of many examples of conflict between the interests of old and New France.

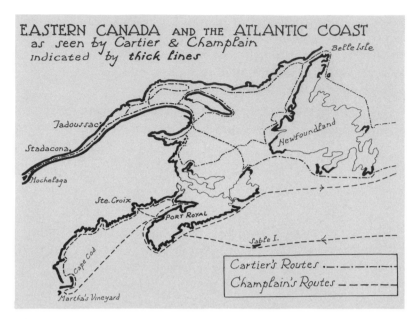

Belle Isle

Tadoussac

Stadacona

Newfoundland

Hochelaga

Ste. Croix

Port Royal

Cape Cod

Sable I.

Martha's Vineyard

Cartier's Routes _._._._._._.
Champlain's Routes _ _ _ _ _ _

COURTESY OF THE PUBLIC ARCHIVES OF CANADA.

Cartier taking possession of New France.
COURTESY OF THE NEW YORK PUBLIC LIBRARY.

28

Samuel de Champlain. COURTESY OF THE NEW YORK PUBLIC LIBRARY.

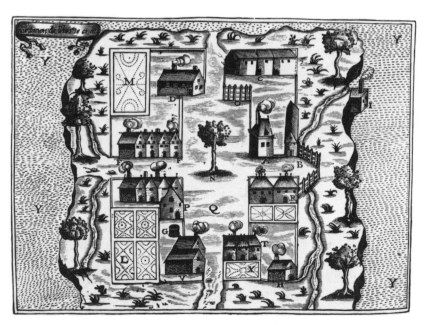

Ile Ste. Croix, the earliest Champlain settlement, 1604.
From Champlain's drawing. COURTESY OF THE NEW YORK PUBLIC LIBRARY.

The Champlain map of 1632.
COURTESY OF THE PUBLIC ARCHIVES OF CANADA.

Champlain's fortified residence at Quebec.
COURTESY OF THE NEW YORK PUBLIC LIBRARY.

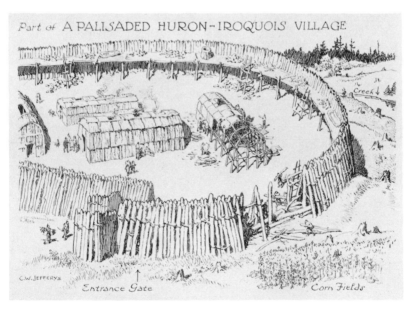

A reconstruction of part of a typical Huron-Iroquois village.
COURTESY OF THE PUBLIC ARCHIVES OF CANADA.

"French Canadian Habitants Playing at Cards."
A lithograph of a painting by Cornelius Krieghoff.

COURTESY OF THE PUBLIC ARCHIVES OF CANADA.

"The Habitant Farm" by Cornelius Krieghoff.

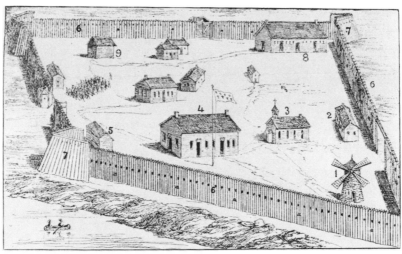

A typical seigneurial fort, Fort Remy, Lachine, 1671. I. Mill, 2. Priest's House, 3. Chapel, 4. LaSalle's House, 5. Barn. From Girouard's *Le Vieux Lachine*. COURTESY OF THE PUBLIC ARCHIVES OF CANADA.

The arrival of the brides at Quebec, c. 1667.
COURTESY OF THE PUBLIC ARCHIVES OF CANADA.

The Founding
of New France

Henry IV was a practical king, an imaginative king—
and a diplomat. He respected his treasurer, Sully,
whose financial genius had rescued France from the brink of
bankruptcy to which Henry's spendthrift predecessors had
brought it. All the same, he did not agree with Sully's write-
off of North American exploration.

He was aware of Jamestown, the colony the English had
established on the bay of the Chesapeake River during the
same year he had canceled de Monts's monopoly. He knew
that the Dutch East Indian Company had engaged an Englishman, Henry Hudson, to explore the river that now bears Hudson's name. He was familiar with Spanish occupation of parts
of the West Indies, Central and South America. He didn't
want France left out of the race.

So, twelve months after revoking de Monts's charter, he renewed it; but in order to pacify Sully, the hatters' guild and traders who wanted a slice of the action, he granted the new rights for one year only. De Monts interested two rich merchants in Rouen, Messieurs Collier and Legendre, in the investment. He gave Champlain command of the expedition and sent Dupont Gravé with him. Their destination was the Saint Lawrence. A separate ship was dispatched to reestablish Port Royal. De Monts remained in France to keep an eye on his interests.

For the next quarter century the story of French North America is the story of Samuel de Champlain. He established the first permanent colony at Québec and became its governor. He is considered Canada's founder.

Neither a businessman nor a politician by nature, he was forced to learn and practice both trades in order to guarantee the survival of his colony. A lover of peace, he was caught up in hostilities between warring Indian tribes. Taking sides with tribes who controlled the riverways was the price of freedom to explore, also the price of obtaining furs, a necessity for financing the exploration.

The beginning was slow and difficult. His base for operations was Québec, where he erected three connecting buildings and a storehouse, manned by twenty colonists. Unfortunately, the cost of their upkeep mounted higher than the profits from furs. Collier and Legendre were soon disgusted. They insisted that de Monts buy out their interest. But de Monts did not have money enough himself to keep the colony going. Champlain returned to France to see what he could do.

He found that certain nobles at court could be interested in backing him if they could see sufficient rewards for themselves in his plans. He selected one such noble, Henri de Bourbon, Prince de Condé, as his patron. The mother and regent of the boy king, Louis XIII, who had succeeded Henry IV, gave Condé the title of Viceroy of Canada. With the title came the award of a twelve-year monopoly on the fur trade above Québec and the right to sublet the contract.

For Condé's pay-off, Champlain organized the merchants of Rouen, Saint Malo and La Rochelle into the Compagnie du Canada, which leased the monopoly from the Prince. The terms made Québec headquarters for fur collection. The settlement was to be supplied by the company with six families of colonists per year.

The first of these was a Parisian druggist, his wife, three children and brother-in-law. The druggist, Louis Hébert, had been a member of the first Port Royal settlement, and Champlain had known and admired him there. At Champlain's urging, the Compagnie du Canada offered Hébert six hundred livres (about $2,880) a year for three years, ten acres and living expenses as an inducement to move his family to Québec.

Hébert accepted and sold his Parisian home and shop. He and his family were about to board ship when the company's shareholders welshed on their agreement. They bribed the ship's captain into refusing to take the Héberts unless a new agreement was signed.

The new one offered only half the former income, in return for which the entire family was to work exclusively for the company, turning over to it all profits from produce they raised. At the end of the three years, Hébert was to sell his produce to the company only, at the going prices in France. The company was to have his services for life. He was forbidden to trade in fur. With home and business sold in Paris, Hébert had little choice but to sign.

More trickery was to come. When the family landed in Québec, they found only five of the promised ten acres available. Nevertheless, the Héberts weathered their hardships. Louis found and was able to acquire on his own an adjacent five acres. He kept the acreage well tilled, producing ample crops of vegetables. He surrounded the garden with apple orchards and grapevines. The cows were content in his stable and his family was as comfortable as settlers could be in the large stone farmhouse that he built for them.

After eleven years of labor, he died in an accidental fall from a ladder. The colony had, as yet, no doctor, or his life might have been saved. Doggedly, his family carried on.

The shoddy treatment of the Héberts was typical of the attitude of French private investors toward colonization. The businessman's sole interest was profit from the fur trade. He didn't propose to dilute that by bearing the costs of establishing permanent settlements. In fact, he did everything he could to discourage them. He didn't really want settlers snooping into his dealings in fur. These were not always carried out according to law, and the fewer witnesses, the better.

Champlain bitterly protested this philosophy. Although his primary interest was exploration, he was also very much the patriot. He dreamed of the Québec colony as a monument to "the glory of God" and "the renown of France." He tried to sell this point of view in a memorandum that he wrote to the Paris Chamber of Commerce describing his vision of a Québec-to-be as "a city filled with noble buildings, the capital of a vast region watered by the Saint Lawrence and abounding in rolling plains, beautiful forests, fat cornfields, rich mines and rivers full of fish . . ." With an enthusiasm that warms his writing only in spasms he adds: "From here the heathen are to be converted and a passage discovered to the east. So important a trade route will it become that from the tolls alone there will be revenue to construct giant public works."[3]

The memo drew a sarcastic snort in reply. "Canada," it proclaimed, "is a land of nothing but barbarians, bears and beaver."

Eventually Champlain triumphed over the cynics, but at the expense of much time and trouble. He persuaded the Duke de Montmorency to look into the Compagnie du Canada's neglect of its promise to send colonists. The Duke de Montmorency had bought from the Prince de Condé the title of Viceroy of Canada and the leasable fur monopoly that went with it. As a result of Montmorency's investigation, the lease was taken away from the Compagnie du Canada and awarded to William and Emery de Caën of Rouen. The de Caëns gave the old company 5/12 of the shares, but kept the controlling voice. Arranging these negotiations cost Champlain many trips back and forth from Québec to France.

During all this time he was also engaged in Indian wars. The banks of the rivers Champlain wanted to explore and the areas where the most lavish supply of fur was to be had were controlled by the Algonquin and Huron Indians. The Algonquins and Hurons were at war with a league of tribes known as the Iroquois League of Five Nations. It combined Mohawks, Oneidas, Onondagas, Cayugas and Senecas. To gain the goodwill of the Hurons and Algonquins, Champlain agreed to help them in their battles with this League. The agreement won the French the undying hatred of the Iroquois, but also gave them the Hurons and Algonquins as faithful allies against the British during a century-long struggle for mastery of much of the North American continent.

In 1609 sixty Algonquins led Champlain and two French companions by canoe through the Green Mountains of Vermont, the Adirondacks of New York, also Lake George and Ticonderoga. They took him to that long lake that straddles northern Vermont and New York, reaching into Canada. The explorer named it for himself, Lake Champlain.

The price of the journey was Champlain's promise to join the Algonquins in battle with the Iroquois tribe of Mohawks who lived on the lake's shores. His journal of the trip gives a graphic account of the battle that took place near Ticonderoga, and of the ceremonies that preceded and followed the fight.

> We met . . . the Iroquois about ten o'clock in the evening, at the extremity of a cape, which extends into the lake on the western bank.[4] They had come to fight. We both began to utter loud cries, all getting their arms in readiness. We

withdrew out on the water and the Iroquois went on shore, where they pulled up all their canoes close to each other and began to fell trees. . . . Thus they barricaded themselves very well.

Our forces also passed the entire night, canoes drawn up close to each other and fastened to poles, so that they might not get separated and that they might be in all readiness to fight. We were within arrow range of their barricade. . . . We dispatched two canoes . . . to the enemy to inquire if they wished to fight, to which the latter replied that they wanted nothing else, but they said that it would be necessary to wait for daylight, so as to be able to recognize each other and that as soon as the sun rose they would offer us battle. This was agreed to by our side.

Meanwhile the entire night was spent in dancing and singing on both sides; with endless insults and other talk, as, how little courage we had, how feeble a resistance we should make against their arms, and that when day came, we should realize it to our ruin. Ours also were not slow in retorting, telling them they would see such execution of arms as never before. . . .

When day came, my companions and myself arranged our arms. . . . We each took an arquebus and went on shore. I saw the enemy go out of their barricade, nearly two hundred in number. . . . They came at a slow pace toward us, with dignity and assurance. . . . Our men also advanced in the same order, telling me that those who had three large plumes were the chiefs . . . and that I should do what I could to kill them. I promised to do all in my power. . . .

I marched some twenty paces in advance of the rest until I was within some thirty paces of the enemy, who at once noticed me. When I saw them making a move to fire at us, I rested my musket against my cheek and aimed directly at one of the three chiefs. With the same shot, two fell to the ground; and one of their men was so wounded that he died some time after. . . . When our side saw this shot so favorable for them, they began to raise such loud cries that one could not have heard it thunder. . . . The Iroquois were greatly astonished that two men had been so quickly killed. This caused great alarm among them. . . . They lost courage and took to flight, abandoning their camp and fort and fleeing into the woods. . . .

After gaining the victory, our men [took] a great quantity of Indian corn and some meal from their enemies. After feasting sumptuously, we returned . . . with the prisoners. . . . Toward evening they took one of the prisoners to whom they enumerated the cruelties which he and his men had already practiced toward them without any mercy [saying] that in like manner, he ought to make up his mind to receive as much. They commanded him to sing, if he had the courage, which he did, but it was a very sad song.

Meanwhile our men kindled a fire, and when it was well burning they each took a brand and burned this poor creature gradually, so as to make him suffer greater torment. Then they tore out his nails. . . . Afterwards they flayed the top of his head and had a kind of gum poured all hot upon it; then they pierced his arms near the wrists, and drawing up the sinews with sticks, they tore them out by force. . . .

I remonstrated, saying that we practiced no such cruelties, but killed at once and that if they wished me to fire a musket shot at him, I should be willing to do so. They refused, saying that he would not in that case suffer any pain. I went away from them. . . .

When they saw that I was displeased, they called me and told me to fire a musket shot at him. This I did, without his seeing it and thus put an end . . . to all the further torments he would have suffered. . . . This is the manner in which these people behave toward those whom they capture in war. . . .

After this execution we set out on our return. I went with them in their canoes as far as Tadoussac in order to witness their ceremonies. On approaching the shore, they each took a stick to the end of which they hung the heads of their enemies who had been killed, together with some beads, all of them singing. . . . [On shore] women undressed themselves . . . and swam to the prows of the canoes to take the heads. . . . They hung them around their necks like some costly chain, singing and dancing meanwhile. Some days after, they presented me with one of these heads . . . and also with a pair of arms taken from their enemies, to keep and show to the king. This, for the sake of gratifying them, I promised to do.

During Champlain's absence with the Algonquins, Dupont Gravé was in charge of the Québec colony. He was again in charge for the several years which Champlain spent among the Indians, living, traveling and fighting with them, lining up channels for the fur trade and pursuing his chief objective, exploration.

He discovered the Ottawa River, which an Indian guide whom Champlain called '"my liar" had told him flowed into a salt body, raising anew the hope of a Northwest Passage. Despite Champlain's disappointment in his guide, the discovery had great value in the French push to the west, for it allowed Champlain and future explorers to bypass the rapids at Montréal that had stopped their predecessors. A branch of the Ottawa flows into the Saint Lawrence just above Montréal, while the river itself flows into the Saint Lawrence just below it. Thus Champlain was able to push on to Lake Ontario and portage overland to Lake Huron.

These discoveries were the result of his usual compromise with the Indians—you take me there, I'll help you fight. In 1615, the Hurons claimed they could no longer bring furs to a trading market that had been established near the rapids. They claimed that Iroquois enemies, the Onondagas, made their route too risky. However, if Champlain would help them defeat these enemies, they would round up a two-thousand-man war party for him to command and would show him many fine lands on the way to the Onondaga stronghold. Champlain agreed.

The war party was rounded up on the shores of tiny Lake Simcoe between Lake Ontario and Georgian Bay, which is a part of Lake Huron. The group proceeded to Lake Ontario and on to little Lake Oneida, north of the present-day city of Syracuse, New York. Here they hid their canoes in a forest and stole on foot a few miles south to a palisaded stronghold of the Onondagas.

The technique with which Champlain planned to have the Hurons lay siege to the stronghold was strictly European. Champlain had by now acquired some facility with Indian languages, but not enough to explain fully his plan of attack. The plan required building a movable scaffolding, thirty feet high, which was to be pushed up against the palisade. Indians protected by wooden shields were to scale this palisade and fire a fusillade into the fort. Meanwhile other Indians were to set fire to logs that they had piled against the bottom of the palisade, thus destroying it.

The palisade climbers threw away their shields and were shot down. The log burners gathered too few logs and set those in such a position that the wind blew the flames away from rather than toward the palisade. Confused, the Hurons broke ranks and ran wild, screaming and yelling. Champlain could not regroup or control them. Two chiefs and fifteen warriors were wounded, and Champlain himself was shot in the knee and leg.

One of the Hurons carried him to their village on his back. The Hurons said they had no spare canoe in which he could be sent on to Québec and he was in no condition to try to reach home on foot. The truth very likely was that in spite of their defeat, they trusted him and wanted him at their councils as they planned further attacks. So Champlain wintered with the Hurons and spent his time writing *The Voyage of the Sieur de Champlain to New France Made in the Year 1615*.

It is a remarkable document, lavishly illustrated by the author's own drawings. In these, every vein of every leaf of every tree is distinct; the anatomy of Indian bodies shows every sinew—but by some quirk all the Indian faces are European and so are the haircuts! Portrait artist Champlain was not.

The text, understated as was the author's habit, gives an uninspired but nevertheless extensive catalog of the Indian way of life. From Champlain's pages the Indians emerge as people who have learned how to put their environment to work for them without destroying it. For example, he shows how, in the felling of trees, the Indians were careful not to deforest an entire site. Rather, they cut the oldest trunks, thereby making room for saplings to reach toward the sun.

He stresses how skills unknown to Europeans had been developed deep in the woods where Indians depended solely on their own resourcefulness for food, drink, shelter and security.

Living among them, Champlain himself began to develop this resourcefulness. He tells about getting lost when he broke away from a hunting expedition. He was chasing a parrotlike bird that interested him when he suddenly realized he didn't know where he was. He spent three nights alone in the forest, killing game for food and searching for a brook that might lead him to the river along which he knew the hunting party was encamped. He says:

> Having resolved upon this plan, I followed it out so well that at noon I found myself on the border of a little lake . . . where I killed some game which was very timely for my wants. . . . I proceeded along the border of this lake to see where it discharged and found a large brook, which I followed until five o'clock in the evening when I heard a great noise. . . . I concluded that it was a fall of water in the river which I was searching for. I proceeded nearer and saw an opening, approaching which I found myself in a great and far-reaching meadow, where there were large number of wild beasts, and looking to my right, I perceived the river, broad and long. . . . Walking along the meadow, I noticed a little path where the Indians carried their canoes. Finally, after careful observation, I recognized . . . that I had gone that way before.
>
> I passed the night in better spirits than the previous ones,

supping on the little I had. In the morning I reexamined the place where I was, and concluded from certain mountains on the border of the river that I had not been deceived and that our hunters must be lower down by four or five good leagues. This distance I walked at my leisure along the border of the river, until I perceived the smoke of our hunters, where I arrived to the great pleasure, not only of myself but of them.

It was May of 1616 before the Indians were willing to part company with Champlain. During the course of the winter he had counseled the Indians as requested and had also been at pains to visit as many Indian villages as possible, setting up relations for fur trading. To Champlain's and the Indians' mutual pleasure, he had successfully arbitrated a dispute between Hurons and Algonquins over an Algonquin killing of a Huron. Had the dispute, already at the brawl stage, escalated to war, the French would have been in an almost impossible position, for both of their tribal allies would have demanded aid from them. By no means, therefore, did Champlain consider his Indian winter a lost season.

It was to be his last season in the wilderness. The rest of his life would be spent governing the colony, politicking with the French court and sweating out a term of exile in England.

His administration of the colony was plagued by the impact of religious wars, which had again erupted in France. The colony's sponsors, the de Caëns, were Huguenots, a name for Protestants that the French took from Besançon Hugues, a Swiss protester against the Catholic Church. England had intervened in France on the side of the Huguenots, and Champlain feared that Québec, which despite its Huguenot sponsorship was a Catholic-populated colony, might suffer English raids. The English had already taken over French colonies at Port Royal and what is now Mount Desert in Maine. So he asked the de Caëns for funds to further fortify Québec.

The de Caëns refused to come up with money that would be used against Hugunot allies, the English. Champlain strengthened the fortifications anyway, but could not afford to do so to the extent he felt necessary. He then sent a report to the Duke de Ventadour who had succeeded the Duke de Montmorency as Canada's viceroy. The report put the de Caëns in a most unfavorable light. De Ventadour took it to Cardinal Richelieu.

Cardinal Richelieu, Louis XIII's chief minister, was a shrewd Catholic statesman who could see the value of Champlain's "capital of a vast region" in the New World. He abolished the de Caëns' charter and formed a new company, the Company of One Hundred Associates, to sponsor the colony. The Associates were a broad cross section of people: nobles, wealthy merchants, small traders. Richelieu's own name headed the list.

The Company's charter gave it a fifteen-year exclusive on the fur trade, provided three hundred settlers were sent to New France every year. Catholic settlers only. The Company must maintain three priests in each settlement. The Associates were prepared to come up with funds for fortifying their investment, but it was too late.

In the spring of 1628, Champlain sent watchers, as was his habit, to the highest point of "the rock," as the cliff that towered above the colony was called. Louis Hébert had established his family on these heights, but the homes of most colonists still clung along the riverbank at the bottom of a sheer 360-foot drop. The winter coat of thick ice had finally melted from the river. Once again its currents divided in swirls around the Île d'Orléans, opposite Québec, pushing their way out to the Gulf and the sea.

The watchers were waiting to sight supply ships that should be arriving any day from France, their holds filled with lemons and oranges, sugar, spices and salt, olive oil and vinegar, rum, wine and brandy, molasses and flour, muskets and powder, knives and beads for trading with the Indians, tools for building.

Sure enough, ships were sighted. One of the watchers was

dispatched down cliff to bring the good news to the anxious colonists. But when the vessels arrived at Lower Town, the good news went sour. The ships were English. Their commander, Lewis Kirke, demanded surrender of the colony. Champlain refused.

Lewis Kirke had been dispatched from Tadoussac, some eighty-four miles down river, by his brother, Sir David, who was engaged in raiding the fur trade headquarters maintained there by the Company of One Hundred Associates. The Kirke family had received orders from Charles I, King of England, to do as much damage as possible to the French colony. On his way to Québec from Tadoussac, Lewis had paused at Cap Tourmente, an agricultural settlement, to seize cattle and destroy crops.

When Champlain refused to surrender, Lewis decided on starvation and deprivation as the best means of doing "damage" to the colony. In the Saint Lawrence Gulf he and Sir David captured all the French supply ships, and the colony starved, but it did not surrender. And finally Lewis Kirke left.

Meanwhile King Louis XIII, on advice from Richelieu, had revoked the promise by which Henry IV had brought religious peace to France. Henry had promised certain Huguenot strongholds that they could govern themselves independently, keeping their religion. One of these strongholds was the city of La Rochelle. After Henry's successor broke this promise, the English Lord Buckingham landed an army on the Isle of Ré, near La Rochelle, in order to protect it. But when Richelieu besieged the city, Buckingham deserted. La Rochelle fell, and Richelieu marched his king triumphantly through its gates.

As a result of this episode, Sir David Kirke's orders were strengthened: he was told not merely to damage, but to capture Québec. When, in July 1629, he sailed up the Saint Lawrence and called a second time for the colony's surrender, Champlain had no choice but to give in. Not only was the colony starved; it had no ammunition.

Champlain was transported to England and forced to remain there for four years. His colonists were given the choice of remaining under English rule or being taken home to France. Louis Hébert, in his farm on the rock, was among the few who remained. The English burned most of Lower Town to the ground.

What neither Champlain, nor his colonists, nor the Kirkes knew was that ten weeks before the Kirke conquest of Québec, England and France had signed a peace treaty in which the two countries had agreed to restore to each other any territories seized after the signing. This time-lapse provision was necessary in days when news traveled by horseback. Transatlantic voyages were infrequent and took even longer.

Consequently it wasn't until three years later that Québec was returned to the French. The following year, in 1633, Champlain came back to the colony. He was sixty-six years old, and this crossing of the Atlantic, his last, was his twenty-third.

His arrival coincided with that of a grand gathering of Huron Indians who had made their way to Québec to barter furs. As soon as he put foot on land, the Indians crowded around him in welcome, crying, "Ho! Ho! Ho!" in an ascending crescendo. This was the Huron form of glad greeting. Gifts were showered on Champlain, accompanied by long speeches from several chieftains. "When you were absent," said one of them, "the earth was no longer the earth, the river no longer the river, the sky no longer the sky; but on your return everything is as before. The earth is again the earth, the river is again the river, the sky is again the sky."

The returned governor at once set about policing the Great Lakes area, sending French soldiers to marshal Indian allies against the Dutch and English and discouraging the Hurons and Algonquins from trading with them. Immediately after the release of Québec from the English, the Company of One Hundred Associates, renamed the Company of New France, resumed active fulfillment of its obligation to provide colonists and clergy. Black-robed Jesuit priests began accompanying fur traders far into the wilderness to set up missions. The colony itself was expanding along the Saint Lawrence to the northeast and southwest. Champlain personally established a thriving new settlement, Trois Rivières, about halfway between Mont Royal and Québec. In Québec he built a chapel for the one hundred souls who lived there. He named it Our Lady of the Recovery, in thanksgiving for the restoration of Canada to the French.

He was buried in his chapel in 1635. On Christmas Day of that year, he died. He had been paralyzed since October, probably by a stroke. Father Le Jeune, one of the Jesuit missionaries, delivered the eulogy. He said simply: "On the twenty-fifth day of December, the day of the birth of our Savior on earth, Monsieur de Champlain, our governor, was reborn in heaven."

A few months earlier, in August, Champlain had addressed a long "state of the colony" message to Cardinal Richelieu. The message was burdened with exaggerated flattery, a wangle Champlain had learned to use with the touch of an expert. But disregarding the diplomacy, the message might well have been his epitaph, for it reflected the dream of that "capital" founded "for the glory of God" and "the renown of the French" to which thirty-two years, almost half his life, had been devoted. He wrote, in part: "The state of this country is such that it stretches out more than 1,500 leagues [2,755 miles] accompanied by one of the best rivers in the world, into which a number of other rivers more than 400 leagues [1,000 miles] long empty themselves. . . . [These rivers] embellish a countryside inhabited by an infinite variety of people,[5] some living in villages built of wood . . . others who are wandering huntsmen and fishermen. The beauty of these lands cannot be over-esteemed nor overpraised, whether for fertility of soil, diversity of woods . . . opportunities for hunting game and fish . . . [the latter] in abundance and of monstrous size. All hold out arms to you. Monseigneur. [It] seems that God has reserved it for you . . . in order that you may bring forth from it a progress pleasing to Him, more than any of your predecessors have ever made."

He goes on to press the importance of defense against the English, whom he still sees, and quite rightly, as a threat to the colony's future. He would like to get rid of rivals before rivals try to get rid of the French: "Monseigneur, please pardon my zeal if I tell you now that your fame has reached the East, it should be better known in the West, and that it would be most prudent to begin by chasing the English from the countryside. . . . We need only 120 men, lightly armed. Having these, with two or three thousand Indians as our allies, we will chase our enemies, whether English or Dutch, and take away their trade with the Iroquois. In a year we can make ourselves master . . . and that will increase both the spread of religion and an unbelievable trade."

Champlain had given New France its start. The future rested in the hands of his successors.

A People Grow

Regardless of Québec's governors, sometimes good, sometimes bad, regardless of aid from home, occasionally generous but more often miserly, New France would never have flourished without its *habitants*. They were the colony's backbone and blood.

Most of them worked land on *seigneuries,* estates granted to nobility of medium rank. Others acquired their own farms. In the habitant's way of life, whether the land belonged to him or to his *seigneur* really made little difference. In either case, the French Canadian farmer was pretty much his own man. If he was a tenant, he paid a small annual rent, in currency, produce, or both. Even that might be waived for the first few years, when he was making his start.

Once a tenant had established himself, the seigneur decided

in what form the rent was to be collected. In a year when
prices were low, he opted for cash. When prices were high, he
chose whatever farm products commanded the highest. In
either event, how little these payments amounted to can be
judged from seigneurial records. A record from an average-
sized farm near Trois Rivières shows that each tenant was
obliged to deliver "one fat fowl of the brood of the month of
May," or twenty sous for each one-and-a-half acre of river
frontage. A sou was slightly less than a penny. A large farm
might pay as much as ten to twelve sous plus a half-dozen
chickens or one bushel of grain. The largest recorded total
sum collected was the equivalent of eight dollars—this total
made up of payments from twenty-five tenants.

The seigneur had certain other privileges. He had the right
to take stone, sand or firewood at will from any of his land,
but he was expected, in return, to make a gift to its occupant.
He was entitled to one of every eleven fish a habitant caught,
though in practice he rarely demanded or received this bounty.
He did claim six days of free labor annually, for which he supplied the tools, and during which he fed the workers. He operated a mill, which habitants were required to use for grinding
their grain, giving the seigneur 1/14 of the amount ground.
Actually, this mill was a greater convenience to the habitant
than to the seigneur.

If a habitant sold his lease, which he was permitted to do,
he had to pay the seigneur 1/12 of the sale price, but it was
customary for the seigneur to return one third of this share.
Each settler was obligated to farm at least an acre and a half.
Generally, he fared well enough to farm more.

The advantage to the seigneur in this arrangement was that
the habitants' work fulfilled the law under which seigneurial
grants were made. To get and keep an estate, a seigneur had
to colonize and cultivate it.

The habitants raised almost all their own food, built
their own homes, made all their own house furnishings, produced the materials for their clothing, did their own weaving

and sewing. Women wove flax crops into fabric for clothes, curtains, bedspreads. In the sub-zero Canadian winters, the whole family wore jackets of caribou hide, coats of wolf and bear fur, pelts of animals brought down by men's rifles.

The habitant particularly liked to shoot wolves. They were a constant threat to his herd of sheep. So heavy was their ravage that wool became a precious commodity. It was not used for outer clothing, but reserved for *au corps*—next to the body—and also for blankets.

Some was set aside for the *tuque,* a hat worn by both men and women and important to both for more than warmth. The tuque was a varicolored cone-shaped creation, with strands of yarn hanging from the peak. It truly was a creation. The color combinations were chosen by each family and each tried to make sure of a combination different from those of the neighbors. A family who lacked sufficient wool for tuques made them from wool and fur combined or, if necessary, from fur alone. The latter, however, had to be made of several different kinds of fur, an imitation of the different colors of wool. And always the tassel must be wool. The tuque was to the habitant what a coat of arms was to nobility. It was a way of proclaiming his identity.

Except for the wolf-threatened sheep, the habitants were successful breeders of livestock. They did well with pigs, cows, poultry and horses, which they raised for transportation. By 1671 Canada's governor informed the king of France that he need no longer send livestock to his colonial subjects. They were raising plenty of their own.

To clear fields for crops and pastures for cattle, the habitants hewed down the forest that fringed the riverbanks and clad the land far into the foothills of the world's oldest mountains, the Laurentians. They used the chopped wood to build and heat their homes. Over wood fires they cooked their meals. They carved barrel staves, which they shipped to the West Indies, where they were made into barrels for rum. The habitants were, in the pithy words of one governor, *"colonisa-*

teurs percherons"—workhorse settlers, on whom much of the welfare of other classes of society depended.

Their ability to team up was part of the secret of their production. Although fiercely independent in defense of their rights and their whims, they knew the value of helping hands when a job was to be done. Neighbors took turns helping each other plow and harvest, husk corn, shear sheep, round up cattle. After a day's work, they relaxed together over the huge meal their womenfolk came together to prepare. Afterwards, they exchanged news, opinions and gossip until the night sky was dark enough to show the stars.

As time went on, however, the security of the habitant was threatened by seigneurial greed. More colonists arrived, seeking land. Choice pieces became less and less available. The once comfortable relationship between landlord and tenant broke up when the landlord discovered he could command higher returns for his land and invented devices for doing so. Some demanded a "bonus" on top of the rent, waiting to push this demand until crops had been planted. Then the habitant faced the choice of paying up or losing his crops. Other landlords refused to rent their best pieces. Instead they sold them —at sky-high prices.

When the king of France got wind of this gouging, he issued edicts putting a stop to it. Any seigneur who disobeyed the edicts could forfeit his entire estate to the government. A number of landlords chose to risk the forfeit, but the majority conformed. Once again the habitants, reasonably sure of independence, could plow all their strength into the land.

For the most part, their lands bordered the Saint Lawrence, stretching back from it in a long, narrow rectangle. Waterfront footage was not only desirable but very nearly essential. In early French Canada the river was the main means of transportation, the route for shipping produce out and bringing necessities in.

Close to the river bank stood the wooden farmhouse. It was small, averaging about twenty-four feet long by fifteen feet wide. The barn, attached to the house, was big; usually a good sixty feet long by at least twenty feet wide. During the six to seven month winter, not only the farm animals, but also all their food must be sheltered inside.

The style of construction for both house and barn was designed to cope with the snows and below-freezing temperatures of the Canadian winter. Before leaving France, the habitants had lived in stone houses. In their new land they built from wood. Wood was more bountiful in Canada, but they chose it for another reason, too. Stone conducts cold; wood does not. Stone was used only for the shallow platforms on which homes rested. The platform was larger than the house, the extra space being used to pile up hay and dirt around the building's base in winter. This provided some insulation from the cold. Hay was also stuffed between the two layers of planks that formed the walls. The roof above sloped sharply to prevent snow from accumulating. It was reinforced with stout rafters inside.

The inside was one room. It served for cooking, eating, entertaining, sleeping. In a corner, under a six-foot-high canopy, stood the fourposter bed of the mother and father, surrounded by the smaller beds of the children. Sometimes a platform was built into the rafters for the children's beds. They climbed a ladder at night to sleep aloft.

Scattered around the room were straight-backed chairs, made from pine or yellow maple, the seats webbed with reeds. Chests of the same woods doubled as benches. A great clothes cabinet stood against a wall, and in the center of the room a broad-planked dining table.

The habitant and his wife did their best to make these quarters attractive. She embroidered the coarse turkey-red bedspread with needlepoint. He planed and polished the furniture until it was as smooth and shiny as honey. He carved elaborate designs on the doors of the clothes cabinet. She brightened the floor with hand-braided scatter rugs in which she combined strands of soft blue and rose, now and then intertwining strands of purple and turquoise.

The heart of the room—and of the family—was the stone fireplace, which served as furnace and stove. On shelves above and to each side stood wooden and birch bark dishes, some burnished pewterware and a few treasured pieces of pastel-colored pottery, bearing designs of leaves and flowers. Iron and clay pots hung from heavy hooks driven into a low rafter above the fireplace.

The action in this room varied according to season. It was gayest in the bleakest season, winter, when outdoor work was impossible. During the growing and harvesting months the whole family, children as well as parents, worked the fields, sunrise to sunset. Except for the celebrations that capped a team job, meals, though hearty, were incidental. They were eaten individually, at odd hours, depending on who could be spared from the fields. For children, a bowl of sweetened milk with croutons floating in it stood all day on the central table. In the growing season, home was a place to eat when one could, and fall into exhausted sleep when darkness fell.

In winter, on the other hand, the house hummed with activity. It was a time for the man of the house to draw up his chair to the fire, as he whittled toys for the children, made corncob dolls, carved a cradle for the new baby, built an extra chest for storage. Seated across from him, his wife spun flax and wool on her spinning wheel and wove it into cloth on her loom. Occasionally she went to the fireplace to stir the pot of dye made from berries, in which she would dip material for spreads and curtains. She cut the still good parts of worn-out garments into squares and sewed the squares into new clothing. She taught her children— and sometimes her husband— to read and write. And she let her imagination have its way with her cooking, inventing new recipes and serving huge meals.

For each member of the family she baked at least two oval-shaped loaves of bread per week, each loaf weighing six or seven pounds. Thick slices were eaten with soup or dipped in milk or brandy. She brought down from her shelves the preserves she had put up in summer: raspberries, gooseberries, wild cherries, mulberries and blueberries. She took from rafter hooks sides of smoked bacon and strips of smoked eel. From her barn, a natural freezer, she selected at will from caribou, deer, ducks, hare, doves, partridge and woodcocks. These had been shot just as winter came on and hung in the barn's granary section where they froze solid. Cod, shad, haddock, sturgeon and salmon were similarly frozen, or else salted. Frozen foods were defrosted near the fireplace.

Sometimes she dipped into her sacks of cornmeal, which Indians had taught her how to grind between two stones. She boiled it as dumplings with fish, roasted it with game, mixed it with vegetable broth or pea soup, used it in pancakes. When she had leftovers, she mixed them all together in a grand *tourtière,* a game or fish pie to which anything tasty mighty be added.

For vegetables she drew on her stock of dried peas, lentils and broad beans and the pumpkins stored in her root cellar. Sometimes, though, she missed her springtime asparagus and the summer cucumbers, which she served as dessert, drowned in thick, fresh cream.

Of a winter evening, families often visited each other, snowdrifts permitting. The host family provided the feast. Several different kinds of meat, fish and vegetables followed each other on the polished table. Forks and spoons were laid out, but no knives. Guests were expected to bring their own. There was plenty to drink as well as eat: fizzy, hard cider from last summer's apple crop, beer made from spruce sap and *bouillon.* Bouillon wasn't broth; it was whiskey. The liquor was made by mixing fermented corn or wheat with water and allowing the mixture to ripen in wooden casks. On special occasions wine, imported from Bordeaux, France, might be served, weakened with much water to make it go round.

The feast lasted from seven to eleven. Then came the time for dancing, singing, storytelling. Singing and dancing went together. Often the dancing took the form of a contest, with partners inventing new steps. The couple performing the most original steps received a prize—a fat ham, maybe, or a side of bacon. The singers were the dancers' orchestra. Their accompaniment was provided by a fiddler. Almost every settlement had a fiddler. He made his own fiddle and bow, choosing from the forest with great care the woods he considered right for his instrument. Originally, the songs he accompanied were French. Gradually, reflections of the Canadian scene crept into them. Finally, these reflections took over, creating an entirely French Canadian folk music. This music dealt most often with *le terroir,* which, literally translated, means the soil. But the settlers used the term in a more specific sense. To them le terroir was *their* soil, the land they had wrested from wilderness and cultivated with sweat.

The terroir songs were often plaintive. They silhouetted the settler as a small figure against the vast landscape of the American North. One such plaint begins:

> *Mon pays, ce n'est pas un pays, c'est l'hiver;*
> *Mon jardin, ce n'est pas un jardin, c'est la plaine;*
> *Mon chemin, ce n'est pas un chemin, c'est la neige.*

> My country is not a country, it is winter;
> My garden is not a garden, it is the plain;
> My road is not a road, it is the snow.

Other songs dealt with fishing, planting, harvesting, in fact most aspects of habitant life. Some twenty thousand of these have been collected and preserved by Canadian museums, universities and students of folklore.

For children, the best part of the evening's entertainment was the storytelling. The storyteller was always an elderly man, known as "the old one." For the most part his stories were drawn from myths common to the folklore of the world, but he adapted them to current, local situations. Instead of relating what characters had done, he became the characters themselves, acting out their parts. He could bring a prince or princess, live, to the party.

When the festivities broke up, guests who lived within a few miles hiked home on their *raquettes*—snowshoes—which they had learned from Indians to fashion and use. Others, who had greater distances to go, rehitched their horses to their sleighs. They made their way home sleepily, but still with an ear cocked for the distant baying of wolves.

Two other festive events occurred in spring and fall, just before planting time and just after harvest. The spring event was the May 1 raising of the maypole in the seigneur's front yard. At dawn every habitant, from grandparents to toddlers, appeared there. Some of the men carried a tall pine from which they had lopped the branches and peeled the bark to within a foot or two of the top. Long strips of bright material were attached to it. Greenery-crowned and with strips flutter-ing, the tree was set in the ground, at which point the seigneur and his family came out of their house. They seated them-selves in large high-backed chairs to watch the ceremony.

Muskets volleyed a *feu de joie*—a fire of joy—and from every throat came cries of "Long live our king, long live our seigneur!" After that the dancing began. Young men and women danced around the pole, winding, unwinding and re-winding the colorful strips. The dance finished, all were in-vited indoors for refreshments. Every so often some habit-ant would dash outdoors again to fire a shot at the maypole. By noon it was thoroughly blackened, and a good many habitants were thoroughly tipsy from nonstop imbibing of the seig-neur's brandy. The crowd departed after much handshaking and well-wishing, the feet of the young still breaking into dance steps, the muskets of the men still firing salvos.

The fall event fell on Saint Martin's Day, early in Novem-ber. This was the day when all habitants came to the seig-neur's house to pay their annual rent. The harvest was in; poultry had grown fat from feeding in the stubbled fields.

The seigneur's yard was filled with carts and wagons. The seigneur himself received each of his farmers, counting off the copper coins they poured from their wallets, inspecting the squawking fowl, presented with their feet tied together, and offering brandy to all comers. Inside the house, the air filled with smoke as both men and women lit their pipes. Children, left to their own devices, snatched cakes from basketfuls laid out on the tables.

As the habitant's children grew older and could supply more skilled labor, the habitant himself could afford some time off. He often used it to go fur trapping, plowing any profits he made into the purchase of new farm equipment, imported from France. At the age of fifty, he made a signed, sealed and notarized contract with his youngest son, giving him his house and land. In return, the son agreed to feed and shelter his father and mother, should they become too feeble to work for themselves. Rarely did this happen. The habitant and his wife kept on working until they dropped dead. Few lived long enough to become incompetent.

The greatest of their fears was an Iroquois attack. Québec, high on its rock, suffered least from such attacks because the cliff safeguarded Upper Town and permitted a long view of the river from which any attack on Lower Town had to be made. Canoes could be sighted a long distance off, and fired on as soon as they came within range. Trois Rivières and especially Montréal, a colony founded at the foot of Mont Royal by a group of priests in 1642, bore the brunt of the Indian wars.

The Canadian National Archives contain an account of an Iroquois attack on a settlement about twenty miles from Montréal, Verchères. It was written by a fourteen-year-old girl who signs herself only by her first name, Marie-Magdeleine. She was alone with her twin twelve-year-old brothers when the attackers surprised her. Her father had gone to Québec on business and her mother to Montréal.

She heard gunshots and, almost in the same moment, saw

forty-five Iroquois running toward her. Hand-in-hand with her brothers, she ran through a meadow toward a fort about three miles from her house. Though under fire from the Indians, by great luck the three reached the fort unharmed.

Inside they found only two soldiers crouching in a hideout. The others had gone hunting. Several women and children and one eighty-year-old man from other nearby settlements had also reached the fort. They told her the Iroquois band was on the warpath.

The little group would have to remain in the fort until help came. Meanwhile, it was quite possible the Iroquois would try to capture it. Marie-Magdeleine began to inspect the defenses. She found several broken-down places in the walls through which an enemy could enter. Lifting a rock to block one of these, she ordered the two soldiers and her brothers to do likewise with other openings. "I spoke in such firm tones," she recorded, "that the soldiers obeyed me, without regard to my youth or sex. I discovered that when God gives one strength, nothing is impossible."

With the breaches repaired, she went about organizing means to hold the fort. By day, she, her brothers, the two soldiers and the eighty-year-old man kept constant fire trained on the surrounding Iroquois. One at a time, they snatched an hour's sleep now and then. Occasionally she commanded the soldiers to fire the fort's cannon. "Not only," she confesses, "to frighten the Iroquois and make them believe we could easily defend ourselves, but to occupy the soldiers, who were more than eager to try a getaway."

By night, the little band, sleepless, manned the lookouts. Hourly, from one lookout to the next and on to the sixth, then once more round, the sentries called loud and clear: "All's well." The idea was to give the impression of an alert and sizable guard.

The women in the fort weren't much help to the young commander. They wept all the time. "I told them," she wrote, "that their cries were putting us in much danger, as they were loud enough to be heard by the Iroquois above the noise of the shooting. I ordered them to quiet down, so as not to give our enemies the idea that we despaired."

Twice, Marie-Magdeleine left the fort. Her first venture out was to warn a family whom she saw from the parapets canoeing down river. She helped them to the relative safety of the fort. The second was to rescue her washing. She remembered she had left clothes on the line when she ran for the fort. She wanted to collect them before the Iroquois burned the village, which they soon did. Both times she begged that one of the two soldiers accompany her. Both times both refused.

Eight days passed before help came. A young man of Verchères, who had escaped the massacre and burning, had made his way by night to Montréal with news of the Iroquois occupation of the area. Troops were dispatched to drive away the Indians and rescue the group holding the fort. Marie-Magdeleine's vigil was over.

Forts, such as the one Marie-Magdeleine held, of necessity dotted the landscape of New France wherever settlers clustered. On the seigneuries, the seigneur was responsible for the defense of his habitants and the mill was usually built to double as a fort. Some took this and other responsibilities more seriously than others. Often those who shirked their duties were born nobility who inherited their titles. Those who fulfilled their obligation were generally men who had won their titles as a reward for their performance in New France. There were other basic differences between these two types of seigneurs.

The born nobles were younger sons who, with titles but without the land or wealth customarily conferred in old France on the eldest brother, had been brought up to do nothing. Oh, they might become officers in the army, or join the clergy; they certainly knew how to flounce the gilded lace trim at their cuffs, but they hadn't the faintest notion of how to run a grist mill or judge a hog. They could adapt, somewhat grudgingly, to urban life in New France, but they were at a complete loss in the countryside. Unfortunately, the largest seigneurie grants, some of one hundred square miles, went to this type of man.

Intensely disliking the role of gentleman-pioneer, but hopeful of gaining profit from his grant, such a seigneur often tried to operate from Québec, or even from Paris. When the king vowed to void the grants of absentee landlords, they were forced to move in. They then set their sons up in the fur trade and survived on their shares of the profits, paying little attention to their habitants except to extort bonuses from them.

The self-made nobility, the nobility of the New rather than the old France, was an entirely different breed. They, too, wanted money, but they expected to earn, rather than extort it. And they founded families that were as much the blood and backbone of the Canadian colony as were its *colonisateurs percherons*.

The Le Moyne family is a good example. In 1641, seventeen-year-old Charles Le Moyne, son of an innkeeper in Dieppe, France, heard stories about fortunes to be made in the Canadian fur trade. He came to Canada to try his luck. But he didn't depend on luck. Wisely, he decided that the Indians, native to the land, must know about as much as was to be known about fur trapping. He spent four years living with Hurons, learning and applying their methods.

When he had finished his apprenticeship with the Hurons, he applied for and received a land grant on the south bank of the Saint Lawrence, just opposite Montréal. The land lay directly on the route used by Iroquois nations in attacking Montréal. Nevertheless, he cleared and colonized it, according to the terms of the grant. For seven years he divided his time between fur trapping and defending and managing his estate. His earnings from fur he used to improve the estate. At twenty-eight when he married, he had done so well with his grant that the governor gave him a wedding present of more land. A few years later the king gave him a minor rank in the nobility.

He and his wife, Catherine, had eleven sons, all of whom distinguished themselves as civil servants and defenders of the colony. Five died at the hands of attacking British or Iroquois.

One son, Charles, the oldest, became a lieutenant governor of Montréal. He turned his seigneurie into a model for all others. The best mill in all the countryside was his, the most beautiful chapel for community worship. He saw to it that his habitants lived in well-built, comfortable homes, big enough to accommodate their big families. The King made him a baron, a rank higher than the title he had inherited from his father.

When Baron Le Moyne occupied his special pew in the chapel he had built, or when his was the place directly behind the priest in religious processions on church festival days, or his the carriage that had right of way at the crossroads, no habitant grumbled. The Le Moynes had earned their honors.

Not necessarily so, the colony's governors. One duty that irked seigneurs and habitants alike was providing hospitality during governors' tours. When a governor took an inspection trip up the Saint Lawrence, he traveled with a retinue of soldiers and servants. The upriver voyage, Québec to Montréal, was by land. Downriver, the retinue canoed. Going or returning, the governor and his party expected to be housed in the seigneuries en route. An advance man, a *voyageur,* was sent ahead to be sure all was in readiness. If late snow blocked the roads, the habitants had to get out and shovel it. At each stop they were required to don their best clothes and come to the seigneurie to kneel before the governor as deputy of the king. Not all governors required this ceremony, but enough did to rile the countryside.

The seigneur, upon receiving his land grant, was also obliged to render homage on bended knee. For that purpose he had to travel from his domain to the governor's court at Québec, no matter how great the distance. Pomp and ceremony were the warp and woof of Québec court life. All officials were sworn into office in the great hall of the governor's residence, the cavernous Château Saint Louis. On such occasions many toasts were quaffed to the king of France and many speeches delivered as wine and brandy loosened tongues.

Friendly Indians, the Hurons and Algonquins, were often invited to these ceremonies. The first time a band of Hurons participated, they were so thunderstruck they asked the governor to repeat the whole affair the next week. He agreed and they fetched a large number of their tribe to witness the goings-on. It wasn't long, however, before Indians started aping French manners. They dressed for court with tribal pomp and bent low to kiss the hands of women.

For ceremonials, the governor's guests donned the most dazzling raiment they possessed. The women's tight-waisted, bouffant-skirted dresses, made of damask, velvet or silk, were embroidered with pearls. The neckline was low cut, sleeves off the shoulders. Ropes of gems glittered on their semi-bare breasts. They wore gold or silver slippers, sequin trimmed.

The men wore knee-length waistcoats of silk, satin or taffeta, with matching knickers. Sometimes both were ruffled at the hems. Their linen shirts were often lace cuffed. One governor, the Marquis de Vaudreuil, had twenty-two such shirts in his wardrobe, along with twenty-three flowing silk ties and fifty-four pair of embroidered socks. No wonder the Indians blinked at first. Everything worn in Québec's official circle was imported from France. People were known to stint on food in order to afford luxurious wardrobes. Style was that important to them. The architecture of their houses was also French in feeling. Spurning the habitants' wood, they built from stone, two stories with dormered windows.[6] The inside walls were plastered and whitewashed. Tables were set with china and silverware shipped from France.

But these aristocrats, as they liked to think of themselves, were residents of Québec's Upper Town. In Lower Town small merchants, laborers and craftsmen lived in a jumble of narrow houses built from the black stone of the riverbanks. These gloomy facades they brightened with bits of garden. Most of them had to scrounge for a living, working on one job, moonlighting on others. Locksmiths also made knives; the weaver was a tailor and a milliner; the saw maker doubled as a carpenter. Many worked in the shipyard besides. They had learned their trades in a school run by priests in Upper Town.

The more prosperous merchants lived in Upper Town, hobnobbing with society. So did the clergy and officers of the army. Look in this doorway. A government official and a hooded, black-robed, black-caped priest have just ducked into it. They are dodging muddy water splattered from the cobblestones of the narrow street by a passing captain's mount. The doorway is that of a prosperous supply shop for *coureurs de bois*, runners of the woods, hardbitten, devil-may-care men who make their living by canoeing and camping in the wilderness for months on end, collecting furs.

The door opens, a coureur, his equipment order for the next trip placed, comes out. He wears calfskin moccasins and goatskin leggings, which he has himself embroidered with mottoes and pictures to suit his whims. His cuffed breeches are made of coarse linen; he can turn the cuffs down and fit them into the leggings to protect his legs from the fierce mosquitoes of woods and swamps. His linen shirt is bright red or orange; the highly visible hue is his protection against bullets from other hunters' guns. Slung over one shoulder is his fringed caribou jacket. The visor of his cap is turned up in front. He is puffing on a long, slender clay pipe.

All three men in the doorway are on their way to the harbor; the priest to bless, the government official to welcome and the coureur to look over a shipment of *Filles du Roi,* daughters of the king. This name has been given to marriageable young women, some one thousand of them, being sent to New France over a ten-year period by Jean Baptiste Colbert, King Louis XIV's finance minister and minister of naval affairs. Their arrival has been much heralded. Priests have been announcing it from pulpits for weeks. Bachelors from way-out settlements have converged on Québec, hoping to find a mate among these fifteen- to twenty-five-year-old orphans chosen to meet Colbert's rigid standards: they must be "industrious and religious." Shipments of girls and young women to the colony are not uncommon, but the Filles du Roi are considered superior to all others.

At the Château Saint Louis they will be presented to the governor and his court. Then they will be sent to live with families, or in convents or hospitals in Québec, Trois Rivières, Montréal and outlying settlements. When asked to marry, they will sign marriage contracts. On their wedding day they will receive a dowry from the king, another from the local government, plus repayment of their overseas passage. Some time is allowed to pass between the contract signing and the wedding. In that period either partner can decide to annul the contract. The arrangement suits the colony and the girls. As they come off the ship's gangplank, they are greeted with cheers.

The sponsor of this venture, Jean Colbert, took a keen interest in New France as a bastion against the English, always provided that the bastion didn't burden the king's treasury, with which he was extremely thrifty. The families started as a result of his first two shipments, each of one hundred Filles du Roi, more than doubled the population. Colbert reasoned that an increase in workers would help the colony become more self-sufficient, less dependent on aid from home.

Another event that drew crowds was also Colbert's doing: the annual Montréal Fur Fair. The fair came into being when Colbert persuaded the king to forbid coureurs from trading for furs with Indians outside the colony. Instead, he said, the Indians should bring their furs in. A number of reasons prompted the edict. The main one was that settlements and forts tended to spring up along trails blazed by the coureurs.

Colbert didn't want the borders of New France expanded to a point that would require expanded military aid. He also felt that the considerable sums needed to equip trading expeditions would be better spent on improving the farms. Let the Indians do the traveling.

Montréal, rather than Québec, the capital, was chosen as the site of the fair because it was the business center of French North America. The Montréalais of those days had a saying: *"Pendant que Québec administre, et que Trois Rivières somnole, Montréal s'affaire,"* meaning that while Québec governed and Trois Rivières drowsed, Montréal made money. It was a town of hustlers. Shopkeepers didn't wait for customers to come to them; they went to the customers. Daily, the wooden steel-rimmed wheels of vendors' horse-drawn carts clattered and clanged over the cobblestones, a vibrant accompaniment for the singsongs in which each merchant cried his wares. The most seductive cries drew housewives from their gossip on the benches on either side of their front doors. They stepped down to the wooden sidewalks to inspect the offerings.

Coureurs, too, often found better deals on provisioning in Montréal than in Québec, though they habitually had their canoes made in Trois Rivières. The artisans of that sleepy town had at least one corner on the market: they built the finest birch bark canoes a man could buy. When coureurs paddled these to Montréal, stocked them and were ready to depart, the Montréalais gathered in the taverns to wish them well. Candles burned late. A similar celebration hailed their return.

But hails and farewells to coureurs were as nothing compared to the goings-on at the Fur Fair. The grounds were on an islet separated from the town by a meandering offshoot of the Saint Lawrence, spanned by a bridge. Would-be traders obtained licenses to set up booths where they displayed beads, knives, hatchets, blankets, pewter pots, muskets and other goods desired by the Indians. The Indians, some four or five hundred strong, circled from booth to booth with furs. Both French and Indians sought to strike the best bargains.

Before the bargaining began, the Indians had been feasted as guests of the governor of Montréal in the courtyard of the Montréal hospital. The nuns who ran the hospital prepared a favorite Indian dish: cats and dogs. The animals were simmered in huge iron cauldrons for half a day. Then corn, grapes, raisins and seasoning were added and the mixture boiled for another two hours. When it was done, the chieftains were served by the nuns. The other Indians helped themselves, filling wooden bowls which had been set out for them. When all had finished, they belched in chorus to show their appreciation. Then to the islet for the business at hand.

Between the stalls of merchants and the crowd of Indians, the armchair of Montréal's governor was set up. Several tribal chiefs advanced to him, offering peace pipes. Indian pipes, known as calumets, were of two types, peaceful and warlike. Both were made of polished red stone and hung with feathers. On war pipes the feathers were red. While pipes were being puffed at the fair, another chief stepped forward to deliver a long speech. In concluding, he made the governor a gift of some precious pelts. After that, the haggling began. It continued for two or three days.

Nighttimes, the Indians frequented Montréal's taverns. They had never tasted liquor until white men introduced them to it, and few of them had learned to drink moderately. They often became raving drunk and started fighting with each other. While they were quarreling, French merchants were not above stealing back the goods they had traded during the day for furs. Every year, the cheated Indians, feeling none too hale and hearty after their carousing, swore they would never return. But every year they did, until a godson of Louis XIV, Louis de Buade, Count de Frontenac, made such a farce of the fair that Colbert had to have it discontinued.

Actually, the fairs were beginning to die a natural death before Colbert put a stop to them. The Indians resented the extortions practiced and they were also preoccupied with planning defenses against threats of war from the Iroquois. The number attending was shrinking. The year the fair was cancelled, the Indians had heard false rumors of smallpox in Montréal and might well not have showed up had the fair been held. Certainly they were not put off when the end came.

To the Mississippi

I t was autumn, 1672. Patches of crimson-leaved maples,
white trunks of birch, slender as arrows, broke the somber
green cloak of pines along the shores of the Saint Lawrence.
Past Cartier's Anticosti and Île d'Orleans, Louis de Buade,
Count de Frontenac, a man of small income and large ambitions, sailed up river for the first time to Champlain's Québec.
At Lower Town his ship sidled to dock. The journey had
been hard. For weeks contrary winds had kept the vessel close
to the coast of France, "like an involuntary coast guard," as
Frontenac, the newly arriving governor, described the delay.

The disembarking governor, with a crippled right arm—
the result of a battle wound—looked bedraggled. The drear
shambles of Lower Town didn't lift his spirits, as he saw to
the unloading of his eighteen bales of baggage. Still, he had

obtained a great deal by coming here. He was deeply in debt in France. Despairing of being repaid, his creditors had been about to seize all he owned, though that wasn't much. With his new appointment, they had been told by the king's Council of State to wait awhile—giving him a chance to recoup his finances in New France.

The curious Québecois who gathered at the dock when word spread of their new governor's arrival saw a tall, big-framed man of fifty-two. Despite the wear and tear of travel and the limp right arm, the man's vigor was apparent as he descended the gangplank, issuing orders concerning his luggage.

The stride with which he broke through the crowd was arrogant, but there was charisma in his manner, too, as he doffed his plumed hat, waving it with his left hand in response to his subjects' cry of *"Bienvenu,"* welcome. His thick, gray hair, his own, in a day when wigs were customary, curled on his shoulders. His smile, between close-clipped mustache and trim, pointed beard, was quick, but his eyes, under bushy brows, sized up the scene, even as he smiled.

What would be the chances of making money here? Eventually those postponed debts would have to be met. Besides he had a wife, Anne, to support at the court of France. She was a rich man's daughter, but her father had cut off her inheritance when she married Frontenac, of whom he disapproved. It would be necessary to send most of his salary as governor to Anne. Other income he would have to earn by moonlighting. In the fur trade, hopefully. He was, therefore, more than a little aggravated to find that Montréal and François Marie Perrot, who had governed that town for thirty-two years, had the lucrative fur trade well sewed up.

He set out to change that arrangement. Not only did he take over the Montréal Fur Fair, but within a year after his arrival he had substantially short-circuited Montréal's trade with Indians in the region of the Great Lakes. This he did by building a fort at Cataraqui on the northwest shore of Lake

Ontario, where the Canadian city of Kingston now stands; the fort doubled as a trading post. From this fort, traders willing to split their take with the governor had direct and easy access to Indian trappers. They got the furs before the Montréalais could reach the Indians or vice-versa.

The way Frontenac financed the building of the fort was deft. He knew there was no use seeking help from home: Colbert would have none of it. But there was an institution in New France called the *corvée,* a draft of habitants to work on public projects. Corvées were usually soon over; they might last a couple of weeks at most. Frontenac called a summer-long corvée to build his fort. His labor was free. To cover the cost of materials, he leased the fort on a short-term basis to a pair of fur trade rivals, Montréal merchants by the name of Le Ber and Bazire. While leasing to them, he also offered the outpost as a gift to the king, sending to court a man he counted on to get the gift rented back to him as a concession.

He could well count on his messenger, Robert Cavelier, sieur de La Salle, for he had been in charge of the building of the fort and was allowed to deliver goods to Seneca Indian villages and receive furs in return. The Senecas had previously been trading with the English in Albany, which meant they had to canoe and portage more than two hundred miles. They were glad to get out of the arduous journey.

The cut-off of the English was a compelling argument for Cataraqui. In New France, however, François Marie Perrot quite naturally objected to this interference with Montréal's access to fur. When Frontenac brushed this objection aside, Perrot held up a shipment of supplies being sent from Québec to Fort Frontenac, as the new outpost was called. Whereupon Frontenac threw him into the dungeon of the Château Saint Louis for "defying the governor of Québec, thereby defying the king, the governor of Québec being His Majesty's representative in New France."

On Easter Sunday, 1674, a staunch friend of Perrot's, the Abbé Fénelon, mounted the pulpit in Québec to preach a sermon that, while not mentioning the governor by name, was an obvious attack on him. La Salle was present. He rose from his pew to object. His protest, though loud, made only a small ripple in the congregation. In most of the pews people were asleep.

After the Abbé's attack on Frontenac, La Salle hastened to the Château Saint Louis, where he quoted Fénelon to Frontenac. Frontenac asked Fénelon for a copy of the sermon. Fénelon refused to deliver it. Frontenac then ordered him to appear before the Sovereign Council, to be tried on charges of sedition, the penalty for which was death. Fénelon showed up at the trial, but refused to answer the questions, maintaining that the Council had no jurisdiction over him. He would submit to their questioning only if so ordered by his bishop, who was then in France.

Meanwhile, the Sovereign Council, which combined the functions of a high court and a legislature, was also trying Perrot. Fénelon continued to agitate for Perrot's freedom, and the Montréalais got up a petition in his support. Perrot hired an extremely able lawyer who convinced the Council that they lacked authority to convict his client. He was sent to France for the judgment of the king. There, on Colbert's advice, he was reinstated as governor of Montréal, but told to apologize publicly to the governor of Québec. Feeling the unmistakable direction in which the wind of official favor blew, Perrot subsequently went into the fur business as a partner with Frontenac.

Fénelon, who had also gone to France, was forbidden to return to Canada. Frontenac was warned that he mustn't interfere with the affairs of districts outside Québec without first giving notice to the presiding official.

The whole rumpus was the product not only of Frontenac's temper and highhandedness, but of the unwieldy structure of the colony's government. Though the governor of Québec, as the king's representative, was supposedly the top official, the governor of Montréal, the governor of Trois Rivières and the intendant, a sort of watchdog appointed by the king, all had independent powers. So did the Sovereign Council. Disagreements among them, which were frequent, were referred to France. The Saint Lawrence being navigable only in summer, a year could elapse before a decision came back to the colony. Meanwhile each disputant went his own way, lining up his own supporters. For ambitious colonists, choosing sides could be a matter of great importance. Their careers, indeed their livelihood, could depend on it. La Salle chose to line up with Frontenac.

La Salle was interested in Cataraqui not merely as a base for fur trade. He needed that—but only to finance his real interest—exploration. He saw this fort as the first in a series that would stretch southward. He had given up a hope he had long held of finding a Northwest Passage to the China Sea. In fact he had sarcastically given to the rapids at Montréal the name they still bear, Lachine—China—his epitaph for a dream. What he hoped to find instead was a passage to the south, one that would remain open for shipping year round. He knew of Colbert's concern in this area. "The worst thing about Canada," Colbert had written, "is the entrance to the river, which, being so far north, allows ships to enter only a few months of the year."

La Salle had not easily given up the lure of the northwest myth, however. During the winter of 1668 he had sheltered some Seneca Indians at the seigneurie he then owned. They told him of a large river they called the Ohio, meaning beautiful water. They claimed it flowed from the rising to the setting sun, emptying into a distant sea. Ottawa Indians also boasted to him of another great river, which they called Missi-sepe, meaning big water. Might one of the two lead to the China Sea? La Salle decided to sell his seigneurie and use the proceeds for equipping an expedition that would find out.

The expedition of fourteen men in eight canoes left the seigneurie on July 6, 1669. La Salle had previously received permission from the governor and the intendant for the trip. He had been authorized to explore "the woods, rivers and lakes of North America," and permitted to select his traveling companions from among French soldiers quartered in Québec. He was to be accompanied by Father Dollier de Casson, a Sulpician priest who had recently wintered among the Indians between Lakes Huron and Ontario.

The Sulpician father added three more canoes to La Salle's eight, seven more men and one portable chapel. In La Salle's lead canoe were the Senecas who had spent the winter with him.

The trip was rough. The party had to portage around many rapids. They ate mostly boiled corn, since La Salle was not willing to waste time hunting en route. Before they reached Lake Ontario, almost half the men were sick. De Casson wanted to make for a Sulpician mission on the Lake shores, where they could recuperate. La Salle refused. He said de Casson and his men might rest at the mission if they pleased. He and his men would continue. De Casson went along.

The group paddled parallel to the south shore of the lake as far as the Oswego River. Leaving de Casson there with a few men, La Salle and the others hiked upstream to a Seneca village. There they asked to borrow guides who could lead them to the Ohio River. Their request was refused. Moreover, the Senecas threatened that dire perils would beset La Salle if he sought the Ohio. Later he tried to buy a prisoner the Senecas had captured from another tribe, but this attempt also failed. Eventually he found a Seneca out hunting and fishing who agreed to guide the party, but whose knowledge of the region was decidedly sketchy.

A route to the Ohio River flows out of Lake Ontario, but La Salle's party missed it. Instead they paddled straight across the lake to the Niagara River, within earshot of the roar of Niagara Falls. Between Lake Ontario and Lake Erie they met Louis Jolliet in Tenaouata, a small Indian village. Jolliet had La Salle's itch to make known the unknown. When the two met, he was returning from an unsuccessful search for copper around Lake Superior. He informed the Sulpicians with La Salle that the tribes on the south shore of that lake had never been reached by missionaries. The Sulpicians were gleeful. Here was an area where they could be first. Jolliet laid out the route to the Lake Superior tribes. It led north. La Salle wanted to travel south. So the two sections of the expedition parted company, with de Casson carrying his portable chapel toward Lake Huron. The little group was overtaken by a violent storm in which the chapel was destroyed. The priests, fearful of venturing among strange tribes without its protection, returned to Montréal.

Some of La Salle's men who had been frightened by the Seneca warnings deserted. They reached Montréal in November and were greeted with jeers—not for having deserted their leader, but for having forsaken the Sulpicians. La Salle pushed south until he encountered, at last, the Ohio River. He followed it to the junction with the Mississippi. Eighty-four years later, in 1755, the French claimed the Ohio valley on the basis of this trip. But when La Salle returned to Montréal in the summer of 1671, he received a cool welcome. People were saying that he had accomplished nothing, since he hadn't found a route to the China Sea.

What he had found was more valuable: the sure conviction within himself that no such route existed. He based his belief on his observations of the way land sloped and the rivers flowed, and on much lore given him by Indians. The Mississippi, he was certain, flowed south. Even in the face of criticism, however, he kept his certainty to himself, probably because he didn't want to tip his hand to other explorers, like Jolliet.

He stayed in Montréal only long enough to reprovision for another trip, from which he returned shortly before Christmas. He was off again in the spring of 1672 and didn't return until October of 1673. At some time between the summer of 1671 and the winter of 1672, he reached the Mississippi by way of the Illinois River. He named the Mississippi the Colbert—in honor of the man whose patronage he needed and whose interest in a year-round waterway he knew.

Unfortunately, La Salle seems to have kept no personal record of the Illinois voyage. An account of it is contained in the writings of one Abbé Renaudot, to whom La Salle gave a verbal description in France during the visit to support Frontenac and to round up support for further exploration. While he was there, Jolliet and a Jesuit priest, Father Jacques Marquette, reached the Mississippi by way of the Wisconsin River and traveled downstream to the Mississippi's junction with the Illinois and beyond. They canoed to within 700 miles of the Gulf of Mexico.

The southernmost section of the river had already been explored by the Spanish, beginning with Hernando De Soto, in the preceding century. Spanish galleons were active in Gulf waters and Marquette and Jolliet had no wish to tangle with them. France and Spain were frequently at war. Therefore the pair did not pursue the river to its mouth. They had gone far enough, however, for the Jesuits to celebrate. When Jolliet returned—he had left Marquette to set up a mission— he was welcomed by the order with the ringing of church bells and the singing of a *Te Deum,* a chant of praise and thanksgiving. Jesuits, they claimed, had discovered the Mississippi!

Not so, said La Salle, nettled. Jolliet and Marquette had located the Colbert, which *he* had discovered and named a year earlier. The truth was that Marquette and Jolliet were the first to enter the Mississippi from the Wisconsin, La Salle the first to enter it from the Illinois. His entrance preceded theirs, but they covered more distance than he. And De Soto had preceded them all.

The Marquette-Jolliet expedition provided, in the notes of Father Marquette, the most detailed and lively information to come from any of the Mississippi's explorers. Father Marquette had been sent by the Jesuits to convert the Indians of New France to Christianity. At the Jesuit school for missionaries in Trois Rivières, he spent two years learning Indian languages. Then he traveled westward to begin his work. So knowledgeable did he become, not only in the languages but in the cultures of different tribes, that another Jesuit priest said of him, "Although he was a Frenchman with the French, he could be a Huron with the Hurons, an Algonquin with the Algonquins, one with any among whom he lived and worked."

Marquette was delighted when Jolliet was ordered by the Jesuits to take him along on a hunt for the Mississippi, for he was eager to encounter new tribes to the south. His long diary of the voyage begins: "I embarked with Monsieur Jolliet, who had been chosen to conduct this enterprise, on the 13th of May, 1673, with five other Frenchmen in two bark canoes. We laid in some Indian corn and smoked beef for our voyage. We first took care, however, to draw from the Indians all we could concerning the countries[7] through which we designed to travel, and drew up a map on which we marked down the rivers, nations and points of the compass to guide us on our journey."

The pair set out with their companions from Marquette's mission on the island of Saint Ignace in Lake Superior, crossed the lake and portaged south to Lake Michigan, skirting that lake's northern shores. At Marquette's urging, they traded with Indians along the way for the remainder of the crop of wild rice harvested the preceding fall. Marquette, who was extremely fond of this dish, gives in one of his letters to Jesuit headquarters in France a step-by-step account of how the Indians gathered and prepared it. He describes them pushing canoes through the swamps in September and shaking the rice down. "Dried over a slow fire," he reports, "it is packed in skin bags and trodden under foot. When winnowed, the rice is either pounded into flour or boiled in water and seasoned with fat."

On Lake Michigan he and Jolliet paused at Green Bay to obtain information and borrow guides. Again they portaged, this time to the Wisconsin River. "We have left behind the waters that flowed toward Québec," Marquette recorded, "and entered those that flowed toward the Mississippi." The current grew stronger, canoeing more difficult. For seven days they paddled, with might and main, until they entered a wind-whipped expanse of waves and sighted the Mississippi.

Along the shore, one of the guides spotted human footprints. They dragged their canoes on land and followed the footprints to an Indian village. The Indians turned out to be friendly Illinois, to the explorers' great relief. The Illinois were equally relieved to find that the white men came as friends. Uncertain until Marquette addressed them in their own tongue, they had made no preparations for the elaborate ceremony that their etiquette called for in the way of welcome. To gain time for such preparations, four old men walked at a snail's pace toward the visitors. Two of them carried handsomely decorated peace calumets, which they waved in the air. More time was consumed in the all-around smoking of these pipes. Then the elders conducted the party to the village.

In front of the first lodge, a naked Indian with arms outstretched gave a short recitation: "How beautiful is the sun when you visit our abode, O strangers from beyond the sea! The village awaits you and beneath our roofs you shall rest in safety and peace." Inside the lodge more pipes were smoked, first by the French, then by assembled braves and squaws. Silence prevailed except for an occasional murmur of "How good it is, our brothers, that you should come to us."

Silence was an Indian mark of respect. After an hour of smoking, the French were conducted, still in silence, to a second cluster of lodges up the hill for a council meeting and a feast. When the council was assembled, Marquette presented the chief with four gifts, making an oration, Indian style, with each.

In the first he said that he and his companions were journeying to visit the nations dwelling by the great river and hoped to follow this river to the sea. In the second he spoke of the God who had made white men and red and willed that all should know and worship Him. In the third he described Frontenac as a great warrior sent from France. In the fourth he asked for all the guidance his hosts could give him about the land and people of the river valley.

The chief replied with a speech overflowing with superlatives, thanking the French for the blessings accompanying their visit: "Never has our corn flourished so greenly . . . our tobacco tasted so sweet . . . our river been so calm as now." His exaggerations spiraled as he warmed to his subject. He even went so far as to declare that the river had never been so clear of rocks, which the French canoes must have brushed away in passing!

He then presented his visitors with the gift of one of his sons, also a calumet, which he said would be immediately recognized as a special token of friendship, not only by Illinois, but by all tribes along the Mississippi banks. After these formalities, on with the feast!

Cheered by this warm reception, the band of explorers continued down river. Soon they passed between walls of rock, eroded into weird shapes. Indians had painted these shapes to resemble fantastic beasts. "They are big as calves," wrote Marquette, "and have antlers like deer. Their faces are rather like the faces of men, with tigerish mouths and red eyes, hideous to behold. Their bodies are covered with scales, and their tails are so long that they pass over their heads and down between their legs, terminating like the tails of fish. The colors used are red, green and black." From later records, we know that traces of the paintings remained on the rocks for another half century.

Not far beyond this display, the Illinois and Missouri Rivers roared into the Mississippi. When Jolliet and Marquette reached these junctions, full summer had arrived. The days steamed with sodden heat. The cooler dusk swarmed with mosquitoes. They lit fires to smoke the insects away, but with small success. Any exposed skin was soon swollen with bites.

They paddled on. Eight days past the river junctions, they were startled by savage yells from the wooded shore. Almost immediately Indians armed with bows, arrows and tomahawks crowded the banks. The paddlers stopped paddling and grabbed guns. Marquette waved the precious calumet that he had been told all Indians on the way would recognize. These seemed not to. A club zinged passed his head. Canoes full of Indians surrounded the seven.

Jolliet told his men not to fire. He was familiar with Indian attacks. They were usually stealthy. Behind the bluster of this one, he detected fear. The Indians were, he believed, only trying to frighten intruders away from their village.

He was right. A small group of elders, their eyes trained on the calumet, paddled a short distance from the bank, laying down their bows as they did so. They made signs for the French to land. On shore, Marquette tried one language after another. The Indians understood none. Finally an old warrior was summoned who spoke Illinois. With him as an interpreter, Marquette was able to make clear the peaceful nature of their mission. Then he produced the customary gifts. He records in his journal that relief replaced wariness in the Indians' eyes. Through their interpreter, one of the elders explained that they were a small tribe of Michigameans. They would be honored if the visitors would sup with them and spend the night in their village.

The next morning ten Michigameans escorted the French to a village of Arkansas Indians. Word must have been sent ahead to expect guests; a reception had been prepared. The party was greeted by a warrior with a calumet and a cake of Indian corn. While they ate the cake, "the warrior sang most agreeably," Marquette commented. Then they were led to the chief's lodge where they found elders, young men, squaws and children sitting in circles on the floor, waiting for them. After Marquette had presented his gifts and explained his mission, the chief warned that the way ahead was perilous. He said the Indians were well armed and hostile to white men.

His own village, alas, was surrounded by tribes who would not permit his people to trade with white men on pain of death.

As a result, he apologized, his people were poor. He had no need to say so. Their poverty was apparent. The feast consisted only of dog and sagamité. As soon as their guests had been served, the Indians scrambled for the food in such haste that Marquette believed that even this meager fare must be an improvement over their daily menu. Their clothing and housing were primitive. The women had no ornaments; their garments, made of hide, were tattered. The men wore only loincloths. The lodges were built of bark, raised slightly from the swampy earth.

When their chief added to Marquette's and Jolliet's concern about hostile Spaniards the further threat of hostile Indians, the two decided it would be more prudent to return than to continue. They had proved that the Mississippi flowed south; they had made valuable charts and maps. Were they to be captured, either by Spaniards or by Indians, this information would be lost to the French government. They pointed the prows of their canoes to the north.

They regained Green Bay in late fall and spent the winter at a mission there, organizing their maps and reports. In early spring, Jolliet started for Montréal with three boatmen and the little boy who had been presented to the explorers by the Illinois chief. All went well until they reached the Lachine Rapids. The snows that winter had been deep; the Saint Lawrence ran high with their melting. Moreover, in July, as Jolliet paddled toward Lachine, strong winds rose. Despite winds and torrents he reached the center of the rapids. There a swift and sudden gust spun the canoe like a merry-go-round, then capsized it.

The Indian child and two of the boatmen drowned. Jolliet and the third boatman managed to scramble onto a rock from which some fishermen were finally able to rescue them. Jolliet's reports and maps were lost in the current. He wrote to Frontenac: "I had escaped every danger. I had suffered no harm from Indians. I had passed many rapids. I was nearing home, full of joy at the success of a long and difficult voyage. I lost . . . men and my box of papers when I was in sight of Montréal, which I had left two years before. Nothing remains to me but my life and the ardent desire to employ it in any service you may please to direct."

To Monseigneur Laval, Bishop of Québec, he wrote a different kind of note. It was a lament for the death of the little Indian, for whom Jolliet had seen great possibilities in life: "He was ten years old, quick-witted, diligent, and endowed with an excellent disposition. He had learned to speak French and was beginning to read and write that language."

Fortunately Marquette's journal, even though a far less explicit geographical guide than Jolliet's, remained. And Jolliet was able to recall much of what he had written and mapped. In the long run the accident didn't harm his career. The lack of detailed documents did prevent him from getting a fur trade monopoly with which he had hoped to finance fort building and more Mississippi exploration. But as he went on to distinguish himself in other ways in the service of New France, he reaped well-deserved rewards. Marquette was ordered by the Jesuits to establish a new mission at the junction of the Des Plaines and Illinois Rivers, which he set out to do in the autumn of 1674.

While missionaries like Marquette, explorers like Jolliet and companies of fur-fortune hunters were opening up northwest America, New France's Governor Frontenac held his strong left hand on the colony's helm in Québec. Too strong for the liking of other officials in the colonial capital. The governor fought with his intendant; he fought with the Sovereign Council; he fought with the Church. Decision on the winner in such tussles came from France where no one quite understood the needs and problems of New France. Off and on the verdicts favored Frontenac. Often, they did not.

Brandy caused one of the bitterest disputes between Frontenac and the Jesuits. To the courtier, brandy was to be inhaled, savored, sipped, after a repast. To the colonists, it was the currency that bought the best beaver from the Indians and the most economical coin for the purchasing of quantities of other furs.

The best beaver was considered to be a pelt that an Indian had worn until the hide was greasy from contact with his flesh. The suppleness of this greasy beaver commanded high prices from Europe. Just one jug of brandy could buy as much as fifty of these pelts. It could also buy one hundred pounds of dry (unworn) beaver, or other furs. By contrast, a blanket, another staple trade item, could be exchanged for only four pounds of fur. With a few jugs of brandy a coureur could strike a better bargain than with whole canoeloads of other merchandise. And the lighter load meant fewer canoes for transport, fewer paddlers to hire, fewer livres to invest.

The root of the bargain, for the coureur, was the Indian craving for the "firewater" to which the white man had introduced him. The coureurs did all they could to encourage this craving. Indeed they might be compared to today's dope peddlers. And like today's dope addicts, the Indians were of two minds about the stuff. They wanted it, but feared the effects. A jug or two sent them on wild binges, then into collapse. Knocked out, they were unable to hunt or fish or tend their corn. Their families came near starving. They also lost their ability to calculate. An unscrupulous trader could do a drunken Indian out of a whole winter's catch of furs. Knowing this, Indians sometimes begged officials for protection against their own weakness. One Ottawa chief, returning with his tribe from Montréal, asked the governor for escorts to prevent anyone along the way from beguiling them with brandy. His request was not uncommon.

These pleas were taken to heart by the Jesuits. They and the coureurs lined up on opposite sides of the liquor issue. Jesuit bishop François de Montmorency de Laval led the battle against brandy. Frontenac led the coureurs' fight to continue the trade.

The bishop won the first round in the brandy battle with an edict from the king forbidding anyone from carrying it to an Indian village, also forbidding French settlements to sell visiting Indians enough to make them drunk.

Frontenac won the last round by simply not enforcing the edict. He counted on the profits the trade brought to vineyard owners in France to keep Colbert from insisting on enforcement or calling the lack of it to royal attention. The trade remained illegal—and continued to flourish.

In his battles with the Jesuits, Frontenac often had the support of Colbert, who had no love for clergy. An economist, he complained that although they owned one quarter of France's material resources, they contributed nothing to them. He also thought little of their doctrine of celibacy for the priesthood, saying: "They not only shirk the labor that would aid the common good, but also deprive the public of all the children whom they could produce to serve useful and necessary functions." The latter comment applied especially to Canada, where Colbert was anxious to increase the population. To Frontenac he wrote: "If they wish to carry ecclesiastical authority further than it should extend . . . it is necessary to give them gently to understand the line of conduct which they must observe, and if they do not mend their ways, adroitly to oppose their schemes . . . without any rupture, and to advise His Majesty of all that occurs that he may impose the proper remedies."

Frontenac was not above applying this mandate to the pettiest details; for example, his right to enter the church before the clergy on high holy days. His interpretation was upheld in France, but when Frontenac stretched it to include every Sunday, Colbert balked.

Of greater importance to the king's minister was the occasion when Laval attempted to hold services in the king's warehouse in Québec's Lower Town. Laval's idea was to save people from climbing the hill to the church in Upper Town, especially in bad weather. He sent a priest down to conduct mass, who, on orders from Frontenac, was barred from the building by soldiers. Laval's protests to Colbert and His Majesty received no reply. Not even a bishop of the Church, and from Colbert's point of view, especially not a bishop of the Church, could take over royal property without authorization.

As the Frontenac-Laval feud heated up, the governor did all he could to hinder Jesuit missionary work. He claimed that their missions in Indian villages were fur trading posts in disguise and insisted that priests must apply for passports in order to travel to them. Most likely the Jesuits were not directly engaged in the fur trade, but inadvertently their work forwarded it. The coureurs were quick to take advantage of the friendly relations between Indians and Jesuits and often established their trading posts near Jesuit missions. During the war with the Iroquois that struck New France in the late 1680's, Jesuit missionary work paid off for the whole colony. The mission villages remained friendly to the French.

Frontenac's efforts to block the Sovereign Council and intendants received less support from home than his bridling of the Church. At one point during the absence of the intendant, who presided as chairman of the Council, and of its powerful member, Laval, Frontenac simply took over the Council's court functions and tried cases himself. "Without proceedings, without records and without experience, I can settle in one day more cases that the Council can try in a month," he boasted. His boast was probably true. But it flew in the face of the system of colonial government that the king had ordained. To defy Frontenac was to defy the king, but for Frontenac to defy the king's institutions was also a defiance of royal authority. To check him, the king gave more power to the office of intendant. The man appointed to fill it at this time was Jacques Duchesneau, the previous holder of the office.

Frontenac was furious. Attempting to elevate his own position above that of Duchesneau, he claimed that as governor he was also president of the Council. The colony's attorney general questioned the view. Whereupon Frontenac booted him to France, telling him to explain to the king by what right he had questioned the authority of the king's representative. Two Council members who had supported the attorney general were packed off with him. Finally Frontenac dissolved the Council, refusing to reconvene it until members were willing to recognize him as their superior officer.

These actions brought a series of warnings from the king and from Colbert. The self-created title of council president was taken away. "I admonish you," the king wrote to Frontenac, "to strip yourself of all the personal animosities which up to now have been almost the sole incentive of all your actions . . . nothing being more inconsistent with the duty which you have to discharge for me in the position that you hold." And again the king warned: "Monsieur le Compte de Frontenac, I was astounded to learn of all the new disputes and new divisions that have occurred in my province of New France. . . . My edicts, decrees and proclamations have made my wishes so clear that I have all the more reason to be astonished that you, of all persons . . . have advanced claims that are completely contrary to them." Colbert informed Frontenac bluntly that unless he changed within a year, the king would remove him from his post.

Frontenac's wife, who was well connected at court, commenced a campaign to save him. But she campaigned against tremendous odds, not the least of which was her husband's stubborn pride. Jesuit clergy, seeing their chance to get rid of the man who was obstructing their progress in North America, plotted ways to add to the damage that Frontenac was already doing to himself. Influential nobles at court began receiving letters from men eager to take Frontenac's place.

The king played his hand evenly, however. The indignant Duchesneau was also warned. No matter how justified his indignation, he was told, he would have to change his way of expressing it or also face removal. An intendant, in a dispute with the governor, was permitted only to lodge a protest with the governor, sending a copy to the king, meanwhile submitting to the governor's orders. The governor, as long as he was governor, was the king's man.

During the early part of this ruckus, La Salle was in France. He had gone there to seek royal permission to search for the mouth of the Mississippi and to build forts en route, all at his own expense. The project had Frontenac's backing. The governor's survival was important to La Salle—the two shared a fur monopoly around Cataraqui—and the explorer did his utmost to defend Frontenac while pleading his own suit.

Well armed with maps, and having made a reputation for himself in the management of Cataraqui, he was in a position to be an impressive pleader. With the king's permission, he had made land grants to Recollets in the neighborhood of the fort. He had also made grants to a few colonists. As a result, an Iroquois and a French village grew up. The Recollets taught the Iroquois to read and write French; the Iroquois taught the French to breed cattle. A school and a church served both villages. Traders used the outpost as a take-off point and stored their trading goods there. Fort Frontenac hummed with profitable activity.

Furthermore, La Salle had created this wilderness community against considerable odds. The Jesuits had been determined to prevent its success. There were a number of reasons for their opposition. They were irritated by his grants to the Recollets. Most important of all, they wanted to delay the westward push of New France until they had sufficient strength to control the missionary aspects of it. Marquette was one of their own, a means to this end. La Salle was too independent for them. He would work with anyone who could help him find the next river leading to the next river. Their plan of attack on La Salle had been carefully thought out.

Their missionaries told Iroquois to the north of the fort that it was to be used as a base to attack them. They told La Salle, Iroquois were planning to attack *him*. Naturally, he tightened his defenses. Then the missionaries said to the Iroquois: "See, here is proof he is planning to make war on you."

When these tactics produced no immediate results, they planted an ally inside the fort as an employee. The employee made off with all the fort's canoes, one tied to another and loaded with as much ammunition and trading goods as he could pile into them. La Salle's men eventually found him, hiding on a plank suspended under a bed in the house of the missionary who had recommended him for employment. The stolen goods were retrieved, but when La Salle complained to Bishop Laval, there was no response.

The Jesuits even tried to involve La Salle in a sex scandal. A certain Madame Bazire, the alluring wife of one of the Montréal fur traders to whom Frontenac had briefly leased Cataraqui, was an ardent Jesuit supporter. She agreed to try to get La Salle into bed while her husband waited in a closet. No use. When she made her first pass, La Salle bolted from the room and her house.

Having survived these plots, the explorer had still one more to cope with before he could present his requests in Paris. The Jesuits sent a special envoy to Paris with a twofold assignment. He was to rouse support for Colbert's opposition to westward expansion, and he was to spread the tale that La Salle was a madman who ought to be confined. He did his work so well that Colbert refused to see La Salle.

Only by bribing His Majesty's director of commerce to the tune of 16,000 livres (close to $10,000) did La Salle finally gain access to Colbert. Then he was able to tell his side of the story. Colbert took him to the king.

The results were more than La Salle had hoped for. He was given permission to construct his chain of forts. He was ordered, not just permitted, to explore "the great and mysterious river of the west down to the sea, where . . . there would be a harbor for His Majesty's vessels." He was to have seigneurial rights over whatever lands he might discover and colonize and was to become governor of them. His expeditions were, of course, to be without expense to His Majesty's treasury (one overhears Colbert's whispered reminder in His

Majesty's ear at this point), but he was to receive a fur monopoly as a means of finance. The monopoly was to extend to all the lands he explored.

On July 14, 1678, a jubilant La Salle sailed from La Rochelle for Québec. His ship was loaded with materials he would need for a Mississippi voyage, from beads for Indians to canvas and rigging for the ship he intended to build. He had thirty men on board; skilled workmen who would build his forts and his boat, priests, would-be explorers, the ship's crew. The vessel cleared the sheltered harbor where fishermen's skiffs rocked gently at anchor and headed for the open Atlantic. The crossing was easy. By mid-September La Salle was in Québec.

He was delayed there, purchasing more materials and supporting Frontenac in some of his battles. It was almost Christmas before he managed to reach Cataraqui. He settled in impatiently. Snow drifted as high as the fort's palisade. Ice locked the lake. Spring, opening the way to the "harbor for His Majesty's vessels," was in the future.

To the Gulf
of Mexico

The ice had barely melted when La Salle set out to begin the series of forts that would serve as bases for exploring and trading posts for fur. The first sites he chose lay on the Saint Joseph River, close to Lake Michigan, and on the Niagara River. On the way to the Saint Joseph, he paused between Lakes Ontario and Erie to leave on the Niagara three trusted companions. They were Father Louis Hennepin, a small, wiry Recollet priest with a slakeless thirst for finding new rivers, Lamotte de Lussière, a skilled builder, and Henri de Tonti. Tonti was known as *Main de Fer,* or sometimes *Gant de Fer*—Hand or Glove of Iron—because he had an artificial iron hand.

Tonti and de Lussière were in charge of a crew of men La Salle left with them. The crew was to build another fort, to be named Niagara, and the boat with which La Salle intended to navigate the Great Lakes. Hennepin had instructions to make friends with the Iroquois in the area. La Salle proceeded to the Saint Joseph. By November the fort built there, which he called Miami, was habitable. Returning to Niagara he found that Tonti and de Lussière had made similar progress.

However, distressing news also awaited him. A canoe loaded with provisions for the fort builders had foundered on the southern shore of Lake Ontario. He hastened to the spot to see what could be salvaged. Very little was left. Fresh supplies would have to come from Fort Frontenac. There was no hope of canoeing there, for Lake Ontario was already beginning to freeze. Only one way to reach the fort remained: on foot. With two men and a dog La Salle walked the 250-mile stretch, much of it over ice.

Again he had to fume through winter. In early spring of 1679 he was back at Niagara. Tonti, Hennepin, de Lussière and their crew had used their wits to survive. They shot game along the river banks and strung guy ropes on which they hung the meat to freeze. In early fall they had gathered wild grapes, letting them ferment in birch-bark buckets. Father Hennepin contributed altar towels for strainers, and they pressed the fermented grapes through these. The strained liquid was stored in gourds, a wilderness wine.

Before La Salle's arrival, work had already commenced on the ship. In May she was blessed by Hennepin and, with the last of the wilderness wine purpling her bow, was christened the Griffon, after a breed of hunting dog. Frontenac's coat of arms contained a griffon, which prompted La Salle's choice of the name. A somewhat grotesque image of the dog served as the Griffon's figurehead. With La Salle himself at the wheel, the vessel sailed into Lake Erie, her square, wind-billowed sails the first to be seen on the Great Lakes. Her hull had been hewed from deep forest, the planed planks seamed with fir fibers and pitch. Her sturdy masts were fir trunks. She was broad of beam and staunch of keel.

Crude, perhaps. But when, on August 27, 1679, she anchored off Michillimackinac, at the entrance to Lake Michigan, she seemed a vision to the crowd of Indians, sunburned coureurs and black-robed Jesuits who gathered to gape at her from the shore. A fleet of twenty Indian canoes came out to meet the "floating fort" as the Indians called her, or as some said, the "great canoe." La Salle fired a cannon salute in return for their welcome.

Michillimackinac was a Jesuit mission serving Ottawa and Huron villages. Waiting there were a number of men La Salle had previously dispatched as scouts to the Illinois valley. They had come this far and quit. Their excuse was that they heard it would be too dangerous to continue. Six others had deserted, taking with them several thousand livres worth of furs. La Salle wrote off the loss and went on to Fort Miami.

At Miami he found greater encouragement. The loyal band holding down the fort had assembled a great stock of fur. He had it loaded onto the *Griffon* and sent the ship back to fur storage warehouses on the upper Niagara River. The quantity and quality of fur would easily pay off the debts he had incurred in equipping his expedition.

He himself, with fourteen men in four canoes, paddled south on Lake Michigan through rain alternating with early wet snow. The winds mounted. At the foot of the lake the canoes ran into a gale so violent that the party was forced on shore. Fresh moccasin prints indicated that Indians lived nearby. La Salle posted a sentinel and told everyone to be very quiet. The wind howled, the rain slashed. So loud was the tempest that the sentinel failed to hear Indians removing supplies from the beached canoes until all but one of them had left.

The one Indian was seized as a hostage for the return of the stolen goods. The next day a great number of his tribe swarmed toward La Salle's camp in search of their brother. Taking only five of his fourteen men, La Salle climbed a height where he could be prominently seen, and stood waiting their advance calmly, gun in hand. The amazed Indians admired his cool. The hostage and the stolen goods were exchanged without further ado.

The party continued south on the Saint Joseph River, pausing when necessary to hunt for food. Chasing a stag one late afternoon, La Salle lost track of the way back to the riverside to camp. The sun sank; dusk increased the difficulty of finding the river. He detoured a marsh and reached the shore, but the spot wasn't where the camp was. Surely the site must be nearby. He fired shots, seeking an answer from his companions. No reply. Then he saw a fire on a nearby height. Thinking it to be the camp, he hurried there, only to discover a lonely Indian sentinel who fled at his approach. He spent the night on the Indian's grass mat. Looking about at dawn, he found his mat circled and recircled by moccasin prints. Curious Indians had prowled around him through the night. Later in the morning he met Hennepin who was out hunting for him.

The adventure had not been without profit. La Salle suspected, and rightly so, that the marsh he had skirted bordered the Kankakee River, which he knew to be a tributary of the Illinois. He decided to follow the Kankakee. Despite more marshes, thick with rush and alder that hampered the canoes, the route proved to be a short cut.

The weather, though cold, was not as inhibiting as the Canadian wintertime. The party canoed on through December. On New Year's Day of 1680, they reached the headquarters of the Illinois Indians, located about where the city of Peoria is now. There was the usual feast and powwow. La Salle obtained the Indians' agreement to let him build a fort there, also a boat for Mississippi navigation.

The goodwill was short lived. A Jesuit priest ministering to a nearby Miami village sent an Indian emissary, well loaded with presents, to persuade the Illinois that La Salle was their enemy. His real purpose, suggested the emissary, was to form alliances with Mississippi nations hostile to the Illinois.

Abruptly, the Illinois presented to La Salle a threatening picture of perils on the Mississippi. Six of his party, terrified by the Illinois talk, deserted, carrying with them a large share of provisions. "Anyone else who wants to leave," said La Salle, "leave." No one did. But someone tried to poison his soup.

The six men who deserted were sawyers. Their loss slowed down the building of both fort and boat. La Salle himself took saw in hand, coping as best he could with this new delay. How he felt about it can be judged from the name he gave the completed fort: Crèvecoeur—Broken Heart.

Meanwhile he had received no word of the *Griffon*. Where *was* that ship, loaded with the furs, which were almost his sole source of finance? Not only that—she was also needed to fetch supplies and bring them to Fort Miami, from which point they could be canoed south. When March came and there was still no news, La Salle could stand the suspense no longer. He decided to go back north and see what he could find out.

He left Tonti in charge of the Illinois camp and sent Father Hennepin, accompanied by two other men, to explore the upper Mississippi while he was away. Hennepin was overjoyed. This expedition, though small, was the first he had ever commanded. La Salle headed up the Illinois, taking four men with him.

It was dead winter still, but the river was not entirely frozen. By wading waist-deep in the bone-numbing water, the five men could shove their canoes through the ice floes. Where a stretch of ice had firmed, they skittered the canoes across it. By night they slept, blanket-wrapped, on layers of twigs, hoping that their wet clothes, draped over branches, would dry without freezing. If the clothes froze, they thawed them over fires and donned them wet.

Finally the river ice turned solid all the way. They abandoned the canoes and took to foot, plodding across the prairies, knee-deep in the slushy snow. On March 24 they arrived at Fort Miami, exhausted.

No news of the *Griffon* was to be found there. They went on toward Fort Niagara, clearing their way through forest where thorns and brambles grew so thickly that their clothing was tattered and their flesh was torn. "Our faces were so covered with blood," La Salle wrote later, "that we had difficulty recognizing each other."

Where waterways were semi-navigable, they built rafts and canoes. On April 21, they reached Fort Niagara. Three of the five men who had made the journey were desperately ill. Small wonder. In fifty days they had traveled a thousand miles through untracked wilderness; they had been soaked to the skin and frozen to the bone; they had built and discarded three canoes, and built and discarded six log rafts to pole across swirling, swollen streams.

And still the news that greeted La Salle was bad. There was no word of the *Griffon,* but there *was* word that La Salle's creditors had seized what little property he had retained, as partial payment for the debts he owed them for equipping the Mississippi expedition. To see what could be done to settle with them, La Salle went on to Montréal. But before leaving, he sent Fort Niagara's commander to the Illinois village with materials for building the Mississippi ship. No matter what, the exploration must go on.

With Frontenac's help, La Salle quieted his creditors. Then he hastened to Cataraqui. There he was confronted with more disturbing information. A message from Tonti warned him that the men working on the Mississippi boat had deserted, taking with them quantities of pelts, trading goods and ammunition, and were on their way to Fort Frontenac. They hoped, Tonti's message revealed, to find La Salle there and kill him.

La Salle set watches over the accesses to the fort, taking one of the watches himself. The first of the deserters arrived while

La Salle was on duty. He forced their surrender and jailed them at the fort. The next day more came. Two were killed, three more were jailed and eight escaped. But almost all of the stolen goods were retrieved.

In July La Salle prepared for his return trip to the Illinois valley. He sent ahead the rescued trading goods and ammunition, as well as other necessary supplies. The pelts he entrusted to coureurs for delivery to Frontenac, part of his debt settlement. Then he set out with twenty-five skilled workmen who were to continue work on the Mississippi boat. He was determined to launch it.

Seven months before he had sludged his way north through ice and snow. Now the prow of his canoe parted swarms of midges and mosquitoes. He and his companions paddled and portaged, river to lake, lake to river.

In an Indian village northwest of Lake Ontario, he finally learned the fate of the *Griffon*. The ship had been caught in a bad squawl in the upper part of Lake Michigan. Winds had whipped the water until the whole lake was white, the Indians said. They told the *Griffon's* pilot to pull into shore. He replied: "My ship does not fear the wind." The Indians watched the vessel enter the straits of Michillimackinac, all sails but two furled as she struggled against the wind. Neither ship nor men had been seen since.[8]

La Salle had lost pelts worth the equivalent of $42,000. Yet he pushed on. When he reached Lake Erie, the men he had sent ahead with trading goods, ammunition and supplies were nowhere to be found. He pushed on to Fort Miami. There he was told that Tonti was dead and that all those with him in the Illinois village to which La Salle was returning had fled. He pushed on.

On December 1 he reached Fort Crèvecoeur. It was empty, half-crumbled. Nailed to its doors were human heads. More heads were spiked on poles. They were mostly skulls; birds had pecked off the flesh. Within the fort, charred bones were

heaped. The fields around were strewn with half-eaten car-
casses. Over the putrid remains, crows fought by day and
wolves by night.

The hull of the Mississippi boat, partly finished, listed on
shore, the iron nails ripped from the sides. Carved into one
plank below the gunwale were the words *"Nous sommes tous
sauvages ce jour,* A . . . 15, 1680." We are all savages (the
French word for Indians at that time) this day, A. . . 15,
1680. The illegible letters after *A* were obviously *o-û-t,* spell-
ing *Août,* August. La Salle interpreted the inscription as a
message from Tonti meaning that he was going to live with
the Illinois. At least there was hope that Tonti was alive.

Inspecting the boat, La Salle decided the dismantling was
the work of the French—to prevent the Indians from using it.
Moreover the heads were clearly Indian. He concluded that
the French had been caught in a crossfire of fighting between
the Illinois and the Iroquois.

He spent the winter at Fort Miami. Meanwhile, Father
Hennepin's little group had reached the Mississippi by way
of the Illinois on March 7, 1680. They paddled north to the
river's junction with the Wisconsin, and on nearly to the site
of present-day Minneapolis. They were the first Europeans to
explore this particular section of the river. Their aim was to
reach its headwaters, but they were prevented from continuing by a band of Sioux Indians, who captured them and took
them to the Sioux village. The Indians also appropriated the
twelve hundred pounds of trading goods the three were carrying.

One of the Hennepin party spoke Sioux and argued so
strenuously with the tribe's council that the goods were returned. The three were guided to Montréal by a highly accomplished coureur, Daniel Greysolon Du Lhut, who was at that
time in Frontenac's employ. Du Lhut happened to be hunting
near the Sioux Village and was able to persuade the tribe to
release their captives.

Father Hennepin hurried from Montréal to France. He

wanted to establish there credit for being the first upper Mississippi explorer. He wrote a long report, abundantly embellished with his own imagination. As La Salle, who was very fond of the gutsy little priest, remarked wryly: "He is inclined to speak more in accordance with his wishes than in accordance with his personal knowledge."

La Salle heard the good news that Tonti was alive and had returned to Fort Miami, on his way back to Montréal in the spring of 1681. He sent messengers to bring Tonti to the fort. In Montréal he received an account of the Hennepin voyage from one of the men who had accompanied him.

Neither at Fort Miami nor at Fort Frontenac had trappers and traders been idle during La Salle's absence. Both forts were well stocked with fur, on all of which La Salle's monopoly permitted him to collect a percentage of the profit. The money helped with his mounting debts, although to the end of his life the explorer was never debt free. In Montréal he had to spend considerable time persuading merchants to underwrite his next expedition. He finally succeeded, but it was December 19, 1681, before he regained Fort Miami, the appointed meeting place for all who were to accompany him.

Assembled there with Tonti were twenty-two of the ablest and most experienced men who had accompanied him on earlier trips. With them were thirty Mohegan and Abenaki Indians who had settled around the fort. They were accompanied by their squaws and children. La Salle's reasons for having them were sound. First, they knew the Indian way of fighting. If attacks had to come, they would be invaluable in driving them off. Secondly, they were skilled huntsmen. They could keep the party supplied with game without wasting time. Thirdly, some of them spoke the languages of tribes to the south. As La Salle traveled southward, he added to this band. Through his Abenaki and Mohegan interpreters, he requested guides from other tribes, also offering to buy prisoners taken in tribal warfare. The guides introduced him to tribes friendly to their own, and to prisoners captured by hostile tribes, in each case making clear that La Salle's mission was peaceful.

The group started out from Fort Miami without waiting for spring. The Saint Joseph River, the normal route to the Illinois, was frozen, but the southern waters of Lake Michigan were not, nor was the Chicago River. By this detour they arrived at the Illinois. It was sheer glass. They attached to their canoes thin, broad planks, bent up in the front, turning them into toboggans. Then they slid down to Fort Crèvecoeur. There the ice disappeared and the canoes became canoes again.

On February 6, 1682, they reached the Mississippi. While waiting for the Indian families, who had proceeded on foot, they made new birch bark canoes, hunted and fished. On the thirteenth they launched their new canoes on the river. To the veterans in La Salle's company, who had endured so many misfortunes with him, the smoothness of this voyage seemed unreal. The current made paddling effortless, sometimes unnecessary. The waters provided more catfish than they could eat; the shores abounded with wild turkey, woodcock, deer and buffalo. In the lee of small islands, wild swans drifted.

In the section between the Mississippi's junction with the Missouri and its junction with the Arkansas, the line of canoes traveled in a long *S* as they navigated the river loops. By day the sun shone and the soft air was sweet with the scent of peach trees in bloom. By night the black water reflected the stars. Owls hooted from the shores and tree frogs piped. Feeding carp flapped and splashed. Some of the men were sure they were dreaming.

On March 12, they reached the Arkansas's mouth. They were warmly welcomed there by Arkansas Indians, with whom they spent three days. La Salle invited the chief to become a subject of the king of France, in return for which the king was to accept responsibility for the protection of the tribe. When the chief accepted, a *Te Deum* was sung and the French flag hoisted. La Salle claimed for Louis XIV "possession of Louisiana and . . . all the lands of the . . . Mississippi River."

On the three-week stretch from Arkansas to the mouth of the Mississippi, traveling conditions were less dreamlike. Indians on shore were hostile. Fish and game disappeared. The men lived mainly on alligators.

But these relative hardships were forgotten when the explorers caught their first sight of the sea. On April 6, they separated into small groups to follow the river's various channels through its delta. Three days later they came together on the Gulf of Mexico. There La Salle dedicated his discovery to his God and claimed it for his king. He had the king's coat of arms painted on a tree, with the inscription: "The great Louis, King of France, reigns, this ninth of April, 1682."

The same inscription was scratched on a copper plate and buried at the foot of a cross that La Salle had erected. Standing beneath the cross with his drawn sword in his right hand, his commission from the king in his left, La Salle said: "In the name of the most high, mighty, invincible and victorious prince, the great Louis . . . this month day of April 1, by virtue of His Majesty's commission, which I hold in my hand. . . . I have taken and do now take in the name of His Majesty and of his successors to the Crown, possession of this country of Louisiana, the seas, harbors, ports, bays, adjacent straits, and all nations, peoples, provinces, cities, towns, villages, mines, minerals, fisheries, streams, and rivers within the said Louisiana, from the mouth of the great River Saint Louis to the east, otherwise called Ohio . . . as also along the Colbert[9] and the rivers issuing there into, from its source beyond the country of the Sioux . . . as far as its mouth at the sea, or Gulf of Mexico."

He went on to name all the Indian tribes in the areas he had mentioned and avowed that the claim was being made with their assent and their "assurance that we are the first Europeans who have descended and ascended the said Colbert River." At the end of his speech psalms were sung and three salvos fired. Except for a thirty-eight year interval, Louisiana remained the property of France until 1803, when the French Emperor Napoleon sold it to the United States for $15 million.

The return trip from Louisiana was uneventful. The explorers spent the winter of 1682–83 just southwest of Lake Michigan where they built the last in La Salle's permanent chain of forts, Fort Saint Louis. The site was a miniature of the Québec rock, some 600 feet in circumference, towering 125 feet above the Saint Joseph River. This fort would be much easier to defend than the crumbled Crèvecoeur, which it replaced. Taking advantage of the protection offered, friendly Indian tribes flocked to settle at the fort's base. A community of some twenty thousand soon flourished there.

La Salle now knew his way down the Mississippi from the Great Lakes. He wanted to locate its mouths from the sea. His chance came in 1684 when the king of Spain barred France from sailing in the Gulf of Mexico. Two French ships were seized for defying the ban. Taking advantage of this humiliating situation, La Salle proposed to Louis a project that would strike at the Spanish in Mexico, where they had rich holdings. At the same time the proposal would let La Salle fulfill his own urge.

The plan was to seize the northern part of Mexico, riddled with gold and silver mines. To accomplish this, La Salle told the king, he would sail up the Mississippi from the Gulf as far as the Red River and build there a fortified settlement that would serve first as a base for attack, later as a commercial port. He would need from the king 200 men, a thirty-gun ship, food, arms and ammunition. He promised to recruit 5,000 more men from the settlement around Fort Saint Louis and from Saint-Domingue[10] in the West Indies. Such a number would, he vowed, be more than enough to overcome the "four hundred effeminate and indolent Spaniards" and their troops, who were scattered about Mexico.

La Salle had no problem selling his formula to Louis. He

was given the ship *Joly,* bristling with thirty-six guns, manned by a crew of seventy. He was presented also with the *Belle,* a small frigate, one hundred soldiers, a year's wages for them, supplies for nine months, eight cannons for the fort he was to build, plus ammunition for all the artillery. The commission signed by the king made La Salle governor of all the territory he should conquer.

He was also handed a ticklish problem: a divided command. To a certain Sieur de Beaujeu went command of the ships "in what concerned maneuvers," but "concerning the route to be followed" La Salle was the authority. When La Salle was on shore, Beaujeu was supposed to "provide him with all the succor he might require, exception being made for orders that would be against the safety of the ship and of navigation."

If La Salle was willing to make the best of the two-headed command, Beaujeu was not. He was a man of overweening vanity, a snob, a fanatic on the subject of ancestry. He couldn't take being put on an equal basis with La Salle, whose noble title had been conferred rather than inherited. He complained that the explorer "smelled of savages." Beaujeu was particularly put out by being kept in ignorance of the secret purpose of the expedition. The secret was known only to the king, La Salle and the Marquis de Seignelay, Colbert's eldest son, who, when his father died, succeeded him as Minister. Beaujeu interpreted the withholding of information as an insult to what he considered his superior status.

He was, then, from the start determined either to get full command of the expedition or else to wreck it. His complaints constantly crossed Seignelay's desk, full of trumped-up errors, which he laid at La Salle's door. When this tactic bore no fruit, he took direct action. He refused to let La Salle exercise any authority over the soldiers on board the *Joly,* claiming that the ship's security would be endangered by his "interference," even though the soldiers were passengers, not crew. He called the crew of seventy inadequate and drafted additional crew from among the soldiers. He did what he could to see that the soldiers, recruited in France, were the least qualified for what lay ahead of them. They were in bad physical condition; they were inexperienced. Some were beggars seized from church doorways.

By the time the sails were set for the voyage, La Salle was already worried about the undertaking. But it was too late to pull out. So on July 24, 1684, the small fleet cruised out of the harbor of La Rochelle. There were the *Joly* and the *Belle,* also the *Aimable,* a vessel chartered by La Salle from a La Rochelle merchant and laden with food, ammunition and supplies. There was the *Saint François,* a small ketch that would carry food as far as Saint-Domingue. La Salle's brother, the Abbé Jean Cavalier, and his nephew, Moranger, were among the passengers, also a few families who would form the nucleus of a colony.

A short distance out of La Rochelle, the *Joly's* bowsprit split in half. The four ships swung about, heading back to harbor. August 1 they were on their way again. Off the island of Madeira, Beaujeu suggested a stopover for water and provisions, though the fleet already had more than enough. What he really wanted was opportunity for his officers to sell merchandise to the islanders, gouging them for a steep profit. La Salle refused to dock.

A few days later he discovered that Catholic sailors on the *Joly* were insisting that the Protestant sailors be baptized as Catholics or else pay off the Catholics with either liquor or money. La Salle put an end to this extortion. His integrity had now antagonized all the ship's officers and most of the ship's crew.

In the West Indies, La Salle and Beaujeu agreed to reprovision. Seignelay had told the governor of Port de Paix, a French community on the northwest coast of Saint-Domingue to watch for the little fleet's arrival. The island was partly Spanish held, partly French, and it was most important to give the Spanish territory wide berth. Fully aware of the need for caution, Beaujeu nevertheless sailed past Port de Paix and down to the southwest, taking with him the *Saint François.* The *Saint François* was captured by the Spanish, the first but by no means the last loss of the expedition.

Beaujeu returned to Port de Paix to find a fever raging. La Salle, among others, was brought down by it and taken ashore. He was not expected to live. When sailors saw a priest enter the house where he was, to give last rites, they gathered under his window and danced. That great was their resentment of this man who had interfered with their baptismal racket.

But they didn't know their man. The illness delayed him for two months, during which time several men deserted, but then the little squadron, minus one vessel, started once more westward. For this part of the trip La Salle moved from the *Joly,* on which he had been sailing, to the *Belle.* He trusted the *Belle's* Captain Aigron no more than he trusted Beaujeu and felt it was time to keep an eye on him.

In mid-December the three ships entered the Gulf of Mexico. On the twenty-eighth they saw land to the northeast. In Saint-Domingue, La Salle had picked up information about a strong west-east current in the Gulf that drew ships eastward. Logs floating in the Gulf waters signaled he must be somewhere near a Mississippi mouth, but remembering the Saint-Domingue advice, he calculated that he probably still needed to sail about five hundred miles westward. Actually his ships had already passed the delta.

He gave orders that the *Aimable* and the *Belle* should skirt the shore, while the *Joly* paralleled them in the open sea. Every so often he landed scouts. Fog set in and the *Joly* disappeared. The surf became too rough for landing. By then La Salle was convinced he had somehow missed the Mississippi, but he had to find the *Joly* so he continued westward. On January 19, he caught up with her.

It was no accident that she had disappeared. Beaujeu had in mind luring La Salle to the west end of the Gulf and leaving him there. When La Salle climbed aboard the *Joly,* he found the ship's officers and pilot near mutiny. Knowing that the *Aimable* carried their food, they feared the separation of the ships, which their captain seemed bent on accomplishing. Supplies on the *Joly* were running low. La Salle offered Beaujeu sufficient food for two weeks. Not enough, said Beaujeu. He claimed some eleven hundred additional pounds of meat, plus corn and wine, which he maintained he had borrowed from his sailors' rations to feed La Salle's soldiers.

La Salle removed his soldiers from the ship. He gave them supplies, landed them and told them to walk to the first great river they saw. There he would meet them. The *Aimable* and the *Belle* poked along the coast until they reached a point just west of the mouths of the Colorado River. A channel led from the river into Matagorda Bay. Soundings showed that the channel's depth was ample for the *Belle* and might well accommodate the *Aimable.*

As assurance that the *Aimable* could make it, La Salle suggested lightening her weight by transferring cargo to the *Belle.* Captain Aigron refused the transfer and even refused the services of the *Belle's* pilot, a man who knew the channel. Then he deliberately ran the vessel aground, ignoring the markers La Salle had laid in the channel and the warning of a sailor in the fore lookout. When the sailor shouted "Pull to port," the captain pulled to starboard. The ship grated on the shoal.

"Drop anchor!" cried the *Amiable's* pilot.

Aigron countermanded the order. Had the anchor been dropped, there might have been time to clear the cargo. "Of all who were on board, there was none who did not believe the accident to have been premeditated," wrote an eyewitness. His statement was later confirmed by sworn documents from the pilot and sailors. One of these documents pointed out that Aigron had ordered all his personal belongings moved to the

Joly before taking the *Aimable* into the channel. *"All,* even to his jampots," the sailor swore. Later, their statements sent Aigron to jail on grounds of treason.

La Salle did his best to save the ship's cargo while Aigron did his best to drift it downstream. In the midst of the struggle, a storm broke. The rain deluged; the wind whipped. Of all the supplies only a few barrels of pork and flour were salvaged. Beaujeu, with La Salle's best landing launch on board, set sail for France, leaving La Salle and company with almost no food, ammunition or tools. Aigron sailed with Beaujeu.

One on the heels of another, misfortunes dogged the deserted group. La Salle sent some of his men to an Indian village to negotiate for the return of blankets which had drifted ashore from the wreckage of the *Aimable.* Instead of negotiating, the men raided the village, grabbed the blankets and stole all the pelts they could find. On their way back to La Salle they were attacked by the understandably irate Indians, who killed two of them and wounded two others.

La Salle's intent, despite misfortunes, was to continue his sea search for the Mississippi outlet, but he dared not leave the others without protection. He built a temporary fort and put it under the command of a man name Joutel, one of the few he trusted. Then he set out to find a suitable site for a permanent colony. In June, he sent back word that he had found one, north of Matagorda Bay. Joutel was to march the whole group there, bringing as much timber from the temporary fort as could be carried. The company was much reduced. Indians had attacked and reattacked. Scurvy and yellow fever had taken their toll. And as though that were not enough, one man had died of rattlesnake bite.

Doubts racked everybody's mind. Would the new site be any safer? How many would die on the way? But, dubious though all were, the raggle-taggle band obeyed Joutel. And they all made it alive. To their surprise, the new site did turn out to be an improvement. Fish and buffalo were abundant. The fort they built had six rooms, with surrounding cabins.

Compared to the way they had lived at sea or on shore for almost a year, Fort Saint Louis, as La Salle called it, was a cas-
tle. Only the Indians continued to be a threat. No colonist
strayed far from the fort's palisade.

As soon as the fort was complete, La Salle set out in the
Belle, followed by five canoes, again hunting for the Mississippi's meeting with the sea. When he found no sign of it, he
decided to search on foot, taking with him only the most cap-
able of his crew. This time, according to his official report to
the king, he found the delta and built a small palisade there.
The time was mid-February, 1687.

Elated, he returned to the spot where he had left the *Belle,*
intending to sail her up river. The *Belle* was nowhere in sight.
He and his men walked back to Fort Saint Louis, reaching it
on March 24. News of the *Belle* had preceded them.

Five men had taken off from her in a small launch, seeking
fresh water. When they didn't return, two more took off on a
raft. They didn't return either. The pilot, desperate and drunk,
tried to take the *Belle* to shore and ran her on a shoal. A Recollet priest, the Abbé Chefdeville, and four others had made
their way to the settlement on foot, bringing the bad news. In
all, fifteen men had perished. The *Belle's* provisions were
totally lost, along with any hope of sailing her to Saint-
Domingue for replacements.

Only one chance remained. Somebody had to go to France
for aid. La Salle decided on his brother, the Abbé Jean Cavalier. The abbé was to go down the Red River to the Mississippi and up that river to the Great Lakes and Canada, from
which he would sail for France. La Salle set out with the
abbé and his party, intending to lead them as far as the Mississippi. Partway along he sent ahead four men, two brothers by
the name of Duhaut, an Indian and a surgeon, to find a cache
of corn he had buried on his site-hunting trip. The men found
the corn had rotted, but they gave the Indian the good news
that they had shot two buffalo. La Salle dispatched his

nephew, Moranger, with the Indian and one other helper to bring the buffalo back. When they caught up with the hunters they found the men eating their kill. Angered by this display of selfishness, Moranger seized the meat. While he slept that night, the surgeon chopped off his head with an ax, also the heads of the Indian and the helper.

Alarmed when Moranger failed to return, La Salle went searching for him, taking along a priest, Father Douay. High-wheeling vultures identified the spot where the buffalo had been killed. La Salle fired two shots in the air to announce his coming and listened for answering shots. Silence. In the long prairie grass, not fifty paces away, the younger Duhaut lay on his stomach, his rifle cocked.

Unaware, La Salle walked toward him, stepping from tuft to tuft of slim, sideways-curving grass blades and separating the feathered vertical shafts with his hands. Parting the grass, he became clearly visible. Duhaut aimed.

La Salle took one more step. Duhaut fired. The bullet pierced La Salle's brain. He dropped. The feathery grass tips trembled for an instant in the movement of air made by his falling body. Then stillness returned.

Some yards behind La Salle, Father Douay dropped on his knees, praying. The two Duhauts and the surgeon found him there. "It's bad luck to kill a priest," said the elder Duhaut, restraining his brother. They stripped La Salle's body and left it for the vultures, the jackals and the wolves. Then they ordered Father Douay to return to the camp with them. They ordered the few there to accompany them back to Fort Saint Louis.

At the fort they forced Joutel out of command and announced their intention to set out for Canada. About half of the settlers went with them, but only six made it to Montréal. The rest murdered each other in violent quarrels, drowned crossing rivers, died of yellow fever and scurvy, or went to live with Indians. The six who reached Montréal were Father

Douay, the Abbé Cavalier, Joutel and three settlers. It is to the abbé that we owe the preservation of most of La Salle's precious records.

The men and women who remained in the fort were killed by Indians. Several infants who had been born during the twelve months of the settlement's existence were adopted by the Indians and later taken from them by the Spanish.

From the start La Salle's last expedition had all the ingredients of doom: a split command between a seasoned, dedicated explorer and an ignoramus status-seeker; and under this command a sorry crew of rabble and desperadoes. Completely unprepared for the ambushes of wilderness life, these bewildered recruits brought with them only the dog-eat-dog way of survival to which they were accustomed at home. The notion of teamwork never entered their heads. Their instincts led them to kill their leader over a piece of meat, and so, in the long run, destroy themselves.

All in all, the 1680's were unhappy years for the whole of New France. While La Salle followed the Mississippi to his death, the pioneers along the Saint Lawrence lived on the edge of terror. Among themselves, they were divided by rival claims to the fur trade; from without, they were menaced by the Iroquois and the English.

To the north the English had taken over and fortified Hudson's Bay, a fur rich area. The Iroquois Five Nations, whose leaders were superior strategists, were playing a cunning game of diplomacy. They were gradually conquering or subverting French Indian allies to clear the way for an attack on the French themselves. At this point, when the colony most needed to be united, the Montréalais and the La Salle-Frontenac fur-seekers were at each others' throats. Fort by fort, the chain La Salle had constructed from Cataraqui to below Lake Michigan, together with the trade privileges granted him by the king, were squeezing Montréal out of the business. The forts were also antagonizing the Iroquois. In the very regions where the new French bases appeared, the Iroquois had been freely bartering for furs with trading goods obtained from the English.

In 1680, La Salle's Fort Crèvecoeur was caught in Iroquois-Illinois crossfire. The action was part of a well-planned design. The Iroquois army, seven hundred strong, invaded most of the territory of the Illinois. The Iroquois had guns; the Illinois had only bows and arrows. The slaughter of Illinois was wholesale. Subsequently the Iroquois went after the Miamis, who, like the Illinois, were French allies.

Frontenac sent messengers with gifts in an attempt to assuage the various Iroquois nations. On one occasion the messenger was La Salle's Tonti. He was greeted by having a dagger plunged in his chest, then led to the chieftain. As Tonti delivered Frontenac's message, an Indian stood behind him, one hand holding Tonti's hair up from his neck, the other holding a poised knife, awaiting the chief's decision. The chief told Tonti he would discuss with Frontenac terms on which the Iroquois would make peace, had his wound treated and sent him back to Québec.

The reply was the usual Iroquois tactic, an effort to disarm and a play for time. Frontenac held several conferences with the Iroquois chiefs, trying to buy them off. To one, an Onondagan, he presented an outfit of clothing encrusted with gold braid and trimmed with lace, also a musket, ball and powder, and a satin gown for the Onondagan's daughter. The chief accepted the gifts suavely, assured Frontenac of his friendship and went home to launch an attack on another of the French allies, the Ottawas.

While trying in vain to halt the Iroquois, Frontenac also tried with an equal lack of success to persuade the French allies, whom the Iroquois were pursuing, to make concessions to their would-be conquerors. He must have known, as did the fearful colonists he governed, that these appeasement efforts would never work. From his experience in the fur trade, he was by then an old hand in negotiating with the Indians. But he probably also suspected that his recall could come on the next ship. He had continued the quarrels for which the king had reproached him, and from which, by nature, he could not refrain. If the Iroquois attacked the French, the problem would be his successor's. This, Québec insiders reasoned, was why the actions of this normally decisive man were so indecisive in answer to the Iroquois threat.

The one positive step he took was to strengthen urban defenses. Château Saint Louis, which doubled as a fort in Québec, was badly in need of repair. There was no fort at all in Montréal, and only a wooden palisade at Trois Rivières. A rapid building program remedied these weaknesses.

But in the countryside, matters went from bad to worse. From a Jesuit missionary to the Onondagas, Father Lamberville, Frontenac received a terse warning: "[The Iroquois] gain every year from our losses. They crush our allies and make Iroquois of them. They do not hesitate to say that, after adding to their own ranks from those we have abandoned, and thus strengthened by those who would have been able to aid us in waging war against them, they will descend . . . on Canada and overwhelm it in a single campaign."

In fact the whole Great Lakes area was being turned into an armed camp. No river was safe; French canoes were subject to constant pillage; an ambush waited in every portage. But Frontenac was busy fighting Duchesneau. "He makes himself think," Duchesneau wrote a friend in France, "that those who oppose him are linked in a cabal, and this he uses to render suspect the most innocent persons and to discredit all that has been done for the good of the country. He flies into temper tantrums when crossed and has taken to beating people with his cane."

One whom he beat was Duchesneau's sixteen-year-old son. An argument had started on the street between the junior Duchesneau and a young man in Frontenac's household. Both boys had called each other some curt names. Frontenac demanded an apology from the teen-aged Duchesneau, and his father, recalling the royal warning that the governor was the king's representative, sent his son to apologize. Instead of which the boy demanded that Frontenac's householder apologize to *him*. Whereupon Frontenac gave a demonstration of his cane-beating technique. Young Duchesneau ran for home, and his father barricaded the house doors behind him. Frontenac sent soldiers to break down the barricade, capture the boy and throw him into the Château dungeon.

Duchesneau Senior followed the routine the king had laid out for him. He protested to Frontenac, sent a copy to the king. The next ship from France brought two letters of recall: one for Frontenac, the other for Duchesneau. Impossible as Frontenac had made it for the king to leave him in office, to leave the intendant victorious over the representative of the royal personage was equally impossible. So New France lost two strong men.

Nevertheless the basic strength of the colony remained. The habitants clung to their land, repelling Indian raids in the fashion of the fourteen-year-old Marie-Magdeleine. And the coureurs and the priests continued their conquests of the wilderness, even though the odds against them were greater than ever.

Hébert's statue of Frontenac at Quebec.
COURTESY OF THE NEW YORK PUBLIC LIBRARY.

Louis XIV. COURTESY OF THE PUBLIC ARCHIVES OF CANADA.

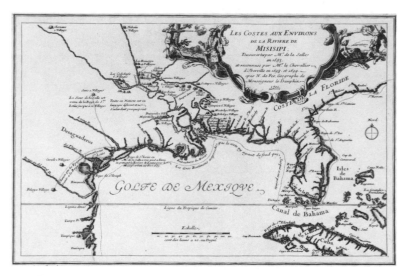

La Salle's last voyage.
COURTESY OF THE PUBLIC ARCHIVES OF CANADA.

The building of La Salle's *Griffon* from *Nouvelle decouverte d'un très grand pays dans l'Amerique* ... by Louis Hennepin, R.P., 1697. COURTESY OF THE PUBLIC ARCHIVES OF CANADA.

A view of the fort at Ticonderoga in 1759.
COURTESY OF THE NEW YORK HISTORICAL SOCIETY.

An old engraving depicting the martyrdom of Jesuit priests among the Indians.
COURTESY OF THE NEW YORK PUBLIC LIBRARY.

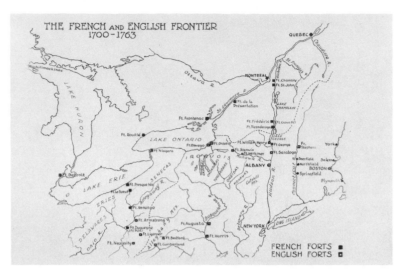

THE FRENCH and ENGLISH FRONTIER 1700-1763

FRENCH FORTS
ENGLISH FORTS

COURTESY OF THE PUBLIC ARCHIVES OF CANADA.

Louis Joseph de Montcalm.
COURTESY OF THE PUBLIC ARCHIVES OF CANADA.

A view of the taking of Quebec, September 13, 1759.
COURTESY OF THE PUBLIC ARCHIVES OF CANADA.

The Priest, the Coureur
and the Indian

In general, the missionaries who sought to convert the Indians of New France did not have an easy lot. Numbers were beheaded by tomahawks, but even they were fortunate compared to those who were tortured. Some were burned alive in their chapels. Others were stripped and chained to stakes, seared with boiling oil, then mutilated, finger by finger, toe by toe, limb by limb, before having their hearts cut out.

The tortures the Indians inflicted on them were no different from those they inflicted on one another. Torture was simply a part of the Indian way of life. From his earliest years an Indian boy was trained to expect it if he were captured in battle. He was also taught that the final measure of a man was how silently he was able to endure such a death. The priests, who knew their Indians well, proved themselves as stoic as their torturers, and won great respect for the courage with which they stood up under intense suffering.

The Roman Catholic Church has set aside a special day, September 26, for services in memory of some of these martyrs, a few of whom have been made saints. Actually, their martyrhood was only indirectly related to their priesthood. For the most part the priests were victims of the Iroquois war on the Hurons. This was especially true of the Jesuits, most of whose missions were in Huron territory. The Iroquois simply massacred everybody in the Huron villages, priests included.

Occasionally the village medicine man was responsible for doing away with a missionary. Practitioners of magic, the medicine men were regarded with great awe as intermediaries with the Indian gods. They realized that if this awe were to be replaced by faith in a god they didn't represent, they would lose their power. Consequently they overlooked no opportunity to blame the gray-frocked Recollet or the black-frocked Jesuit for misfortune. Let drought dry up the crops or floods rot them out, it was the fault of the robed one with his little prayer book, which the medicine men were convinced was a catalog of sorcery.

They saw the crucifix as a sort of hex, and when the priest traced the sign of the cross in the air with his hand, they told their people he was calling down the wrath of the gods upon them. The result could be a hard winter, scarce game or an epidemic. Whatever bad befell, the priest had caused it. When adversity was long drawn out and tempers shortened, the medicine man could sometimes direct the tribal anger at the missionary in their midst.

Actually the medicine men had less to worry about than they thought. The priests' efforts to convert Indians to Christianity were never very successful. The greatest stumbling block was the lack of any Indian concept of a single Supreme Being. They didn't even have a word for such a concept in their language. There was *Manitou* and there was *Oki,* but either of these could be anything from a snake to a painted rock. Theirs was an animistic, or naturalistic faith, in which they worshiped creation rather than a creator.

To give their congregations a sense of one God, the missionaries had to use roundabout terms like "Ruler of all." In time the Indians fitted this new deity into their old scheme of beliefs and began to speak of the "Great Spirit," whom they conceived of as an all-powerful, invisible force, controlling the other forces which they worshiped.

They were especially drawn to the Great Spirit by the chants that were part of the mass. Singing filled many functions for North American Indians. They sang for joy, returning victorious from the warpath. Their prisoners sang to prove that they didn't fear death. The Hurons had a habit of singing to keep their minds off their empty stomachs when crops were bad and game was scarce. What the priest could not get across in words, no matter how proficient in Indian languages he might be, he had better luck communicating through music. Even so, he had to remain alert for the most unexpected stumbling blocks. One Jesuit priest was asked by the Hurons whether Iroquois could be admitted to Paradise. When he replied "yes," the Hurons refused to be baptized. They wouldn't risk a hereafter in which they would again encounter the enemies who had done them so much harm in the here and now.

But conversion, though the missionaries' main goal, was not their most influential contribution to Indian life. The contribution with the greatest impact was teaching the Indians to fertilize soil and rotate crops so that they could become a settled rather than a nomad people. Before the advent of the missionaries, the Indians migrated as soon as they used up the soil's nutrients. The church stabilized village life.

Another benefit that came along with the Church was implements, which eased daily work. For example, priests brought small handmills for grinding corn. The Indian fashion of grinding it between two stones had taken four to five times longer. Priests also gave them clocks so that the hour no longer had to be calculated from the heavens. "Chieftain of the day," the Algonquins called the first clock they ever saw.

Schools were another Church-sponsored advantage. The children were eager students. They learned quickly and enjoyed displaying their knowledge. Many parents asked to be taught also.

If the Indians gained a certain amount of worldly wisdom from the priests, the priests acquired from the Indians the gift of adaptability. They often had to improvise on the spot to carry out their work. For instance some used the clanging of old kettles to substitute for the ringing of steeple bells. The burning of sweet-smelling pine cones could do for incense; cider might substitute for communion wine.

They also had to learn Indian codes of behavior. The earliest missionaries compiled from their own experience rules that were handed down and expanded, generation by generation. These included tips for travel, for social conduct, for mealtime manners. Among them: don't make Indians wait for you when on a voyage; don't offer to paddle unless you intend to paddle all day; don't wear a hat if it annoys your traveling companions; you *must* eat at dawn and sunset, and you must accept and swallow whatever portion is offered you.

When the portion was dried eelskin, acorns and moss, a standard hard-times ration, the priests had some problems. They also had problems with feasts of dog. They could not withstand long periods of famine as easily as Indians, and alternate periods of starving and stuffing wrecked their stomachs. But they carried on.

Honors were frequently given them, the choicest morsels of food at the feast, the best place by the fire. The rules told them to accept these without ceremony. Don't make too many observations and don't ask too many questions, the regulations continued. Be pleasant without being too familiar. But praise young hunters; fondle children; honor the dead.

The missionaries mastered Indian codes well. As a result, in village after village, from the shores of the Saint Lawrence to the shores of the Great Lakes, their log chapels, topped with a cross, were a familiar sight until the Indian wars mowed down the ranks of the wilderness parishes.

A number of the priests, like Marquette and Hennepin, were explorers as well as men of God. By the 1680's a good deal of the Great Lakes territory had been mapped by the missionaries Allouez, Druilettes, de Casson, de Galinée and Dablon. And in 1672 Father Charles Albanel had traced a water route from the Saint Lawrence to Hudson Bay, by way of the Saguenay River, Mistassini Lake and the Rupert River.

Hudson Bay had first been explored by the English. Henry Hudson entered it in 1610 and Thomas James in 1631. A group of English traders moved into the area in 1668 and built forts.

Nevertheless, in 1674, Frontenac had sent Albanel back to Hudson Bay with a letter of introduction to the English governor there, Charles Bayly. Albanel's secret mission was two-fold: to try to persuade the Bay Indians to trade their furs with the French-allied Ottawas instead of with the English, and to swing back to the French side two coureurs, Pierre Esprit Radisson and his nephew, Chouart de Groseilliers who had deserted to the English.

Albanel was a priest and explorer—but no spy: his secrets were all too easily pierced. Frontenac should have known better than to send him. Perhaps he did know better and had a purpose in picking the wrong man for the job. It was not he, but his Montréal rivals who were eager to break into the north. He was much more concerned with his own trade in the west.

In any event, Frontenac showed no great dismay when Governor Bayly packed Father Albanel off to England as a prisoner on the first English ship available. Groseilliers and Radisson didn't return to their compatriots until five years later, when they were assured of pardon for desertion.

In that same year, 1679, Jolliet returned from explorations in the vicinity of Hudson Bay to report that the English had built there three well-manned, well-armed forts. After his return from the Mississippi voyage with Marquette, Jolliet had married the daughter of a wealthy Montréal fur trader. The Hudson Bay trip was made at his father-in-law's request: Jolliet was supposed to look into the possibility of cutting into the English fur trade. The English offered Jolliet money and fur options to remain with them, but unlike Radisson and de Groseilliers, he refused. His loyalty was rewarded with large landholdings on the Saint Lawrence islands of Anticosti and Mignan.

Jolliet's report prompted Montréalais to form the Compagnie du Nord, as a counterforce against the English Hudson's Bay Company. After Radisson and Groseilliers had been pardoned, the Montréal company put them in charge of an expedition to the Bay. When Frontenac got wind of the plan, he tried to prevent the coureurs' departure. They had to work out devious means to escape his watchful eyes.

Using the excuse that he had to go to England to see his sick wife, Radisson sailed out of Québec with Grosseilliers aboard. The pair wintered in Acadia, and in July of 1682, while La Salle was canoeing southward on the Mississippi, they sailed north to Hudson Bay. There they captured two ships, one belonging to the English governor, the other from Boston, and took and destroyed an English fort. They built a trading base where they left an eight-man garrison and returned to Québec with a two-thousand-pound cargo of beaver.

The rivalry over the Bay continued for as long as the French held Canada, with forts and trading posts changing hands from one side to the other, and coureurs raiding the depots of their rivals.

The coureurs, like the missionaries, spent much time living with Indians. They spoke their languages; they knew their ways. They invented clever means to cope with hardships. In summer rains they took shelter beneath upturned canoes. In winter they often built snowhouses. Sometimes at night they converted to tents the daytime sails they had hoisted on their canoes when there was enough wind. Song and tobacco gave them the greatest consolation. They sang as they sailed, usually old folk airs from France, the words and music slurred by the pipes clenched in their teeth. Many were such continuous pipe puffers that they could measure distance by the number they smoked.

One of the aids on which they relied most heavily was the birch tree. From its bark they built their canoes. They used the spongy leaves to wipe sweat from their faces while paddling, and to prevent sunburn. Their journals and records were written with charcoal on birch bark, paper being too heavy to carry.

Radisson and Groseilliers once built themselves an A-frame cabin of birch trunks, the branches interlaced at the top. An early winter had overtaken them on the shores of Lake Itasca, the source of the Mississippi, in what is now Minnesota. All unaware that they were the first Europeans to view the source of that soon-to-be-much-explored river, they beached their canoes. Then they put up their dwelling and furnished it with beds of pine branches and a tree stump table. They built fires on the dirt floor over which Groseilliers did the cooking. Radisson was the provider, fishing through the ice, shooting hare.

In the bush around their winter home they strung small bells which they had brought for trading. If an attacker should approach during the night, his stumbling against the cord would set the bells to jangling like an alarm. Occasionally wild animals tangled in the line, awakening the coureurs needlessly. But the wakening was a small price to pay for the sense of security with which they lay down to sleep.

Soon, however, curious Sault and Ojibwa Indians who roamed the area began to work their way closer and closer to the A-frame. One day Radisson sprinkled gunpowder in a circle at some distance from their shelter. When the Indians came at evening, he threw a hot coal into the gunpowder. A circle of fire immediately surrounded the house.

The effect on the Indians was magical. They assumed that the inhabitants must have superior powers. The coureurs were invited to winter in one of their villages. The two accepted the invitation readily. The Indians insisted on carrying all their baggage all the way to the village. Radisson's journal describes the trip and their reception: "We walked four days through the woods, being treated like gods. They admired everything we did more than the courtiers of Paris admire the actions of their king. On arrival we were presented with their most precious of all gifts: beaver—great stores of it." The coureurs in return made many gifts to the Indians from their store of trading goods.

The spirit was good, but the life was not easy. The winter was severe. There was never enough game to feed the whole village. Radisson and Groseilliers pulled in their belts and starved along with their hosts. What little they could shoot, they shared with their hosts. They expected to share both the bad and the good.

The cracking of the ice came at last and then the spring. The two coureurs brought their rich load of pelts to Montréal, rejoicing, but their joy abruptly changed to bitterness. Their load was confiscated by the regional governor, who declared that they lacked a proper license. Actually the governor would have probably overlooked that detail, were he not vying with the coureurs' sponsors. He wanted the furs himself. It was this bit of unsavory business that prompted Radisson and Groseilliers to switch their allegiance from the French to the English.

The knowledge of the Indians the French gained through the experience of both the coureurs and the missionaries brought bonds of friendship and loyalty, and, of course, furs to the French. But only to a point. Ironically, the knowledge that the Indians gained from the French put the generation of Indians in the 1680's in a much more effective position than they otherwise would have been to pressure the French. The Indians of the late seventeenth century were no longer greeting French officials as they had once greeted Champlain with joyous Ho! Ho! Ho's. The welcome was far more likely to veil a threat.

Part of the problem in the 1680's also came from attitudes that French expansion provoked among Indians who were not friendly to the French. In 1682, the alliance Champlain had made with enemies of the Iroquois seventy-three years earlier bore full-scale results. In the summer of that year, Le Febvre La Barre, the governor appointed after Frontenac's first term, received a letter from a Jesuit missionary, Father Lamberville, at Fort Cataraqui. The letter quoted an Iroquois chief as saying that war on the French would provide "an excellent chance to discover whether or not it was true that their flesh had a salty flavor."

By then the Iroquois had all their enemies well in hand. Their long-contained fury, further fueled by French invasions of their fur grounds and artfully fanned by the English, was about to be let loose.

English
and Indians

The governor at the time the Iroquois nations took to the warpath was Le Febvre La Barre. He was a lawyer and a good administrator, but soldier he was not. He had already shown great reluctance to commit troops to battle in a previous post in the West Indies. He was a sensitive man, a thinker, and his views—far ahead of his time—were pacifist.

Nevertheless, recognizing the Iroquois danger, particularly after Fort Saint Louis had been attacked, he asked the king for reinforcements of 500 to 600 men. He got 150, of whom only 120 were fit for battle. He himself drummed up some 800 raw recruits in Canada.

Still, he hesitated to commit them. Perhaps peace could be negotiated. He decided to call a peace conference at Cataraqui. One of the Iroquois Five Nations, the Onondagas, offered to mediate. Some of his advisers, who knew the Iroquois better that he, warned that calling such a conference would only arouse Indian contempt and provoke more aggression. Whatever promises the Iroquois might make, La Barre's counselors cautioned, they would not keep.

La Barre was not convinced. He proceeded to Cataraqui. There he waited for the Onondaga mediators. And he waited. And he waited. His supplies began to run out. His men came down with the flu. He sent five hundred of them, along with two hundred Indians living at the Cataraqui mission, to La Famine, a settlement across Lake Ontario. They were to hunt and fish there and, hopefully, escape the flu. He also sent one of the Le Moyne brothers who was with him to find out what was happening with the Onondagas.

Word finally came from Le Moyne. The Onondagas would meet La Barre at La Famine. La Barre had flu but he made the journey. When he arrived, he found La Famine also laid low with the epidemic. Le Moyne had caught it and was so ill he could barely walk. But he had done his job of rounding up Indians. Present were Onondagas, Cayugas and Oneidas, three out of the Five Nations. Their spokesman was the Onondaga chief, Hotreouati.

The chief was quite aware that the French were in no condition to fight. They couldn't even get out of La Famine and Cataraqui without his say-so. He was in a position to dictate harsh terms—and he did. The French could take his terms or leave them. It was up to them whether they wanted to stay alive.

La Barre took the terms. The agreement bound the French not to interfere with the Iroquois effort to wipe out the Illinois, the traditional French allies. The French were also to quit their bush warfare against the Senecas. The Senecas would give the French a thousand beaver pelts—damages for the pillaging of French canoes, which had occasioned the warfare. The pelts, of course, were never collected.

After the signing of the treaty, those of the French who

survived the flu made their way back to Montréal. When Louis XIV was advised of the treaty, he was outraged. "For a savage of the American forest to dictate such terms to the monarch of the most respected nation in Europe is unthinkable," he fumed. La Barre was recalled.

The next governor, Jacques René de Brisay, Marquis de Denonville, was supplied with an additional three hundred soldiers, in the hope of preventing another such humiliation. It had taken "a savage of the American forest" to bring to the attention of the great Sun King, as Louis was known, the danger which shadowed his colony. But he and his faraway advisers were still incapable of understanding how much was needed to lift that shadow. The troops supplied to Denonville were badly armed and the royal treasury provided neither food nor pay for them.

Regarded as one of the best officers in all Louis's kingdom, Denonville, by contrast with his predecessor, was a practical man of action. He saw immediately what ought to be done and knew that he would have to settle for what could be done. He realized that to the south, in New York, the English were helping the Iroquois in efforts to drive the French from the west, while to the north, in Hudson Bay, they were depriving the French of fur.

Denonville considered the English the colony's biggest threat, but the Iroquois as the most immediate one. His master plan, the plan he would have liked to have followed, consisted of a double-pronged attack. One prong would attack the Mohawks and Oneidas in the Albany area, at the same time threatening the English there. The other prong would attack the Senecas to the west. The combined armies would then drive the rest of the Iroquois in on the space between the two prongs, ravaging villages as they went. After that, La Salle's old fort at Niagara should be rebuilt and garrisoned. Armed ships should patrol the Great Lakes.

Great plan, but as things stood he had barely enough resources to attack the Senecas alone. He dared not wait for additional aid from France, partly because the Iroquois were creating so much havoc, partly because he was not at all sure what might or might not come from France.

He decided to go ahead on a limited basis: he would attack the Senecas. As he commenced mustering men for the foray, he heard from Father Lamberville that the Onondagas would like to confer with him at Fort Frontenac in Cataraqui. Denonville quickly agreed to a conference, although he had no intention of conferring. He was merely adopting the Iroquois trick of disarming the foe. All preparations for the expedition were kept top secret. Boards cut and planed for building flatboats were stored out of sight. Arms sent to Fort Frontenac were packed in barrels labeled "salt meat," "dried fish" and the like. Even from Father Lamberville the preparations for attack were concealed. Denonville knew that the priest would be distressed by the double play.

Orders went to all seigneuries to build forts and stockades and for every male inhabitant fourteen years old and up to arm himself. Jesuit missionaries were drafted to relay orders to seigneuries and to commanders of distant posts. The coureur Greysolon Du Lhut was sent to Detroit to muster as many more coureurs as he could, and Tonti was sent with him to muster allied Indians. They were to bring their recruits to Fort Niagara by July 6.

On June 10, 1687, 832 French and 930 Canadian soldiers lined up for departure from Montréal. At the same moment a ship docked in Québec carrying 800 additional men from France. Had Denonville expected them he could have carried out his entire master plan. But they arrived too late. Instructions for the forthcoming campaign had by then gone all across New France, and the length of time required to withdraw those and send out others would have caused great delay as well as vast confusion. So the new troops were distributed among the settlements to help defend them from the Iroquois counterattacks that Denonville fully expected.

The day after Denonville and his army left Montréal, they

were joined by some 400 Indians recruited from Jesuit missions. The Indians, who had spent the previous night in war dances, were attired for battle. Naked except for animal tails attached to their buttocks, they had striped their bodies and faces with red and black, overlaying the stripes with animal drawings. In their ear lobes and nostrils they wore metal rings and spikes. These decorations were intended to frighten their enemies and raise their own morale.

The group toiled up the Saint Lawrence. They tugged their flatboats against the current, often in peril of being dashed against the rocks. Around rapids, they portaged. Daily, scouting parties were sent ahead to clear the shores of enemy Indians lurking in the woods. At last the army reached Fort Frontenac.

There, by various means, they made prisoners of 50 Iroquois men and 150 Iroquois women and children. Some had been invited to a feast. After they had eaten, they were clapped into jail. The only Indians released were two Onondagas who had come with Father Lamberville, supposedly to discuss peace. The others Denonville knew he would need for exchange purposes. Many French could be captured in battles to come. An exchange of prisoners would spare them the traditional Indian death by torture.

Meanwhile Tonti and Du Lhut had assembled at Niagara 180 coureurs and 400 allied Indians. Denonville and his troops met them there July 6, as scheduled. Between Niagara and Seneca land the entire army had to clamber through three narrow defiles. Weighed down by shoulder packs of arms and rations, the men edged along, swatting at the black flies that buzzed around their ears and eyes. A pitiless sun kept the sweat streaming down their faces.

Between the second and third defiles, toward sunset, the Senecas struck. At Denonville's command, the whole army took cover. Only the forward battalion returned the Indian fire. The Senecas thought that battalion was all Denonville had. As they advanced, Denonville brought his rear troops to the front. Twenty-seven Senecas fell during the volley they let loose. The rest fled.

Denonville's troops were too tired to move. They camped where they were. The Indians among them were supposed to follow the fleeing Senecas, but they had other plans: they quartered and stewed the twenty-seven dead. Six dead French were buried and stretchers were improvised for carrying the wounded on the next day's march.

The army moved from one Seneca village to another. All were deserted—and obviously in haste. Ashes were still warm in some of the fireplaces and remnants of half-eaten meals lay on the floors of lodges. The French destroyed the villages and burned the corn crops growing in the hills. Then they headed back to Niagara. Denonville would have liked to go on to attack Cayuga villages, but his troops were falling sick and his Indians were slipping away.

He remained at Niagara long enough to rebuild the fort. Then, leaving a commander with a garrison of one hundred, he returned to Montréal in mid-August. In two months he had marched his army into the most distant territory of the most powerful Iroquois nation. By so doing, he had prevented the Iroquois and the English from breaking the French hold on the western fur trade.

Yet the colony was by no means in the clear. Denonville well knew his victory was temporary. The Iroquois would respond, he prophesied, trying to persuade the habitants to move into stockades. He might as well have tried to persuade birds to move into a cage. It was not in the Canadian character to live in a compound.

The Iroquois response came quickly. In a systematic campaign of ravaging the French farms of outlying districts, they killed the farmers and burned their homes, barns and crops. They ambushed supply convoys headed for French forts, bringing starvation to garrisons of critical posts.

Not only Indian raids but also epidemics attacked the colony in the late 1680's. With so many crops burned and with men afraid to venture into the woods for hunting, malnutrition and the illnesses it caused became widespread. And as if home-grown disease was not sufficient, smallpox and measles were transported from Europe by the French supply ships. In the year 1688, out of a population of 11,000, 1,400 perished. In Fort Frontenac the entire garrison of 100 died. Iroquois burned the fort's crops, killed its cattle and very nearly succeeded in burning down the fort itself.

Half the Indian prisoners Denonville had brought back with him were killed by measles, a new disease for North America, to which the native population had no immunity. The remaining half of the prisoners Denonville shipped to France. With them he sent a messenger bearing a request for 4,000 soldiers, 400 to 500 flatboats and supplies for two years. His request couldn't have come at a more unfavorable time. England and France were again on the brink of war: France needed her resources at home. Denonville got 30 men, no boats and no supplies.

He decided to hold a peace meeting. He didn't expect tangible results; he was playing for time. With time he might be better able to plead his cause in France. He sent four of the Iroquois prisoners to invite their chieftains to attend. The governor of New York, Colonel Thomas Dongan, getting wind of the proposed conference, did all he could to prevent it. But the governor was up against a shrewd adversary—Father Lamberville, who persuaded Onondagas, Cayugas and Oneidas to send their chiefs to Montréal. The discussion began on June 8, 1688.

Denonville commenced by questioning whether any negotiation would be possible, since the governor of New York now claimed that the Iroquois were British subjects. Under those circumstances, they could make no treaties without the governor's approval.

Deliberately, Denonville was pricking Indian pride and trying to insert a wedge of anger between the British and the Iroquois. As he hoped, spokesman Hotreouati's reply was indignant. He said that his people recognized no man as master. They had received their lands from the Great Spirit and had never been conquered by either English or French.

Off to a good start, the conference got down to details. Denonville insisted that all French Indian allies be included in the treaty, and they were. The Iroquois present agreed to get the other two nations, the Mohawks and Senecas, to accept the treaty in return for which Denonville would abandon Fort Niagara. He retained Fort Frontenac and the right to garrison and supply it. There was to be a mutual exchange of prisoners, and Denonville promised to arrange the return of those he had sent to France. If any French Indian ally attacked any Iroquois before Denonville was able to spread word of the agreement, this was not to prejudice its final acceptance. The signing by all concerned would take place in Montréal the next year.

Two months later the Iroquois made their most murderous strike up to that time. At Lachine, close to Montréal, they burned fifty-six of the settlement's seventy-seven houses, took ninety prisoners and killed twenty-four. They roasted five children.

Their assault was provoked by four circumstances. First, the English colonies had learned, as the French had not, that the expected war between France and England had broken out. The English immediately passed the word to the Iroquois, who quickly grasped the fact that French Canada would be all but stranded for the duration of the war. The moment to launch a mass attack was ripe.

Secondly, ambassadors sent to inform Denonville that the Senecas and Mohawks had agreed to the treaty were ambushed by the French-allied Hurons. The Hurons were afraid a peace settlement would free the Iroquois to make war on them.

Thirdly, the Iroquois prisoners had not arrived from France. And finally, Sir Edmund Andros, the newly appointed governor of New England, was doing his utmost to disrupt the peace.

To Governor Denonville, the situation was intolerable. He saw no way to get from France what he needed to fulfill his responsibility for safeguarding the colony. He was tired; his health was broken. He wanted out. He sent his good friend Hector de Callières, governor of Montréal, to France with a listless request for reinforcements and an urgent plea that His Majesty appoint a replacement for himself. De Callières wanted the post, and Denonville would have been pleased to have seen him in it. But the man appointed was Frontenac. In October, he arrived on the same ship with Denonville's letter of recall and the Indian prisoners.

By the end of 1689, the year Frontenac arrived, the English had cemented with the Iroquois an alliance that was on the verge of wiping out New France. English ambassadors, speaking in the councils of the Five Nations, sabotaged every peace effort the French made. Indians armed with English muskets, English knives and English hatchets were massacring habitants to the north and west of Montréal. Coureurs were ambushed in the forests. Villages of French Indian allies were being razed.

Frontenac reversed Denonville's policy of attacking the Indians first, as the most immediate threat, and delaying attack on the greater threat, the English. He decided to go to the source of the trouble. Three war parties were organized by the colony's three main towns to ravage fortified settlements on English borders. The Montréal party was ordered to attack Schenectady. The target of the Trois Rivières group was Portsmouth, Maine, while the Québec contingent was to head for Fort Loyal, on Casco Bay, Maine.

In Casco Bay half the garrison was killed in the first onslaught. Then the French dug trenches around the fort and stuffed them with homemade mines. When the remaining half of the garrison saw this operation, they surrendered. The fort was destroyed and its cannons spiked. Homes in the area were burned. At Portsmouth, the French were also victorious. But the scene of their greatest triumph was Schenectady.

The slogan of the attacking Montréal group was "Remember Lachine," and no one suffered any loss of memory. Giving Indians in their party a free hand to slaughter in their own fashion, they made another Lachine out of Schenectady. As the mayor of Albany described it in a Calendar of State Papers: "The Cruelties Committed at said Place no Penn can write, nor Tongue expresse; ye Women big with Child ripped up and down and ye Children alive Thrown into Flames and their Heads Dashed in pieces against Doors and Windows." The Canadians returned to Montréal with fifty horses loaded with plunder and twenty-seven prisoners.

The successful raids gave the English pause—but only temporarily. In the long run the result was the opposite of what Frontenac sought. Prior to the attacks, the English colonies had been bickering among themselves. The French onslaught, and particularly the atrocities at Schenectady, gave the colonists a united purpose, which they expressed in a Latin slogan: *Delenda est Nova Francia*—New France must be destroyed.

While the English were gathering strength to act on this belief, the Iroquois continued their havoc. Some 120 strong, a band of them burned down La Fourche, a French fort on Lake Champlain. They were commanded by an English colonist, Captain John Schuyler, and their ranks were reinforced by twenty-nine Albany militiamen.

Subsequently Frontenac sent two ambassadors to the Iroquois; they burned one alive and turned the other over to the English. The Ottawas were greatly agitated by the French efforts to negotiate. They preferred the Iroquois to attack the French rather than their own tribes. They began considering a separate peace with the Iroquois in return for a promise to help them fight the French. One Ottawa tribe did just that, in the presence of witnesses from Albany.

The threat of a total Ottawa desertion was averted only by luck. A convoy on the way to Michillimackinac with some Ottawa paddlers was attacked by Senecas. The convoy won the fight. The commander shrewdly gave the Ottawas one of the Seneca prisoners. They boiled and ate him. Their action brought to a short stop any further possibility of an Iroquois-Ottawa alliance.

No sooner did this threat recede, however, than the next one arose. In the autumn of 1690, the English assault began. It had been planned as a two-pronged attack, partly by land, partly by sea. The land campaign ran into one difficulty after another. A large force from New York, New England and Maryland was supposed to join some Iroquois at Albany. The ranks turned out to be far fewer than had been promised. On the march toward Lake Champlain smallpox struck. Quarrels erupted. The number of canoes and quantities of supplies proved inadequate even for the reduced number of men. The Indians deserted in disgust, and the English turned back, without firing a shot.

The sea expedition presented the French with a more serious hazard. A fleet of thirty-four large vessels, four smaller ones and an assortment of ketches, barques and brigantines was assembled in Boston harbor under the command of Sir William Phipps. Sailing north, the fleet paused to take Port Royal in Acadia, then headed for the Saint Lawrence. On October 8, the mayor of Québec received word from the French-allied Abenaki Indians in Acadia that the fleet was on its way. Frontenac was in Montréal. The mayor quickly dispatched a messenger by canoe to give him the news. Frontenac's response was immediate. He ordered every man in Montréal, except for a small garrison, to hurry to Québec. He himself hastened there in the messenger's canoe, pausing at Trois Rivières long enough to leave the same instructions he had left in Montréal.

He found Québec panicked. The Ursuline nuns had buried their convent silver and altar ornaments and were about to evacuate. Frontenac told them to dig up their treasure and stay. When the Montréal and Trois Rivières reinforcements arrived, the Québecois' facilities were taxed, but their spirits rose. Morale recovered.

On October 11, three days after the Abenaki warning, the English fleet arrived in Lower Town. A small boat put off from the admiral's ship, carrying an emissary, Major Thomas Savage. Standing in the prow, he waved a white flag. As he stepped ashore, the French blindfolded him and led him up the steepest of the paths to Château Saint Louis. He carried a message from Phipps to Frontenac.

Frontenac was ready and waiting. He had designed what he considered to be an awe-inspiring setting for the receipt of the admiral's message. He had no doubt that it would call for immediate surrender. When the blindfold was removed from Major Savage's eyes, he saw what he later described as "a stately hall, full of brave, martial men." Frontenac had ordered his officers to dress to the teeth. Their hair was powdered and curled. Their hats were plumed. Their shirts were trimmed with gold and silver lace. They were obviously not fearstricken.

The major handed over Phipps's message, which read as Frontenac had supposed. Taking a watch from his pocket, Savage demanded a reply within an hour.

"I shall not keep you waiting that long, sir," Frontenac answered. "Do you really believe these officers—" he gestured toward them—"would accept such a demand?"

The major continued with what he had been ordered to say. "The admiral wishes your reply in writing."

Frontenac stared at him. Not a motion, not a whisper stirred the silence of the room. When the escort advanced with the blindfold, Frontenac spoke. "I have no reply to make to your admiral," he said, "other than from the mouths of my cannons and muskets." The blindfold was adjusted and the major led back down the cliff.

Frontenac had powerful allies: geography and climate.

They, rather than the English admiral, determined English strategy. Phipps couldn't lay a long siege, or he would risk being iced in. The capture of Québec had to be fast—or not at all. He had to land his men, not when he chose, but when the tide permitted. Even so, they bogged down in swampy mud flats. And the sheer rock that descended to the flats offered no easy foothold. From the bush, habitants kept steady fire trained on all who tried to invade. And it was cold. Bitter cold that chilled to the bone, nipping noses and ears, chafing the skin raw.

On the right bank of the Saint Charles River, Frontenac held in reserve the tri-town forces he had recruited. But he never had to use them. On October 24, a storm scattered the English fleet. By the following day, all had sailed off, still storm-pursued. One ship was wrecked on the island of Anticosti, two or three more were lost at sea and a few were driven as far as the West Indies.

So ended that attempt to take over New France. But it was not the end of English ambition to have Canada. Nor did the 1690's bring any decrease in the hardships that the colony had managed to weather in the 1680's.

Hudson Bay
and Louisiana

The 1680's were not a complete loss, however. There were some victories for New France in those years. And some in the 1690's as well. Many of these occurred in the far north, and were in part due to the vision of Denonville. It was he who, with the directors of the Compagnie du Nord, in 1685, decided to launch an all-out effort to add Hudson Bay to the French hunting grounds. Between 1686 and 1697 five expeditions were sent north, all under the command of Pierre Le Moyne d'Iberville.

D'Iberville was one of the eleven sons of the famous seigneur, Charles Le Moyne, who was a founder of the Compagnie du Nord. The first expedition in 1686 included two of d'Iberville's brothers, other coureurs, Indians, engineers, soldiers, workmen and a priest. Their mission was furs and forts. They were to bring back as many pelts as possible and do as much damage as possible to the English forts. They started out toward the end of March. The entire town of Montréal turned out to witness their departure and wish them well. After a church service, they launched their long line of canoes on the Ottawa River, amid cheers from onlookers crowding the banks.

The farther north they traveled, the more laborious the way became. Iced rivers were neither soft enough to permit canoeing, nor hard enough to walk on. One canoe capsized in a combination of rapids and ice. At another point forest fire destroyed all the tents. Further on a load of heavy arms was bogged in drifted snow. Seventy-two days from the time they had left a cheering Montréal, they reached James Bay, the southern tip of Hudson Bay. They arrived at night and made camp. D'Iberville left the camp to do some scouting.

The moon and stars were overcast. Only the display of the aurora borealis, the northern lights, streaked the sky. All was still except for an occasional rumble of ice floes breaking up. Suddenly the moon came out. Thirty feet ahead, d'Iberville saw a black mass—the English Fort Monsipi.

He went back to camp and aroused others to accompany him. Reaching the fort, he and a few companions stealthily scaled the walls. As soon as they dropped inside, they imitated Indian war cries, causing the English to rush to their cannons. While the rush was on, d'Iberville opened the gates to let in the rest of the French. Following his orders, they set up a terrific clatter of arms. The English, believing that a large French and Indian attack had been launched, surrendered. The French escorted them into the fort's cellar for the night.

The next morning they inspected the fort's supplies. They found a tremendous quantity of furs, much food and a great stock of ammunition, all of which they appropriated. They held a feast with some of the food, inviting the English to join them. Afterwards they shut them up in a ship that Radisson had previously abandoned there.

Having learned from their prisoners that the English governor of Hudson Bay had gone to meet a pair of supply ships,
d'Iberville determined to intercept him. Leaving a garrison at
Fort Monsipi to guard prisoners and secure any furs Indians
might bring in, he set out in an English ship.

Near Fort Rupert, between the Rupert and Nottaway
Rivers, he and his brother, Paul de Maricourt, left their ship
for two canoes carrying fourteen men. Sighting an English
ship at anchor, they paddled quietly along side. Only one man
was on deck, and he was asleep. The French climbed aboard
and as the one sailor wakened, they knocked him down with a
sword, but not before his startled cry had alarmed the rest of
the crew below. D'Iberville and de Maricourt killed two who
came topside. The rest took refuge in the captain's cabin. The
French broke open the cabin door with an ax, and the English
surrendered. The whole operation took less than fifteen minutes.

They went on to capture the fort itself in an all-night battle.
Their victory put them in the novel position of being outnum-
bered by their prisoners. How to guard them? D'Iberville took
them to the small island of Weston, in the Rupert River,
gave them lines for fishing, guns for hunting and a warning
not to try to leave the island on pain of death. Should some
emergency occur, they were to send a pair of unarmed men
wrapped in white blankets to Fort Monsipi. When the supply
ships arrived, they would be sent home to England.

And so, on to Fort Kitchichouan, at the confluence of the
Kitchichouan and Alba Rivers. This was a larger and better
defended fort than Rupert or Monsipi. D'Iberville wasn't
sure he could take it, but feeling certain that news of his previous victories would have reached Kitchichouan and, hopefully, discouraged the garrison, he sent emissaries to discuss
terms under which the fort would be surrendered. The governor, who was there, made every effort to prolong the discussion. He had indeed received news of d'Iberville's triumphs,
but he believed the supply ships would arrive at any minute

and help defend the fort. D'Iberville saw through the tactic. Come what may, he would attack.

The first fusillade landed in the governor's apartment, where he was dining with his wife and the fort's chaplain. It broke all the dishes on the table. The governor fled to the cellar. A short time later he came out, offering wine, food and total surrender. The prisoners were sent to the island of Weston, and an abundant haul of furs to Monsipi.

Next on d'Iberville's program was Fort Saint Anne. Here there was no question of terms, no need to fire a shot. The fort's commander welcomed him with wine. Again prisoners were sent to the island. The furs, the richest stock yet, were left at the fort with d'Iberville's brother, de Maricourt, in charge.

The supply ships didn't arrive for some months. D'Iberville made a quick trip to Montréal to reprovision. He was back at Fort Rupert in time to capture the sole supply vessel that finally showed up. Keeping his word to the prisoners on Weston Island, he set them aboard, leaving them enough provisions for the voyage home, but appropriating the rest.

Later a second vessel was found stuck in the ice by three of d'Iberville's men. When they reported their find to him, he said, "Go get her." She appeared to be deserted. But not so. The crew, eight men, were below. As the three French approached, the English fired. One of the three dropped. The other two surrendered. They were taken aboard the vessel for the winter and in the spring pressed into working on ship's repairs, under the watchful eye of a sentinel.

On a day when the sentinel had turned his back for an instant, they killed him. Then they managed to lock the captain in his cabin. They also locked the hatchway, which was the exit from below, and placed the ship's anchor on top, for double security. That should hold the captain down. Then they barricaded themselves behind some heavy rolls of cord. Occupied high in the masts, the English sailors failed to notice what was taking place below.

From behind their barricade the French called out in a mixture of their own language and the little English they knew, *"Allons, en bas, un à un . . .* down, one by one." Nobody moved in the masts.

"One by one," the French repeated. Still no movement topside. Carefully a Frenchman aimed at the sailor swaying near the topgallant, one of the highest of the square-rigger's sails. His aim was perfect. When his rifle cracked, the Englishman catapulted to the deck, a hole through his head. The others descended, one by one. They were tied up on deck. Alone, the French brought the ship back to d'Iberville as they had been commanded.

Although the expedition had brought the Compagnie du Nord the greatest load of furs Montréal had ever seen assembled at one time, the cost of paying and provisioning the men had also been the greatest. The margin of profit was not large enough to satisfy Montréal's merchants. D'Iberville knew he would have to find some form of additional aid to continue the work. For that he had only one hope, the king.

D'Iberville's exploits were well known at the court of France. Seignelay was glad of the opportunity to present him to Louis XIV. The king listened attentively to d'Iberville's pleas, but all he gave him was one ship. Nor, as events transpired, could he make immediate use of even that. By the time he returned from France, the Iroquois had started their raids on the French. He was called upon to aid in the defense of the colony. But in the midst of the fighting, he received such a disturbing message from Hudson Bay that he knew he must hurry back. The English in the one fort he had not taken, Fort Nelson, were attracting Indians from other forts by offering them higher than the going prices for furs. The French, not having received adequate provisions from the Compagnie du Nord, were half-starved and on the point of abandoning their posts.

He obtained leave to return to the Bay and managed to persuade the trading company that their stinginess was going to destroy all possibilities of income. The Compagnie du Nord outfitted two boats for him and grudgingly loaded them with provisions. Once again d'Iberville sailed north. After leaving the provisions at the three French forts, he headed for Fort Nelson, which guarded the entrance of the Nelson River into James Bay. There he sighted three English boats, one with forty cannon. Courageous as he was, he was not foolhardy. He backed off and disappeared. The English thought he had left for France. Actually on a dark night he had sailed to an English fur depot. The officer in charge took off with his men, but set fire to the depot rather than let the precious pelts fall into the hands of the French. D'Iberville was fortunately able to put out the fire fast enough to save most of them. He sailed home, loaded down.

He was thirty-two years old at the time of this adventure. He had spent ten years on and off in the frozen fastnesses of the far north. Its opportunities magnetized him. But there was something else he also wanted: a wife, a family. To found a family was part of the tradition in which he had been reared. He reconciled the two desires by marrying a true daughter of New France, who accompanied him thereafter on most of his voyages. Her name was Marie-Thérèse de la Pocatière. Their first child was born off the coast of Newfoundland in one of the three ships that Louis XIV gave the couple as a wedding present.

Marie-Thérèse was along when d'Iberville finally prepared to lay siege to Fort Nelson. He was heavily armed and manned, but there was no siege. The victory was as simple as the one at Fort Saint Anne had been. The white flag went up as soon as the dreaded d'Iberville approached. The English asked only that they be allowed to remain in the fort for the winter and shipped to France in the spring, from where they would be given safe conduct to England. D'Iberville accepted the terms, and he and his wife spent the winter with the English in the well-provisioned fort. He renamed it Fort Bourbon, the family name of Louis XIV.

In the spring, 150 Indians arrived with canoeloads of fur. They had heard that the French were now masters of the fort and wanted to trade with them. D'Iberville started out for Montréal with the furs, but ran into such adverse winds that he headed instead for France.

He had no need to ask for an interview with the king. He was commanded to appear. The interview was recorded by a secretary of de Pontchartrain, the new minister in charge of overseas activities. The king commenced: "Monsieur de Pontchartrain has told me of his conversation with you, but I want to hear from you directly. . . . Please speak freely."

"Sire," d'Iberville replied, "since you ask for my views, I will give them frankly. Canada is a magnificent country and the Canadians are hard at work to make [it] the most beautiful jewel in your crown. To succeed, they are ready to put forth, without measure, their energy, their intelligence, and even to shed their blood."

"I know that, Monsieur. Continue."

"A problem exists, Your Majesty."

"Be good enough to describe it, Monsieur."

"For a long time New France has been the envy of the English. When we chase them from one border, they come at us from another, so that we are constantly at war with them. Both our agriculture and our business suffer from this state of affairs."

"What do you recommend that we do?"

"Sire, to guarantee peace we must chase the English from areas they have taken from us, which permit them to squeeze us in an iron vise."

"Just how are they doing this?"

D'Iberville, well prepared, had with him a map of Canada. He spread it out on a velvet-covered table in front of Louis and the two men bent over it, Louis seated, d'Iberville standing. He pointed first to Acadia, which included what is now Nova Scotia as well as parts of Maine and New Brunswick. Since the days when Champlain had attempted to settle the region, sections of it had constantly changed hands between the French and English. At the moment of d'Iberville's conversation with the king, most of Acadia was English. His finger traced an arc from Acadia up to Hudson Bay, through the Atlantic Ocean and the English-held island of Newfoundland. He asked, "Does it not seem to you, Sire, that this arc locks Canada in, threatening to cut off communications with France? So long as the English are in command of this arc, we cannot breathe freely."

He might have been echoing Champlain's last urgent plea to Cardinal Richelieu some fifty years before: "It would be most prudent to begin by chasing the English from our countryside. . . . In a year we can make ourselves master."

To Louis, d'Iberville's proposal seemed overambitious. "That is a sizable enterprise," he said. "Just how would you begin?"

"Sire, I would begin in Acadia. The Abenaki Indians who live there are our allies and would be very helpful. Then I would go on up to Newfoundland and finish at Hudson Bay. Thus the iron arc would be broken."

Louis objected. "That is a very costly proposal, Monsieur. It would weigh heavily on the budget of state."

"Less than you think, Your Majesty. The Hudson Bay fur supply is as rich as the gold mines of Peru. As for Newfoundland, the English have a great number of fishing stations there which yield them a profit of more than twenty million livres[11] a year. That sum alone would cover the whole cost of the war."

"Well," said the king, "I will discuss the matter with Monsieur de Pontchartrain and give you my orders in a few days."

He smiled. D'Iberville bowed and backed to the door. The interview was over. Three days later he received the royal go-ahead. With two ships granted by the king and a third that he captured from the British, d'Iberville took Acadia in less than a week. He then took much of Newfoundland, he and his men fighting on snowshoes, sleeping on caribou skins and living on frozen bread, which they cut with hatchets.

His Newfoundland campaign was interrupted by urgent orders from the king to hurry back to Hudson Bay. The English had retaken all the forts d'Iberville had previously taken from them. Three more ships were sent to his aid.

In the king's name, d'Iberville appointed a temporary French governor for the piece of Newfoundland he had conquered and left him with troops to attack the rest. The governor made such feeble efforts that instead of the French gaining more territory, the British recaptured all they had lost. Nevertheless, based on d'Iberville's conquest, France retained fishing rights in Newfoundland until the beginning of the twentieth century.

Soon after the French fleet left Newfoundland for Hudson Bay, the ships were forced apart by storms that iced their sails. D'Iberville, aboard the *Pelican,* arrived in Hudson Strait first and waited there for the others. After a month he thought he sighted them, but as the three vessels approached he saw that they were not his. They were English and heavily armed. The three-to-one odds were a discouraging prospect, but d'Iberville was not a man to be easily discouraged. He addressed his crew: "My sturdy friends, this encounter is going to be perilous, but we have no choice. On one side we are surrounded by icebergs, on the other by the English. But with God's help, we are going to show those English bastards of what mettle Canadians are made." He then gave orders on the strategy of attack, concluding with "Now we strike! Every man to his post."

Masts creaking with the strain of sails jammed on the wind, the *Pelican* sped straight toward the lead English ship, the *Hampshire.* The *Hampshire* fired. As ordered in advance, the French dropped to the deck and the volley passed over them, crippling only the mizzenmast.

Straight on the *Pelican* sailed. The crew aboard the *Hampshire* recognized d'Iberville. For some years the English had dreamed of capturing this man whom they called "the corsair of Hudson Bay." "Finally we have you!" shouted the exultant commander.

The *Pelican* pulled closer, and her boat hooks were made ready to grapple the *Hampshire* in order to pull the two ships together so that the French could board. The *Hampshire's* commander began to change his mind. When the French lifted their battle axes, he ordered the sails reefed so as to come about, then let them out and took off.

D'Iberville wanted to pursue her, but he knew he couldn't maintain enough speed long enough. Instead he sailed hell-bent for high water between the remaining two English ships, his starboard cannons battering one, his port cannons the other. One sank. His own ship was badly crippled: the pumps severely damaged, the mast gone and seven of his cannons disabled. But with 150 men, 30 cannons and a single ship, d'Iberville had defeated three British vessels with 450 men and 118 cannons.

He pulled into an iceberg-sheltered cove and watched the vessel that was left sail away after rescuing the crew from her sister ship. Luckily for him, his own three ships arrived the following day. Abandoning the *Pelican* for the time being, he and his crew transferred to them and went on to recapture Fort Bourbon. The other forts were returned to the French by the Treaty of Ryswick. Under its terms, five European nations, including France and England, exchanged concessions and territory. The treaty concluded an armed quarrel typical of the European squabbling which, from the beginning, constantly plagued the life of New France. The colony was considered a ploy for the advancement of France in Europe, rather than as an entity in itself. Explorers and governors who were most successful in persuading the throne to meet the colony's needs were those who linked their requests to a French objective in Europe. La Salle had known this when he used French-Spanish tensions to beguile Louis into equipping his last Mississippi expedition.

After the Treaty of Ryswick, Louis returned to the idea of a Mississippi colony that would offer competition to the Spanish in Mexico, while at the same time providing a southern port for New France. In 1698, d'Iberville was ordered to pick up where La Salle had left off. He would rather have returned to the icebound north he knew so well—he longed for an appointment as governor of Hudson Bay—but Louis would not have it so. His Majesty sent him instead to find the Mississippi from the sea.

D'Iberville took two hundred men with him, among them Father Douay who had accompanied La Salle and could supply many pointers about the area. D'Iberville himself had poured over La Salle's journal and the records of those who had accompanied him. Still, when he first arrived in the Gulf, he had no more luck than La Salle in finding the Mississippi from the sea.

He decided to follow La Salle's pattern: first found a colony, then embark on the search. He chose a favorable location, about where Ocean Springs, Mississippi, is today, and named it Biloxi, in honor of a local tribe of friendly Indians. With him he had brought seeds, livestock and other necessities for agriculture. As soon as the first harvest was gathered and the colony seemed secure, d'Iberville started on a combined land and sea search for the mouths of the Mississippi.

It's small wonder that both he and La Salle had so much difficulty finding where and how the great river entered the Gulf. The Mississippi delta spreads out over more than a thousand miles of reedy grass and sluggish water. Through still ponds, broad lakes and moss-draped bayous, the river, divided into uncountable creeks and rivulets, snakes to the sea.

Today a man-made channel, marked by beacons and buoys, leads from the Gulf to the port of New Orleans. Ships are piloted through it. But the seventeenth-century explorer had no such aids. His only way of telling that he had found a genuine outlet was to detect current, no easy task in those lazy streams.

Indians told d'Iberville of one which they called "Great Water," because the stream kept changing to a pond and back again. They said Great Water was deep enough for ships. This must be a main mouth, he suspected.

Day after day his search for it continued. Nosing his barque into every opening, sometimes disembarking to wade through bayous, he covered the delta methodically. At last he found faint current. The farther up he followed the current, the more distinct it became. He had started upstream during low tide. When high tide rose, water funneled up the channel, meeting the river current funneling down. The channel overflowed its banks and made a pond.

Some 150 miles up river, after a voyage of several weeks, d'Iberville began to find traces of La Salle. Indians showed him gifts La Salle had presented. A chieftain gave him a letter Tonti had left for La Salle when he had come to search for his friend, not yet knowing of his death. Others took d'Iberville to the spot where La Salle had built his palisade. Floods had rotted out the logs. There was no doubt now in d'Iberville's mind that he had crowned La Salle's work. At almost the turn of the century—the year was 1699—he had found the way up the Mississippi from the sea.

Father Douay celebrated mass. A cross was planted on a mound and the fifty men who had accompanied d'Iberville on the search linked arms and lifted their voices in a triumphant *Te Deum.*

But as the Mississippi had been the death of La Salle, so was it soon to be the death of d'Iberville. On another up-river voyage the following year, he fell ill with yellow fever. He recovered from the first attack, but the fever kept recurring, each bout leaving him more and more exhausted. His response was to work harder than ever. He knew he had little time left and there was so much he still wanted to do.

The King had made him governor of Louisiana. He arranged for a younger brother, de Bienville, to take over for him so that the administration of the colony wouldn't be interrupted when he died. This done, he went off to visit twenty-five Indian tribes, arranging for alliances among them and alliances between the allied groups and the French. His wife and children came to join the growing colony; so did others from Québec and Montréal, among them Tonti. Two priests, Father Davion and Father de Montigny, were dispatched by the bishop. They made the trip in a canoe, establishing the Québec-Biloxi water route by which one could travel from the Saint Lawrence to the Gulf without venturing beyond the borders of New France.

The route was soon well traveled. Fur traders came, seeking muskrats. Workmen and businessmen followed; small industries grew up. Marie-Thérèse d'Iberville's uncle started a tannery for buffalo hides. He bought raw hides from Indians and sold the tanned product to Québec merchants. In 1702 the colony moved, for reasons unknown, to a site near the present-day city of Mobile, Alabama, where it continued to prosper. Other, smaller settlements spread out around it. Governor de Bienville decided there was need for a more gracious capital city than the sprawling Biloxi. He himself designed the layout for what became in 1722 New Orleans, the capital of southern New France.

D'Iberville had meanwhile undertaken for the king one last assignment: an attack on British possessions in the West Indies, which was intended as a prelude for attacks on Boston and New York. He traveled as far as the West Indian island of Cuba. There, at the age of forty-five, the man the English couldn't defeat surrendered to yellow fever.

Like d'Iberville, most of the coureurs were also explorers and frequently warriors. Their knowledge of terrain and of survival techniques made them invaluable in the defense of the colony—especially since most of the regular soldiers came from France and knew nothing about the guerilla-type fighting required for wilderness victories. By no means, however, did all of the coureurs share d'Iberville's passion for New France. They did what they did for money, and many of them would do anything to get it. The shifting allegiances of Radisson and Groseilliers are an everyday example. So, too, is the career of Antoine La Mothe Cadillac, who succeeded de Bienville as Louisiana's governor.

Actually the coureur's name was not La Mothe Cadillac; it was Antoine Laumet. He made up not only his name, but his family tree and had a coat of arms designed to go with his imagined ancestry. That coat of arms appears on Cadillac automobiles today. He had arrived in Québec with his family in the summer of 1691, penniless, but with a letter of introduction to Frontenac from the minister of overseas activities. Frontenac had just returned as governor, and was attempting to deal with the rising tide of Iroquois warfare and the threats of the English.

Cadillac had spent some time in the English colonies and knew their ways. He spoke English as fluently as his native French. Such a man, the minister thought, could play a useful role in the growing contest between England and France for control of North America. He requested Frontenac to "give him some fitting employment." The governor gave him an army commission and the command of a trading post at Michillimackinac. Cadillac quickly gained Frontenac's confidence and became his partner in the fur trade.

From Michillimackinac he operated with a ruthlessness that was equaled only by his ambition. The Jesuits complained bitterly about the barrels of brandy with which he was swindling their Indian converts. Nor was his swindling limited to Indians. He was not above tricking fellow coureurs, as two of them, Moreau and Duran, themselves no angels, discovered early in Cadillac's career. Cadillac's wife had engaged the pair to take trading goods to her husband. Frontenac gave them permission to carry goods of their own besides, but they added a greater load than their permit allowed. At Michillimackinac they contracted for still more goods on credit from Cadillac.

Looking for some means to cut in on their stores, Cadillac had Durand jailed for refusing to pay for an Indian's dog, which it was said he had injured. Durand replied by saying that he no longer cared to buy the items he had contracted for. Moreau also pulled out of the contract, saying he couldn't afford the purchase alone. Cadillac then threw Moreau into jail on the pretext that he had tried to kill Durand.

While the two were locked up, Cadillac helped himself not only to their trading goods, but also to their personal belongings, including their canoes, wine, food and arms. He broke open their strongboxes and found some IOU's, which he claimed were evidence of dealing in illegal goods.

He kept them in jail only a few days, but then sent them into the wilderness unequipped. They managed to borrow what they needed from other coureurs and traded with the Sioux Indians until they had accumulated enough pelts to return to Québec. There they waited for Cadillac.

When he showed up, they presented a petition against him to the intendant. The petition demanded that he pay each of them the two hundred livres (one hundred dollars) he owed in wages, also reimburse them for the property he had seized and pay damages besides. As for the accusation that they were dealing in illegal goods, they noted boldly, but with reason, that they had as much right to smuggle as he did!

In reply Cadillac declared that his right to smuggle went with his office as post commander. He further insisted that they owed him more than they claimed he owed them, since they were liable for costs agreed upon in the contract they had broken.

The argument shot back and forth for some time. Finally an inquiry was set up to be conducted by a certain judge, the Sieur de Dupuy, and two Québec merchants. Frontenac had Dupuy thrown in the dungeon for two days, whereupon the frightened merchants withdrew from the case. It was next referred to the Sovereign Council, who bounced it back to the intendant, who ruled in favor of Moreau and Durand. He said that Cadillac was to pay them the equivalent of $2,560.

Frontenac canceled the intendant's judgment. The intendant then made a new charge against Cadillac for peddling brandy to Indians, which army officers were forbidden to do. Frontenac covered his protegé by saying that he had personally sanctioned the peddling.

At this point in the battle a mysterious stranger arrived on the scene. All that is known about him is his name, the Marquis de Coutré, and that he came from France. He persuaded Cadillac to make a just settlement of the two coureurs' claims. Did the marquis have something to hold over Cadillac's head? Did Moreau or Durand have some strong relationship with him? Was there a pay-off to Frontenac or Cadillac? Nobody knows. We have only the facts of what happened, not the why.

We do know for certain that Cadillac achieved in a relatively short time his prime ambition: to make money. Fourteen years after he arrived penniless, he was rich enough to offer the equivalent of $70,000 for the purchase of a monopoly on beaver pelts.

Despite the shadiness of his techniques, however, Cadillac had his value to the colony. The minister had been right about that. Foreseeing a race with the English for the west, he founded the thriving settlement that was to become the city of Detroit and made a hard-headed peace with all the Indians surrounding it. As governor of Louisiana, he was less successful. He became embroiled in so many quarrels like the one with Moreau and Durand, that the king was forced to recall him. He went home to Gascony, the southeastern province in France, which was his birthplace.

His fourteen years were part of a colorful achievement in the colony's expansion. Frocks and furs, God and Mammon were key chips in the mosaic that New France was laying, inch by inch, to the north, the south and the west of the continent.

Peace and
New Problems

Yet in spite of good years and some victories, old problems remained for the French and their leaders. In 1691, only one of the eleven supply ships scheduled for New France managed to reach Québec before the freeze-up. The colony had little backlog—a warehouse containing large stores had burned to the ground the preceding spring. Heavy rains all through spring and summer had ruined most of the wheat crop. People fished through the ice and as soon as the snow melted, they grubbed for roots.

That was the spring one thousand Iroquois descended on Montréal, Trois Rivières and settlements between the two. The militia had no ammunition for their guns. The people melted lead from their roof gutters and window sashes to make bullets. Somehow they survived until July when the supply ships arrived with food and ammunition.

Besides supplies, good news came with the ships; the French had won a great victory over the English. The archbishop had a *Te Deum* sung and Frontenac ordered a fireworks display. Candles starred the windows of every house, and in the harbor below, the French ships responded to the illumination with booming salutes. A glittering reception and lavish banquet was held at the Château Saint Louis. Disgruntled Ottawas who had come to Québec to protest the rising prices of trade goods were invited to the banquet. They were so impressed by the ceremonies that they forgot to complain!

The celebrating was supposedly in honor of the king's victory; actually French Canadians were expressing their enormous relief at the arrival of food and ammunition. They would soon need the bullets and gunpowder. The festivities were barely over when the English attacked again.

Major Peter Schuyler—of the same family as the captain who had razed La Fourche—led 266 of the Albany militia with 146 Mohawks and Mohicans to Lake Champlain. The newly armed French defeated this force, but with heavy losses. The mauling delivered to the English was still worse, however. So great was the slaughter that no Albany man would ever again venture into French territory—much to the disgust of the Iroquois nations who were beginning to consider the English as poor battlemates.

There was sound reason for the English fear. In the course of these wilderness skirmishes, the Canadians became hardened guerrilla fighters. They ceased to wait at home for raiders. Instead they took the initiative and became raiders themselves. One of the English governors of New York, Governor Fletcher, compared them to wolves. He said, "They lay close, but no man can discover them until they attack. A hare sitting is much easier found in England."

Their secret was a combination of courage, endurance and

wiliness. A 1693 raid into Mohawk territory north of Albany shows these qualities in action. In lightning strikes, a group of Canadians wiped out five Mohawk villages. On their way back to Montréal, Major Peter Schuyler, in command of English troops plus some Mohawks, caught up with the raiders. They gave Schuyler the slip and reached Lake Champlain. There they had cached food, but when they dug it up they found only rot. The snow was so wet, their snowshoes bogged down to the ground. For the whole group to reach Montréal was unthinkable. So they sent four Indians and one Canadian to that city for aid, and prepared to endure hunger until their return. Their only sustenance was a broth that they made by boiling their moccasins.

The five men reached Montréal in record time—five days. The governor, Callières, sent supplies immediately. In the meanwhile several raiders had died of starvation; others were too weak to move. The weak were left, with supplies, in the care of two officers until they should regain their strength. The others struggled north, throwing away their muskets, blankets and parkas to lighten their load. Frontenac's secretary, Monseignat, witnessed their arrival in Montréal. He wrote: "Only those who saw them could realize what they had been through."

He might have added that few outside the borders of New France, and certainly none at the court of Louis XIV, could realize what they had accomplished. Their destruction of Mohawk villages had reduced that nation to stark poverty, leaving it reliant on the charity of other Iroquois nations and handouts from the English. The handouts were grudging; the English were prepared to buy, but not continually subsidize Indian allies. Nor were the other four Iroquois nations happy at the prospect of forever supporting a sister nation.

Moreover the Iroquois were becoming increasingly annoyed at the lack of support they were receiving from the English, compared with the support that they watched the French giving their allies. When Governor Fletcher addressed a council meeting in 1694, urging Iroquois to be more aggressive in attacking the French, a chieftain replied that they expected him first to fulfill the many promises made that the French would be attacked by a great fleet so that "the enemy being assaulted both ways, may be overcome." It was impossible, the chief declared, to take Canada by land alone.

Governor Fletcher was at that moment in the same spot that governors of New France had all too often occupied. He had begged vainly for supplies. The king's Privy Council, preoccupied with European wars, turned deaf ears to the colony's needs. Meanwhile just the opposite was happening in France. French victories over England were relaxing Louis XIV and his ministers: they could afford to arm their colonists, while the English could not.

The result was that the Iroquois began to sue in earnest for peace with the French. When this news reached Governor Fletcher, he robbed his own militia to provide chiefs of the Five Nations with 86 muskets, 800 pounds of gunpowder and presents of 60 gallons of rum, plus beer, salt, hatchets, knives, clothing and tobacco. Receiving these, the chiefs promised to end the peace negotiations with Frontenac. But when they heard he was building 150 flatboats for a fresh invasion of the Five Nations, they broke their promise. They again asked Frontenac for a peace conference. Frontenac would go no further than to guarantee that their territory would not be invaded while any negotiations that might be undertaken were in progress.

At the same time the Iroquois were pressing for peace with the French, they were telling the French-allied Ottawas and Hurons that the French were breaking their promise not to make peace without consulting *them*. "It will be safer for you to make a direct peace with us, yourselves," said the Iroquois ambassadors. By this double negotiation with Frontenac and his allies, the Iroquois obtained temporary security from both. They used it to prepare for the new attack, which they unleased in 1695.

But Frontenac too had been readying for war. He led a force of more than two thousand—the largest the French had ever mounted—into Onondaga land, the heart of Iroquois country. Up front Frontenac was carried in an armchair. At seventy-four he was an old man, no longer the vigorous giant who left a wake of awe behind him when he strode the streets of Québec. But though his body was enfeebled, his mind was as active as ever. So effective was his campaign that the Onondagas begged for peace on any terms. Taking heart from this success, the French-allied Indians turned mercilessly on the Oneidas, Cayugas and Senecas—the rest of the Five Nations, the Mohawks having already been subdued.

By 1698, their endeavors along with those of Frontenac and earlier efforts of Denonville had crippled the Iroquois's fighting strength. Among them all, only a thousand or so warriors survived.

At the same time, England and France settled their hostilities in Europe. This wrote an end, for the time being, to English attacks on New France in North America. For the French, the period of peace that followed was such a new experience they hardly knew what to make of it. No border raids from the English, no Indian attacks, and in the west—safety for their fur trade. Ironically, this freedom to trade came about just as the demand for beaver, the colony's major resource, began to fall off. Beaver-greedy Canadian merchants had glutted the market, sending Europe four times the amount that could be absorbed. Moreover, they began shipping stiff, dry beaver. This was so hard to shape that other furs took preference. By 1700 Canadians were telling Indians to take their beaver to the English!

The decline of beaver did not, however, signal the end of the coureur's function. On the contrary, other furs—the otter, the muskrat, and hides like moose and buffalo—came into their own. With English and Indian warfare disposed of, the coureur had greater freedom than ever before. He was in his heyday as the seventeenth century turned into the eighteenth.

Frontenac, the man who had done so much, even if for selfish reasons, to further the coureurs' profession, didn't live to see the new century. On November 16, 1698, half-choked with asthma, he sent for his doctor. He insisted on being told the truth about his condition. The doctor told him he was dying. Frontenac then sent for the bishop and was given communion, after which he seemed to rally. An officer present compared the comeback to "a lamp that before going out, musters all its forces for one final effort." The effort sustained him for almost two weeks, but on November 28, it gave out. He slipped into unconsciousness and died.

Callières, the governor of Montréal, was made acting governor and shortly thereafter was named as governor in his own right. In the first year of the new century, he called a meeting of 1,300 Indians to formalize in a treaty the peace that now reigned. The agreement was signed after a large feast, attended by Indian nations who had once been sworn enemies. Then the document was sent to France. Louis XIV and his ministers must have been indeed surprised when they first set eyes on it. Many of the Indians, unable to write, drew tribal totems as signatures. Those who could write were not content with simply signing their names. They added lavish drawings of animals.

For the next fifty years or so, the peace held. The French used the time to advantage. New fortifications were built around Québec's Upper Town, enclosing new government buildings. New business ventures started—the export of seal oil from Lower Town; the forging of iron at Trois Rivières. A road worthy of being called a road was built between Montréal and Québec. The population of New France, which had always been small, began to grow. Québec City quadrupled in size.

But the peace was short-lived. About the middle of the eighteenth century a new rivalry between the French and British colonies arose. This was a race for the control of the Ohio valley.

The Ohio valley was a natural highway to the west. In 1749, Céleron de Blainville went down the river nailing to trees signs that reasserted La Salle's claim to the region as French territory. The next year an English colonist representing a trading company followed de Blainville's tracks, seeking sites for English settlements. The Indians along the river banks listened in turn to the French and English, drank the French brandy and the English rum, accepted gifts impartially and said nothing.

Fully aware of English interest in the region, the French began building a series of forts connecting Lake Erie with the Ohio River. At that point Governor Dinwiddie of Virginia sent a twenty-one-year-old major of the state militia to warn the French off lands "known to be the property of the Crown of Great Britain." The major was instructed to deliver this warning to commanders in the new French forts of Le Boeuf and Venango in northwestern Pennsylvania.

At Venango the young messenger was invited to dinner. He recorded in his diary that after the officers "had drunk a good deal of wine, they told me it was their absolute design to hold possession of the Ohio and by God they would do it." This reply was reported to Governor Dinwiddie, and the next year the major was sent back with a small force to turn the French out. He clashed with them and their Indian allies, but was forced to retreat. The French had meanwhile secured the area with another fort—Duquesne—the strategic position where the Allegheny and Monongahela Rivers meet to form the Ohio. The major hastily built nearby the aptly named Fort Necessity, but his garrison wasn't strong enough to hold it. The French attacked and defeated him on July 4, 1754. Twenty-two years later the date of July 4 would hold new significance for this officer. His name was George Washington.

The following year British troops commanded by General Edward Braddock were sent to knock the French and their Indian allies out of the Ohio Valley. Along with his 1,400 soldiers, Braddock was given 700 Virginia militiamen, led by Washington. Braddock regarded the militiamen with utter disdain. Accustomed to war in the bush, they traveled light so as to be able to maneuver easily, dodging from cover to cover. Braddock's men were weighed down with heavy arms and marched in column formation. Washington tried in vain to warn him that his traditional methods weren't suited to the American wilderness, but Braddock refused to listen.

While his column was crossing the Monongahela, he and his troops were mowed down by sharpshooters sheltered behind trees, boulders and bushes. All but 482 were killed, Braddock among them. When the firing ceased to allow Indians to collect scalps, Washington and his militia managed a retreat that prevented the rout from being any bloodier than it was.

The war for the west was different from any other previously fought on American soil. Usually the colonial wars, if not strictly over local matters, were touched off by wars between the mother countries. This time matters went the other way around. The war in America and British-French colonial rivalry in India were powerful contributing causes to the Seven Years' War in Europe. The fighting, which erupted in 1756, stretched from North America to India to Russia, and involved most of the European nations.

From the start it was clear that the outcome would determine whether Canada was to become English or remain French. The mid-eighteenth century was Canada's critical moment in terms of national destiny.

Two strong men, one English, one French, had a profound influence on the question. One was the English war minister, William Pitt, who in 1757 raised an army of 22,000 to send against Canada and sparked the colonies into adding 28,000 more. The other was Louis Joseph de Montcalm, Marquis de Saint Véran, who was sent to Canada in 1756 as major general in command of all North American French troops.

Montcalm found Canada in a sorry state. The intendant,

Bigot, and a circle of his close friends manipulated all the colony's business to their own advantage. Bigot had twisted the governor, Vaudreuil, around his little finger. Vaudreuil was a weak man, vain enough to lap up the flattery that Bigot served to him in lavish doses. The people called the governor the peacock and the intendant the fox.

Bigot's handling of food supplies is an example of his methods of graft. When crops such as grain became scarce, the intendant was supposed to buy and store the commodity, selling only what was needed for the people to eat. The idea was to prevent individual hoarding and make sure that everybody got his fair share. Bigot bought crops all right, but only when there was no shortage and the price was low. Then he sent the store to France, using the king's ships to avoid freight charges. The grain was received by Bigot's allies in France.

Next he persuaded Governor Vaudreuil to inform the king that Canada was starving. The message received, Bigot's friends stepped forward to help out. They offered the king plenty of grain, which he bought—at a high price. It came back to Canada, again free of charge in the king's ships. On this side of the Atlantic, Bigot and friends piled the cargo in their own storehouses. They then sold from those—with another price jump—to the king's storehouse. Lastly, the Canadians bought back at an outrageous cost from the king's storehouse the same stuff they had sold for very little in the first place. Both the Canadians and the king were twice cheated.

Bigot had been involved in similar graft before Vaudreuil's appointment, but on a minor scale. When he discovered how easily he could manipulate the governor, he gave free rein to his greed. Vaudreuil, born in New France, was extremely jealous of officials from old France, unless, like Bigot, they played up to his illusion that he was the greatest man in North America. By doing just that, Bigot could get him to sign any order he chose, no matter how illegal.

Naturally, neither Vaudreuil with his pride nor Bigot with his graft were eager to welcome Montcalm. Vaudreuil had several times protested the appointment to the king, avowing that he himself could command troops from France as easily as the Canadian troops of which he was already chief. There was no need for an extra leader, he insisted. When, despite the protests, Montcalm arrived, Vaudreuil was set to make his task impossible in any way he could.

His first move was with the army. There were five sections of the fighting force in Canada, and Vaudreuil, by virtue of his relationship to them as governor, was in a position to unite at least four of them. He did just the opposite. The last thing in the world he wanted was for Montcalm to have the strength of a unified command. The first of the five sections were the "regulars," professional troops from France, under Montcalm, who was himself, however, under Vaudreuil. The Canadian regulars and the Canadian militia—the latter a kind of National Guard—were also under Vaudreuil. The French sailors were in the hands of their own officers, but the officers were subject to Vaudreuil. The fifth section, the Indian fighters, were responsible only to their own chiefs. The chiefs' allegiance depended on who was winning. They could shift sides in the middle of a battle. They had known for two generations that they couldn't rid themselves of the Europeans; therefore they at least wished to be identified with the strongest of them.

So Montcalm was confronted with a badly organized fighting force, corrupt officials and a military situation that, despite French triumphs in the Ohio valley, didn't look too encouraging for the long run. The year before Montcalm's arrival, Charles Lawrence, an English governor of the Nova Scotian section of Acadia, had deported the last of the French living there. Most of Nova Scotia had been ceded to England in 1713, but some six thousand French farmers remained on their land. Lawrence gave orders for all of them to be herded at bayonet point onto English ships, or driven into the wilderness.

The governor declared that they were "rebels on account

of past misdeeds," and that "all their lands and chattels" were to be "forfeited to the crown." The past misdeeds consisted of the neutral stand that Acadians took for their own protection as domination of the region shifted back and forth between French and English. The people refused to take an oath of allegiance to the English crown; equally they refused to aid French invasions.

Lawrence's order did not mark the first time Acadians had been deported; some had even left of their own volition. But this was the first time deportation had been wholesale and had included the loss of all property. The refugees departed destitute, with little but the clothes on their backs.

In more than a few cases, families were separated. The separation was not deliberate, but the shortage of English ships was such that it wasn't possible to keep all families together as each load went off. Some reached New Brunswick and the Isle Saint Jean where Acadians had previously migrated. Some made their way to Québec and the Gaspé Peninsula. Others were dumped by the English in Pennsylvania, Maryland, Virginia and the West Indies. A number were transported to England. A good many of those put ashore in southern colonies managed to make their way to French Louisiana. Their descendants, the Cajuns, live there today. Fiercely proud of their ancestry, they still speak the dialect of the mid-eighteenth century French Canadian. Most of them make their living on offshore oil riggers.

The agony of separation and the hardships of poverty that the exiles endured inspired the American poet, Henry Wadsworth Longfellow, to write one of his most famous narrative poems, "Evangeline." It is the story of young lovers torn apart in the mass exiling.

The brutality of the operation shocked even the English prime minister. Governor Lawrence was ordered to stop it. He paid no attention to the order. He had his eye on the French fort, Louisbourg, on Cape Breton Island to the north.

When the time to besiege that fort should come, he didn't want any French on his rear flank.

Montcalm, however, did not see immediate danger to Louisbourg. His eyes focused on three other forts—Oswego, Ontario and George—which the English had built where the Oswego River feeds into Lake Ontario. He considered the capture of these three essential to the defense of New France. Although he was in a hurry to be about this business, he indulged his troops in one touch of gaiety on their way to strike. At the entrance to the Thousand Islands, which lie in the Saint Lawrence between New York and Canada, is a peninsula that coureurs named Point Baptism. They chose the name because of a custom of the habitants who lived there: every newcomer was required to pay one of them to baptise him by drinking his health. In Montcalm's army were 1,300 newcomers!

This was the last bit of off-duty his men were to see for some time. The foundation of Montcalm's campaign was grueling work, performed at lightning speed. He sailed with two armed ships to cut off Fort Oswego by water, and sent a band of Indians and Canadians through the forest to cut it off by land. An advance guard prepared and protected the cove where he intended to anchor his ships. Called Sackett's Harbor, it lay about forty miles north of Oswego and provided a position from which he could attack all three English forts. In a single week he leveled them to the ground. His 3,000 men defeated 3,800 English; he pitted two vessels against five English ships, and his 22 cannons against 123 English ones.

He returned to Montréal laden with plunder. Oswego had contained particularly rich stores: powder, shot, cannons, food, two armed ships and two hundred boats. In the cellar were great vats of wine and rum. Montcalm emptied these into the Lake, lest the Indians get hold of them. The Indians protested the dumping and grumbled about Montcalm's firm refusal to let them scalp or torture prisoners, according to their custom.[12] To quiet their irritation, he gave them much tobacco along with other gifts. To the French minister of war he wrote: "I am afraid my promises will be costly, but the keeping of them will attach more Indians to our side. In any case, there is nothing I would not have done to prevent any breach of faith with the enemy."

What really attached the Indians to Montcalm, however, was less his gifts than his victories. These demonstrated his strength. And they allayed the fear of an English takeover around the Great Lakes, which the Indians believed would drive them out of their own country. A year later, after much inter-tribal discussion, representatives of fifty-one tribes came to Montréal to see Montcalm. They had made up their minds that the French were most likely to be the final victors in the French-English struggle. They called Montcalm "the chief who tramples the English to death and sweeps their forts off the face of the earth."

Those who had never seen Montcalm were surprised to meet a short man: Montcalm stood only five feet four and a half inches. "We thought your head would be in the clouds," said an Ottawa chief. But then, looking into Montcalm's eyes, he added: "Yet when we look into your eyes, we see the height of the pine and the wings of an eagle."

With the help of this reinforced Indian aid, Montcalm wanted to strike another massive and immediate blow against the English. But he didn't have enough money; he didn't have enough supplies. Vaudreuil had dipped deeply into both for a misguided raid on the English Fort William Henry on Lake George. Montcalm's victories around Lake Ontario and his growing popularity on both sides of the Atlantic had irked the peacock governor; he was determined to outshine the man he saw as his rival. Without informing Montcalm until his plan was well under way, Vaudreuil sent his nephew with 1,600 men to attack the fort. The first mistake the raiders made was their last. They aroused the fort garrison by striking ringing blows on the iced lake with the back of an ax to see whether it was solid enough to cross. Quickly routed, then attacked by snow blindness, the blind led the blind back to Montréal. The only person who got satisfaction from the raid was Bigot. The actual costs were multiplied by five so that he could get the difference.

Montcalm had to wait until he could gather new resources before he could make a new move. By summer of 1757, he had accumulated what he needed. In August he set out to take Fort William Henry the way it should be taken. It fell on the ninth.

As was his custom, Montcalm wished to dispose of the fort's rum before the Indians could celebrate with it. He told the fort's commander to empty the barrels. Instead the commander turned them over to the Indians. They drank hurriedly, lest Montcalm discover what they were doing, and were soon completely wild. Jubilantly, they scalped some one hundred prisoners and would have scalped more had not Montcalm and his men intervened. Several of Montcalm's soldiers were killed trying to prevent further massacre.

Unfortunately many innocent Indians far from the scene of the holocaust suffered the results of it. Some of the scalps that the Indians took were those of smallpox victims. For the first time the disease spread all through the wilderness.

Blaming Montcalm for this savagery, the English broke the surrender terms under which all prisoners had agreed not to fight again for eighteen months. The story of Fort William Henry spread throughout the English colonies and was effectively used to rouse strong anti-French Canadian sentiment— an emotion Pitt was to find useful within the year.

Officially, however, the year 1757 was looked upon by the English and French alike as the year of the fleur-de-lis. The flag bearing that symbol of the French monarchy flew over the whole valley of the Saint Lawrence, upper New York, the Great Lakes, the Ohio and Mississippi valleys and Louisiana. Louis de Montcalm was perhaps the only man on either side of the Atlantic who knew how fragile was the appearance of French superiority. The security of this vast territory depended on his army. And his army depended on a structure that was rotten to the core.

In the winter of 1758, Bigot created one of his artificial food shortages. The shortage became acute when two thousand refugees from Acadia straggled into Québec. Bread was rationed to two ounces (two medium slices) per person per day. To a people for whom heaping baskets of bread were a major staple of every meal, this ration was at starvation level. Meat was also short. Angry housewives hurled rotten horsemeat at Vaudreuil's door. The army, refusing to eat it, subsisted on salt cod. The men were no longer paid in gold but in paper money that no one would accept, since the paper had no backing. A mutiny broke out, but Montcalm's faithful companion at arms, François Gaston de Lévis, managed to quell the rioting.

Presents sent Montcalm by the king for use in negotiating with Indians were appropriated by Bigot. Montcalm wrote countless letters to the overseas minister describing the situation. In one, he commented: "If all the presents that the king sends out were really given to them (the Indians), we should have every tribe in America on our side." In another desperate letter, he asked for his recall. He never received any answers. The minister never saw Montcalm's letters. His assistant was one of Bigot's friends.

By June of '58 Montcalm was thoroughly agitated. He had found out that the English were preparing to attack Fort Carillon on Lake Champlain, later to be known as Fort Ticonderoga. English war minister Pitt had organized the largest army ever seen in North America. Making full use of the passions aroused by the atrocities at Fort William Henry, he had persuaded the colonial militia to add 9,000 men to 6,000 English regulars. All 15,000 were to march on Carillon.

The fort was badly in need of repair. For two years Montcalm had been trying to push the necessary reconstruction, but he was severely handicapped by the engineers in charge who were part of Bigot's network. They billed for good materials while installing bad ones. They dragged the work out so as to collect more pay. The fort was still in poor shape. Montcalm had one bad fort and 3,000 men to defend Lake Champlain against 15,000 advancing English and Americans. His garrison, originally 4,600, had been robbed of 1,600 men when Vaudreuil, still hoping to rival Montcalm, withdrew them for a futile raid in the Mohawk valley. At the last moment Vaudreuil released half of the troops he had commandeered. They reached Carillon at the height of the battle.

Montcalm had hastened there as soon as he received word of the coming attack. He turned his garrison into laborers, digging trenches and building zigzag log walls all around the fort at some distance from it. He intended to fight behind this barricade rather than from within the fort. His strategy was to keep battle away from Carillon, which was in no condition to withstand an onslaught.

In the front of the trenches, snares of tree trunks were piled, their sharpened ends pointing toward the foe. The zigzag walls behind the trench permitted any who managed to pierce the snare and traverse the trench to be caught in a crossfire. Beyond these fortifications trees and brush were cleared from the land in a wide circumference, so as to leave no cover for advancing troops. Except for a brief rehearsal of positions to be taken in battle, Montcalm's soldiers spaded with shovels and swung axes and picks up to the moment when the blue uniforms of the colonial militia and the scarlet of the English troops were sighted.

While all this work progressed at a feverish pace, a scouting party was sent to locate the English position. The party killed the brains of the attacking force, Lord Howe. Replacing him was the not-very-bright and not-very-brave General Abercromby, who believed, fortunately for Montcalm, that cannons were not necessary to take the fort. He said it could be done with bayonets.

When Montcalm saw the glitter of those bayonets, he raised his hand above his head. Every soldier laid down his tools and took up his musket. Four masses of redcoats, flanked on either side by militia, showed through the trees beyond the clearing. At the edge of the clearing, English officers were repeating Abercromby's orders: "Don't fire, nothing but bayonets." Behind the barricade, Montcalm's officers echoed his instructions: "Don't fire until they reach the stakes."

As the foe came abreast of those tree trunks, Montcalm raised his sword. His colonels raised theirs. "Ready—present —fire!" The volley mowed down the first ranks of the red-coats and militia. But the ranks behind massed on and on and on. Disregarding Abercromby's orders, they fired steadily as they advanced. But as they struggled among the sharpened tree trunks, they were caught in crossfire from behind the zigzag wall.

At last the English and Americans retreated. But not for long. Again they charged and again they were shot down. Occasionally their grenades set the wall on fire. The flames were quickly quenched with buckets of water that had been provided for that purpose. For the third time, the enemy retreated.

Abercromby, who never appeared on the field, sent word that they were to repeat their attack—still using only bayonets! The fourth charge was led by Scottish Highlanders in kilts and high-pointed, plumed hats. It fared no better than the first three. At five o'clock in the afternoon the English and Americans retreated for good.

Montcalm had a cross erected behind the zigzag wall. On it was carved in Latin:

General, soldier, ramparts are as naught!
Behold the conquering cross. 'Tis God the triumph wrought.

The soldiers in whose midst he had fought cried out, "God save the king and Montcalm!" They added some less respectful words about Vaudreuil, saying that he had sold the colony, but they had refused to deliver the goods. The English general Abercromby they rechristened "Namby Cromby."

Vaudreuil dispatched orders to Montcalm to pursue the

enemy. Along with the orders came reinforcements—now that the battle was over. They were men the governor didn't want to have to feed in Québec. At this point, Montcalm had almost no ammunition and very few provisions. He replied to Vaudreuil, "I think it very strange that you find yourself at a distance of one hundred and fifty miles so well able to direct war in a country you have never seen." With the hungry reinforcements, Vaudreuil sent Indians instructed to steal supplies. When Montcalm caught them and stopped the stealing, they complained to Vaudreuil, who reproached Montcalm. The situation of the hero of New France had become wholly untenable. He again asked for his recall.

But shortly afterwards he received news that England's Lord Amherst had captured what Montcalm had considered to be the invulnerable Louisbourg on Cape Breton Island. Amherst had replaced Namby Cromby as commanding general in the English colonies. Montcalm canceled his request for recall. He wrote: "Since the affairs of Canada are growing worse, it is my duty to . . . stave off ruin so long as I can."

He knew this was the beginning of the end.

The Fall of New France
and the Growth of
Two Canadas

The fall of Louisbourg had put the English in a position to control access to the Saint Lawrence. From Newfoundland they commanded the northern entrance through the Strait of Belle Isle; from Louisbourg they dominated the southern entrance through Cabot Strait.

Like Montcalm, Vaudreuil and Bigot could see that it was only a matter of time before English ships would lay siege to Québec. Meanwhile the pair were threatened with exposure of their graft. The cost of colonial government having quadrupled in three years of their administration, the king of France sent an inspector to find out why. Already the king's man had noted in the records extra ciphers, which multiplied actual costs by ten. A 500 livres cost would be registered as 5,000, for example. If he caught onto where the difference went, Vaudreuil and Bigot could face imprisonment. Better an English conquest than a French jail, they decided. They determined to betray the colony.

By 1759 English rule of the sea had a stranglehold on New France. Nevertheless, on May 10 and 11 that year, twenty-three French ships, heavily armed, finally managed to dock at Québec. Some fought their way in; others managed to give the English the slip while the fight was on. On one of the ships was an aide-de-camp of Montcalm's, the Count de Bougainville, who brought news that Montcalm's name resounded throughout France. "Even the children use it in their games," the aide reported. He carried with him a commission making Montcalm lieutenant general to the king, also a letter from Marshal Belle Isle, veteran head of the French army. The marshal's message was an urgent command: "No matter how small the space may be that you can retain, you must keep a foot in America; for once we lose the whole country, we shall never get it back again. . . . You must hold out to the very last, no matter what happens."

Montcalm replied: "I shall do everything to maintain a foothold in New France, or else die in its defense." To his wife, he wrote: "Can we hope for another miracle to save us? God's will be done. . . . I would give up all my honors to see you again. But the king must be obeyed. Adieu, my heart, I believe I love you more than ever."

Of the supplies that the twenty-three ships carried, Montcalm said, "A little is precious to those who have nothing." There were only 326 soldiers aboard, and not enough provisions to last the summer. Of bad news there was more than a sufficiency. The aide-de-camp announced that Pitt was sending his enormous forces to conquer Canada. A combined fleet and army would attack Québec. Another group was to take Champlain, then march on Montréal. A third was to take the Great Lakes. Montcalm's men numbered 22,000; Pitt's were double that figure.

Montcalm sent 1,000 men to Niagara, 1,000 to Lake Ontario, 3,000 to Lake Champlain. The rest he kept on the Saint Lawrence. On May 23, part of the English fleet sailed into the river and anchored at Bic, a port on the north shore of the Gaspé Peninsula, about 165 miles northeast of Québec. Montcalm strove to prevent their advance but Vaudreuil sabotaged his every effort. The ships reached Montmorency Falls, a few miles outside Québec, and landed troops. Montcalm defeated them, but they retreated only across the river, where they laid waste to the south shore. They easily established headquarters at Lévis, a town named for the Chevalier de Lévis, Montcalm's closest companion at arms. Directly opposite Québec, Lévis was ideal for launching the day-and-night pounding of the capital city, which the English undertook next.

Meanwhile Montcalm received word that Lord Amherst had taken Carillon, now called Ticonderoga, and was advancing toward Montréal. Montcalm sent the Chevalier de Lévis with another 5,000 men to help the field officer in Montréal hold the city. The day that Lévis left, General James Wolfe, co-commander with Lord Amherst of the English forces, was informed of the Lévis mission. By Vaudreuil.

Montcalm's army in Québec now numbered only 13,100. Reinforcements sent to other points, sickness, desertion and battle losses had taken the rest of his troops. At the same time his lookouts reported that rank after redcoated rank was being unloaded from English ships at Lévis.

One lookout at a post called the Foulon, on the heights just beyond Québec, reported that English officers were busily examining the cliff through a telescope. The officer in charge there was Vergor, a friend of Bigot's. He had already released 150 of his men to work on their farms, on condition that they also work on his. Wolfe, who had come up against Vergor during the siege of Louisbourg, knew his worthlessness as well as did Montcalm. Montcalm wanted to replace Vergor with an officer he could trust. Vaudreuil refused the request. "Do the English have wings?" he asked scornfully in reply to

Montcalm's prediction of an attack on the Foulon. When Montcalm ordered a reinforcement of 400 to the post, Vaudreuil countermanded the order.

Just before dawn on September 12, Vergor was awakened by redcoats running toward his tent with bayonets fixed. He crawled out the other side and took off in his nightshirt. Wolfe easily took over the post. He and his men had climbed single file, through the night, up a narrow ravine in the cliff which had been spotted through the telescope. Wolfe had counted on Vergor to desert.

At five that same morning, Montcalm's quick ears caught a sound of cannonade unlike the firing from Lévis which had been going on for days. The boom was closer. He dressed quickly, swung into his saddle and galloped his black charger to a height where he could see what was going on. He saw redcoats filing one by one to the crest of the Foulon and spreading out in a long line on the Plains of Abraham, a high, rolling plateau between the Foulon and Québec. Two soldiers were struggling with the cannon he had just heard.

He ordered up all the French and Canadian regulars and all the militia except 2,000. Vaudreuil ordered all except 2,000 of the militia to stay where they were. He also held back a battalion—about 1,000 men—of the regulars.

The remaining troops formed six-deep battle ranks on the Plains. When the formation was complete, a full-throated shout went up: "Long live the king and Montcalm!" These were the voices of men who had fought at Oswego, Ticonderoga, William Henry and Montmorency Falls. Montcalm replied to each battalion, reining his horse as he passed, thanking, encouraging and warning of the gravity of their situation. Then, as he saw some confusion in the English lines, he raised his sword, giving the order to advance. Taking advantage of enemy confusion was his only chance.

His troops were not supposed to fire until his sword went up again, but their confusion was soon considerably greater than any in the enemy line. As they came within musket range of the English, three battalions of militia suddenly fired, then dropped to the ground to reload. Their movement threw out the six-deep block formation. The regulars wavered. There was more wavering when the militia, instead of refilling their assigned positions, fled to the flanks.

Montcalm halted long enough to steady and re-form his ranks, then pressed on. A single English gun peppered the French on the left flank, cutting it down by half, but otherwise the unwavering long line of redcoats advanced pace by pace, without firing a shot. Not until the two armies were within forty paces of each other did the glint of the commanding sword blade flash on the English side. Then their volleys boomed successively, as battalion followed battalion, the men of each shooting in unison. The entire front line of the French fell.

The English reloaded without stopping. At twenty paces, they fired again, this time spreading out to circle the French. The volley took not only the renewed front ranks but the rear flanks. The surrounded French fired madly, in utter disorder. The block broke into a shapeless mass. Montcalm, though wounded, tried to rally his men. No use. The mass swayed, broke and fled. The battle had taken only thirty minutes but half the French lay dead or wounded on the Plains, their bright blood staining green hillocks, puddling green hollows.

On the highest hillock, as Montcalm struggled to hold a small group in line, he was twice more wounded. He fell forward in the saddle. At almost the same moment, Wolfe fell, with bullets in his lungs, stomach and one arm. A lieutenant told him the French were routed. He smiled, nodded and died.

Two soldiers led Montcalm, draped over his horse, back to the city. As they entered the Gate Saint Louis, people lined the street. A woman cried out, "My God, Monsieur le Marquis is dead." Montcalm straightened in his saddle. "It is nothing, it is nothing," he said. A few minutes later he asked his doctor, "How long have I to live?" "The wound is mortal," the doctor replied.

"So much the better," said Montcalm, "I will not see the English in Québec." He died later in the day, having kept his promise to Marshal Belle Isle: "I shall do everything to maintain a foothold in New France, or else die in its defense."

There is a monument to Montcalm and Wolfe, a plain column on a pedestal, which stands in a small garden park just below the Plains of Abraham. Translated, the Latin inscription on it reads: "Valor gave them a common death, history a common fame, and posterity a common monument."

A few months later, in early 1760, Vaudreuil, who had fled to Montréal, surrendered that city to Amherst. Vaudreuil was brought to trial in France, but acquitted. Bigot was likewise tried, imprisoned, forced to restore to the Crown the sums he had stolen, then banished from the land.

The war dragged on for another two years in the west, but the fall of Québec had been decisive. After Montcalm's death, his aide, the Count de Bougainville, requested help from the minister of overseas affairs. The minister, still in the thick of the Seven Years' War in Europe, replied, "When the house is on fire, one ought not to be trying to save the barns." The war on their own continent and in India was unpopular with the French; even more so was the necessity for supporting another war on still another continent. The great French satirist and writer of the time, Voltaire, commented, "I am with the public; I much prefer peace to Canada."

In 1762, therefore, France made a secret agreement with the English. The agreement ceded to the English, in return for what Voltaire called "the sweetness of peace," French territory in India along with all of Canada and French lands east of the Mississippi. Spain, which had been allied with France in Europe, was paid off with the country west of the Mississippi.

The following year the agreement was publicly acknowledged in the Peace of Paris, one of a pair of treaties which finally ended the Seven Years' War. The Louisiana territory which had been split between England and Spain was, however, returned to France in 1800. In 1803 the American president, Thomas Jefferson, bought it from the French emperor, Napoleon Bonaparte, and it became part of the fledgling United States.

Canadians of the 1760's felt no deep regrets over the transfer of government from French to English hands. Like the French abroad, they were war weary. Moreover, English rule offered relief from the corrupt Vaudreuil-Bigot government that had persistently skimmed the cream from their earnings and cheated them out of the livelihood their labors merited.

Besides, in the first years after the conquest, the English bent over backwards to be fair to their new subjects. They ruled without vengeance, without violence. No property was confiscated. Civil rights, including freedom of religion, were upheld. The religious issue was especially important to the Canadians, most of whom were Roman Catholics. Their conquerors were Protestants. In a day when ruling powers customarily decreed the type of religion all subjects must adopt, or else suffer the consequences, English permission of diversity of worship in Canada was a most unusual concession. Elective assemblies were also permitted. In addition, French law, which differed considerably from English law codes, was proclaimed to be the law of the land.

These wise English policies kept French Canadians loyal to their conquerors all through the American Revolution, from 1775 to 1781. In 1775 Benedict Arnold and Richard Montgomery were sent by the Continental Congress, a loose confederation of American colonies, to invade Canada. On New Year's Eve, in a blinding snowstorm, French Canadians defeated the Americans at Québec, wounding Arnold and killing Montgomery. French Canadian loyalty to the English held even after, three years later, the Canadians' mother country, France, sided with the American colonies, giving them substantial reinforcements to help throw the English out.

Actually the French Canadians were at first more bitter toward their mother country than toward their new rulers. Government officials and wealthy French-born seigneurs went back to France: those who remained were the habitants, the small merchants, many of the coureurs and some of the soldiers. They had no funds for transatlantic transportation, and even if they could have afforded it, most of them would not have gone. Except for the soldiers, they were Canadians. They felt that France had deserted them, militarily, economically, emotionally. A distrust of France was born, which has persisted to the present day.

One of the first real problems to arise was the question of language. Conquerors and conquered spoke different tongues. In which one were government affairs to be conducted? In 1792, the first elected Assembly of English Canada met. It was the legislature of Lower Canada. The year before, the English had divided the country into Upper Canada and Lower Canada. The names were misleading. Upper Canada was the western part of the country, now Ontario, populated mostly by English and by pro-English Americans who had fled to Canada during the American Revolution. Lower Canada, Québec, was eastern and mainly, though not entirely, French. New Brunswick and the Nova Scotian Islands were governed as separate colonies.

The first question before the Assembly of Lower Canada was the election of a Speaker, the presiding officer. The French Canadian members nominated Jean Panet, a French Canadian. English members, joined by a few French Canadians, proposed an Englishman. The debate centered on the language question. Which was more important: for the Speaker to make himself understood by the ruling power or by his fellow countrymen? The Assembly's answer was to elect the French-speaking candidate.

Shortly afterward, the question of parliamentary debate and publication of parliamentary documents came up. The English maintained that these should be "in the language of the Empire to which we have the happiness to belong." At that point, a French Canadian member, Chartier de Lotbinière rose and, speaking in the halting English he had learned, said,

"Remember . . . 1775. Those Canadians who spoke nothing but French showed their attachment to their sovereign in a manner not at all uncertain. . . . This city, these walls, this chamber"—and he lapsed into French—*"dans laquelle j'ai l'honneur de parler"*—(in which I have the honor to speak) —then again in English—"were saved partly through their zeal and valor. . . . You saw them repulse attacks, which people who spoke very good English made on this city. It is not, you see, sameness of language which makes peoples more faithful or united."

Pierre Bédard, another French member, rose. "Is it not ridiculous," he exclaimed, "to wish to make a people's loyalty consist in its tongue?" The outcome of the debate was that French became, not officially but in practice, the language of debate in the predominantly French-speaking Assembly. Parliamentary documents were published in both languages.

Thereafter the number of English members declined to the point where, in 1800, one of them wrote home, "There are but one or two in the House of Assembly," as against sixteen out of fifty in 1792. Had more Englishmen chosen to run, some of them could certainly have been elected—the original sixteen owed their seats to French-speaking voters. They chose to stay out of the race rather than learn the language of constituents and fellow-legislators. Nevertheless, up until 1805 the French-English relationship remained unstrained.

Then came the first problems. As is so often true, they had to do with money; specifically with taxes, in this case for prison upkeep. The French didn't oppose the tax, but rather the type of taxation, which they believed was weighted against Lower Canada. They succeeded in revising the formula. Whereupon an English publication, the *Mercury,* sounded the first bugle note of battle. "This province," the journal declared, "is already too French for a British colony. . . . It is essential that we should . . . oppose the growth of the French and their influence."

The following year *Le Canadien* was founded. This French

Canadian journal had one purpose: to counterbalance the *Mercury* and defend French Canadian views from *Mercury* attacks. *Le Canadien* never attacked the English Crown. Its target was those English provincial authorities who opposed French ways. The motto, which bannered the front page, was *"Notre langue, nos institutions et nos lois."* Our language, our institutions and our laws. The publication's leading light was Pierre Bédard, one of the men who had spoken out for the French language in the first meeting of Lower Canada's Assembly.

The two publications argued harmlessly in print for a couple of years. Then an English governor, Sir James Craig, set a match to the dispute. Craig had fought Americans in the Revolution; he had fought rebels against English rule in India and South Africa. His was a strictly military mind. In his opinion *Le Canadien* was a rebel publication: hence traitorous. He dismissed Pierre Bédard from the militia of which Bédard was an officer, also Jean Panet, a colonel. Panet, the Assembly Speaker, was reputedly connected with the journal too.

When this action didn't affect the tone of *Canadien* articles, Craig ordered it suppressed, arrested Bédard, the printer and a couple of others involved. After two months he released the prisoners, but Bédard refused to leave jail without being brought to trial. Lower Canada was so irate over the arrest that Craig didn't dare risk a trial. Bédard was ousted from prison at bayonet point.

The governor who followed Craig did his best to soothe the bad feelings; but the sense of separation, French from English, once alive, was not to be spirited away by diplomacy. In 1812 the Canadian party, all French, was born.

Its leader, Louis Joseph Papineau, was a young man of twenty, recently elected to the assembly. His commanding figure, tall and well built, coupled with his quick mind and eloquent tongue made him a compelling personality. Three years after taking his seat in the Assembly, he was elected Speaker, a post he held for twenty-two years, with one brief intermission. The imprint of his leadership, not only on his contempories, but on future generations, sank deep into the French Canadian character.

One of the aims of the Canadian party was to give the Assembly more power. The colonial government consisted not only of an assembly for each section of Canada, but of a legislative council or upper body, and the governor's Executive Council, the equivalent of a cabinet. The Legislative and Executive Councils, mainly English, were appointed, not elected. The French called them "the Château Clique." They and the governor held the purse strings—in effect, therefore, the true power of government. Nor was money the only source of their authority. Legislation passed by the Assemblies could be and often was thrown out by the superior chambers.

When the party's efforts to reform this system were blocked by the nature of the system itself, the stalemates heightened the hostility with which, increasingly, French Canadians were eyeing the English. In 1832, during the excitement of an election in a district west of Montréal, which was hotly contested by both groups, a riot erupted. English troops, called out to restore order, were stoned by an angry French crowd. The troops fired, killing three French Canadians and wounding two.

The riot was a warning of more violence to come. Two years later the Canadian party, now known as the Patriot party drew up ninety-two resolutions, which called to the attention of the king of England some abuses in government, such as the tyranny of the appointed Legislative Council and the concentration of a variety of public offices in the same person, inevitably an Englishman. But the list also included some unreasonable requests such as Assembly power to impeach the governor, a man named Aylmer, who was at that time striving to keep peace between the French and English.

Presented to the Assembly, these resolutions passed by an almost two to one margin. Those French voting against it because of extremist clauses were not sent back to office in the election that followed on the heels of the resolutions' passage. Their failure to hold their seats was still another symptom of rising tempers.

The resolutions were sent to England, resulting in the appointment of a Royal Commission to investigate French complaints. Governor Aylmer was recalled, though he was not censured. An Irishman, Lord Gosford, was appointed to take his place. He pursued a policy meant to pacify the French.

It was now the English turn to become furious. In Montréal they organized a volunteer rifle corps "to protect their persons and property and to assist in maintaining the rights and principles guaranteed by the [colonial] Constitution." Gosford ordered them to disband. They did, and the conflict seemed to be quieting until the Royal Investigating Commission came out with a report recommending against all of the Patriots' resolutions, and particularly one calling for an elective legislative council, which they found "incompatible with the status of a colony." This was, of course, the clause dearest to the Patriots' hearts.

The House of Commons, the lower body of Parliament in England, backed up the Commission's report and in addition gave the governor power to use tax money without consulting the Assembly. Almost immediately the French began to stage protest meetings all over Lower Canada. No longer did they call simply for reform. They wanted independence.

The favorite time for these meetings was after church on Sunday. With flags and placards, the habitants of the local parishes gathered to call for *"Papineau et l'indépendence." "À bas le despotisme!"* speakers shouted and the crowd echoed them lustily. Down with despotism.

Papineau and his followers had been profoundly influenced by accounts of the American Revolution. Those who spoke English translated the Declaration of Independence and other documents into French. They borrowed phrases of the American founding fathers; they copied their techniques. Thus the pledge of the Declaration's signers to devote their lives and fortunes to the cause of freedom became in Lower Canada a call to "transmit to posterity your just rights, even though it cost your property and your lives." And just as Americans boycotted English goods, notably tea, so did the French Canadians, notably textiles.

When the Assembly met in the summer of 1837, the honorable members were dressed like actors taking part in a play set along the banks of the Saint Lawrence a century earlier. Except for the cut of their clothing, it might have been woven and stitched by wives of the seigneurs and habitants who were carving a civilization from a wilderness of woods and water. Their garments were made entirely from *étoffe du pays*, a rough, home-woven material. Their hats were tuques, the habitant's expression of his individuality. Some were shirtless, having been unable to find shirts of Canadian make.

To enforce the boycott and to distribute literature urging independence, the Patriots organized *Les Fils de la Liberté*, the counterpart of the American Sons of Liberty. Corresponding to American minutemen, whose early stands at Lexington, Concord and Bunker Hill were so important to the further progress of the American Revolution, were volunteer companies of armed Patriots.

By such tactics the Patriots had grown strong enough in the fall of 1837 to attract some six thousand citizens to a rally in the town of Richelieu on the Saint Charles River. The meeting was chaired by a close companion of Papineau's, Dr. Wolfred Nelson, who had the crowd roaring when he announced at the climax of a fiery speech that "the time has come to melt our spoons into bullets." Resolution after resolution calling for independence was passed by acclamation, each one celebrated by a volley from volunteer companies of Patriot soldiers.

A column was set up, capped by a tuque, and each man in the audience marched past, touching the column with his hand and swearing to conquer or die for his Canada. Papineau, the main speaker, advised against the use of force. He thought it should be held in reserve for a later date. He suggested giving the boycott a fair trial before resorting to arms. Much too moderate to suit his followers, his advice went unheeded.

In vain did Governor Gosford attempt to ban such rallies. His bans merely became the occasion for further meetings to protest his action. In desperation he wrote to the colonial secretary in England: "I am disposed to think that you may be under the necessity of suspending the Constitution." He added a request that he be allowed to resign, recommending the appointment of a governor "not pledged to a mild and conciliatory line of policy."

To counter the Patriot meetings, the English in Montréal and Québec held equally heated assemblies of Loyalists. The governor was as helpless to quell these as he had been to quiet the Patriots. Both were headed on a collision course.

The collision came in early November, 1837. Some of the Fils de la Liberté hurled rocks through the windows of Loyalist homes in Montréal. Whereupon the Doric Club, a group of young Loyalists, wrecked the offices of a Patriot newspaper. Ten days later came the Lexington of the Lower Canada rebellion. A band of English troopers was traveling between the villages of Chambly and Longeuil with two French Canadian prisoners accused of disloyalty. They were accosted by a Patriot band who demanded the prisoners' release. The troopers refused and a skirmish followed. Several on both sides were wounded before the Patriots won and the prisoners were released.

On the same day a warrant was issued for the arrest of Papineau and his chief aides. Encouraged by the defeat of English troopers on the Chambly-Longeuil road, the Patriots decided to resist the warrant. They knew that the English would march on Saint Denis, a Patriot stronghold where Papineau and Nelson had gone. They quickly gathered forces there.

The English approached the village under sodden skies, plodding through half-frozen mud in a mizzle of alternate snow and rain. As they came close, they heard church bells sounding an alarm. A blaze of fire cut into their ranks. Using a twelve-pound cannon, they tried for five hours to break the Patriots' defense. At that point their ammunition ran low, while the Patriot guns increased their intensity.

The English commanding colonel ordered a retreat, leaving the cannon stuck in the mud, along with the dead and wounded. He had no transport for either men or machines. When they were sure that all their attackers had gone, the Patriots collected and buried the dead and cared for the wounded. Papineau, who considered the victory a temporary one, fled to Vermont, where the Canadian rebels had many American friends. Nelson later followed Papineau but was captured near the border and sent to prison in Montréal.

The English military, who had at first underestimated the strength of the Patriots, were not about to make the same mistake twice. At the end of November they advanced on another Patriot stronghold, the village of Saint Charles. This time they were heavily armed; the Patriots were not. The stronghold fell after less than an hour's fighting. The troopers then returned to Saint Denis, overwhelmed it easily and burned the entire village to the ground.

The government in England now took Governor Gosford's advice. They suspended the constitution of Lower Canada and appointed George John Lambton, Earl of Durham, as Lord High Commissioner, with instructions to come up with recommendations for dampening the Canadian powder keg. There were two reasons for Durham's appointment. Primarily, the Conservative political party in power wanted to get "Radical Jack," as he was known, out of England. He was an active supporter of the Chartists, a group intent on defending and advancing the rights of English laborers. It was also felt that as a champion of the workingman he might perhaps better be able to pacify the habitants.

Durham arrived in May, 1838, and immediately pardoned almost all the French rebels who had been imprisoned. This act went further than his home government had even dreamed of. He was instructed to take back the pardons. He refused, resigned and issued a proclamation giving the reasons for his resignation. He was, in effect, appealing the home government position to public opinion in Lower Canada. Although this did not prevent his government from accepting his resignation, it did much to endear him to French Canadians of that day. When he left, the streets were lined with people; spectators hung out of windows and crowded rooftops. Everyone was as silent as though his carriage had been a hearse. French Canadian men raised their hats in respect as the English earl passed.

He had been in office only five months, but that had been long enough for him to perceive the colony's basic problems and set them forth in a famous Report on the Affairs of British North America. "I expected," he wrote in the beginning of his report, "to find a conflict between government and people; I found two nations at war within the same state."

He did not allow sympathy for the French to stand in the way of his proposals for stopping this war. His report called for a union of Upper and Lower Canada, a proposal that the fathers of the Patriots he had freed from jail had fought off a quarter century before. Evenhandedly, he also called for the across-the-boards system of elective government, which was a main Patriot objective. "But," he insisted, "Canada must be *English,* at the expense, if necessary, of not being *British.*" He felt that representative government, free of British appointees, would remove French grievances, while union would give English Canadians the upper hand in the voting process.

A number of modern French Canadian historians view Durham's desire to keep Canada English as proof of prejudice against the French. But Durham was, after all, an Englishman. And more than any preceding governor, he had understood and taken into account the aspirations of the French section of English Canada. His report reminded the English monarch that "their nationality is their heritage. They cannot be punished . . . for having dreamt on the . . . banks of the Saint Lawrence of preserving [it] for future generations."

The earl hadn't left the Canadian shore two days behind him when new rebellions broke out. Not only had Papineau fled to the United States, but numbers of other Patriots as well. They were gathered mainly near Lake Champlain, where they received sympathy and encouragement from Americans. Robert Nelson, Wolfred's brother, was among them. He issued a proclamation declaring the independence of Canada under a provisional government of which he was president. Papineau, however, refused to have anything to do with the provisional set-up. He had gone to Washington to talk with U.S. president Van Buren and had learned that friendly Vermonters and New Yorkers to the contrary and notwithstanding, no official support for Canadian rebels would be forthcoming from the American government.

Still, on both sides of the border, ranks of French Canadians were grouping, ready to fight. In the fall of 1838 they numbered altogether some 2,500. Border skirmishes between them and the English Loyalist Canadians were frequent. Usually the rebels were defeated, but they persisted in spite of the defeats. One band of 200 carried a fleur-de-lis flag, which had been fashioned for them by the womenfolk of Swanton, Vermont. They also carried a Vermont-donated field cannon, which they promptly lost to the Loyalists in a brief encounter.

Within Canada, whole villages revolted, but their defiance had only a short life. The commanding English general, Sir John Colborne, was nicknamed "Old Firebrand" because his retaliation for revolt was to burn villages to the ground. After several had been razed, Colborne had only to approach a village to have the white flag go up without a shot having been fired. Even so, he burned.

Nelson himself, and an assistant by the name of Dr. Côté, crossed into Canada with a small force of French Canadian refugees. By prearrangement, they met rebel reinforcements.

They were supposed also to meet sympathetic Americans. The Americans never showed. Discouraged, some of the French Canadians went home. Others, led by Côté, made it to Napierville, a town about fifteen miles north of the border, close to the Richelieu River. It had been proclaimed as provisional headquarters.

After the group was installed there, Nelson and two French officers, Hinderlang and Touvray, went back to the States by boat to collect a gift of 250 muskets offered by an American. But such was the disarray at Napierville that when Nelson and his party returned with their precious cargo, no one was around to help unload it! It took about half an hour to round up five or six sturdy men who would pitch into the job.

At Napierville Nelson made his first—and last—speech as "President of the Republic of Lower Canada." Then he sent Côté back to Rouse's Point, at the northern end of Lake Champlain, to collect more arms from the Americans. On the way Côté met and defeated Loyalist troops, but on his return, they defeated him and captured all his ammunition. At the same time, Nelson in Napierville received word that "Old Firebrand" was advancing on the provisional headquarters. Nelson and his force of 2,000 decided to retreat to Odelltown, just north of the border. But Colborne had foreseen the move. Odelltown was occupied by Loyalist militia. They were small in numbers—only 200—but their commander, Lieutenant Colonel Taylor, was a shrewd strategist and they were well armed. The rebels had more pikes and pitchforks than guns.

The Loyalists were concentrated in a Methodist church. The road leading to it and into the village was fortified by a six-pound cannon. The rebels spread out through the fields around the church and fired from behind barns. But as the return fire crackled, those without guns dropped to the snow, where they remained, Hindenlang later wrote, "as motionless as if they were so many saints hewn in stone."

The defenders made several sallies from the church and then a fresh company of Loyalists closed in on the rebel flanks.

Those who managed to escape went back to Napierville under Hindenlang's command. Robert Nelson deserted his troops and fled for Vermont. Later that day, Colborne took Napierville. The revolt was over. The final episodes had lasted less than a week.

Twelve of the rebels, Hindenlang included, were court-martialed and executed. French Canadian judges, Bédard among them, attempted to have the prisoners tried in a civil court where they would have the benefit of a jury, but the only result of their effort was that Colborne suspended the judges from their offices. Most of the captured rebels were sent to English convict settlements in Australia.

While French Canadians were rebelling in Lower Canada, new settlers in Upper Canada staged a separate revolt. The newcomers were largely Scottish, Irish and American. They resented English domination of politics and business in their section just as strongly as the French did in theirs. What the French called "the Château Clique" in Québec, the new settlers of Ontario called "the Family Compact," since many members of the ruling class were related. Although the uprising in Upper Canada was put down as speedily as in Lower Canada, it was the combination of the two that made possible the beginnings of truly representative government in the whole nation.

After the revolts, England decided to do away with the two Canadas. They were made one, but in a very cumbersome fashion. Now known as Canada East and Canada West, they were allowed to keep their own assemblies, but no law could be passed in either one without the approval of the other. This arrangement permitted the two sections to stalemate each other's progress. Canada West had economic interests that Canada East didn't share. The English wanted to expand territory and connect it with railroads. The French wanted to tend their farms. Canada East refused to sanction commercial development. Canada West refused to support agricultural development.

The only common interest was that of the reformers in both sections. In 1847, this interest bore fruit. Louis Hippolyte La Fontaine became prime minister of Canada East and Robert Baldwin of Canada West. Both had been rebel sympathizers in their sections of the country, but neither believed in armed rebellion. They had served briefly in their prime minister posts in 1842—long enought to grant amnesty to all self-exiled rebels. Papineau returned under this decree, and when Baldwin and La Fontaine were returned to office in 1847, worked closely with them. The governor at that time, James Bruce, Earl of Elgin, aided the efforts of these three to create a government, which with certain administrative exceptions, made public offices elective. At long last, the most important recommendation of the Durham report was put into effect.

Still, the situation was politically awkward and everyone knew it. Here were New Brunswick, Nova Scotia and Newfoundland being governed from London, Québec and Ontario half united, half at odds. The first talk of melding these into a more workable union was heard in the 1850's, but not until 1867, after a series of conferences among all concerned, was the British North America Act, the constitution for all Canada, actually agreed upon.

Like the U.S. Constitution it has been much amended since —so much so, in fact, that it is usually referred to as the British North America Acts. The Act and the amendments— sometimes different amendments applying to different provinces—created a confederation of the provinces. A confederation is more elastic than a federation, such as the U.S. Constitution spells out. In Canada the federal government has less say-so in many matters than the provincial governments. For this reason, the French Canadians were at first delighted with the new set-up. It seemed to permit them to be themselves. But as time went on and the nineteenth century rolled into the twentieth, they began having doubts.

The old sore points—language and money—were laid bare again. The new constitution, while guaranteeing that records and journals of the federal parliament and the Québec legislature were to be published in both English and French, permitted either language to be used vocally in all branches of government, courts included. Though the opportunity for choice sounds fair in theory, the effects wreaked hardships on those of the French who could not speak English.

What could a French Canadian do if he spoke no English, but needed to ask help from a policeman who spoke no French? What did a French-speaking person do when brought to trial in a court where he could neither understand the judge and jury, nor they him? How did he feel when, searching for a book in a public library, he discovered that literature in his native tongue was classified in the "foreign" section? Even English-speaking French Canadians resented being considered foreigners.

Schools were another big issue. Before the fall of New France, schools were run by the Catholic Church, but financed mainly by the government. The English permitted Church schools to continue, but provided no financial aid. They made several attempts to establish public schools, but since these were run almost entirely by the English, in English, with Protestant religious studies substituted for Catholic studies, the French Canadian Catholics refused to let their children attend. The result was that education declined in quality and quantity, until, in 1784, only one person in five knew how to read, and even these few did not necessarily know how to write.

Then, between 1829 and 1832, the English government made a series of changes in school law, which included some financial aid to French Catholic schools and quieted some objections of French Canadian parents. School enrollment jumped. By 1837 it had more than doubled the 1832 figure. The jump occurred despite handicaps under which the French schools labored. Teachers were paid less than farm laborers; consequently the profession attracted mainly incompetents. There was a great lack of equipment; not even enough textbooks to go round. The French revolts put an end to even this limited progress. The English closed all schools, their own included.

When the revolts had been put down, the school section of the report of the Earl of Durham was resurrected. The section had been prepared for him by a researcher whom he had assigned to the problem of education. The upshot of the research was a recommendation for two separate school systems, each receiving equal per-pupil aid from the federal government, while also raising additional funds through local school taxes. In 1841 the legislatures of the two Canadas made this recommendation law. With the founding of the Confederation, Article 93 of the British North America Act made the Durham-inspired school law the law of the land.

But as Canada grew, new problems arose. The guarantee of separate schools for separate cultures was weakened. Québec, where the French were a vast majority, wanted more local control over schools than the law provided. Specifically, the province wanted to withhold, or have returned for school support, a portion of the federal income taxes paid by Québecois. They felt that power lay where the money came from.

A case in point is the selection of textbooks. To read a history of Canada written by a French Canadian author and a history written by an English Canadian author is like reading the history of two different countries. The French emphasis is on the growth and survival of French Canada. The English emphasis is on the growth of English Canada and the survival of the Confederation. The fall of New France is for the English author the beginning. English texts tend to glide rapidly over the long period of French exploration and settlement, devoting three quarters of their space to events that followed the battle on the Plains of Abraham. "New France had fallen at last," or, "A new age had begun in Canada's history, the age of British North America," are typical wind-ups of the quick coverage of the people who carved the land and society that the English took over.

The French history book, of course, does almost exactly the

opposite. Half the space is devoted to the growth of North American French culture prior to the English takeover. The other half opens with such references to the battle of the Plains of Abraham as *"une veritable catastrophe pour notre peuple"* —a real catastrophe for our people. The text may continue with a warning like this one:

> *Notre peuple devait désormais affronter la domination d'une nation puissante, longtemps ennemi, animée de vifs sentiments anticatholiques, dont la politique commerciale ne pouvait guère favoriser le relevèment Canadien. . . . L'opposition d'idées, de sentiments, d'intérêts, devait nous placer dans un péril extrême pour notre survivance. La résistance à l'assimilation . . . se prolonge toujours. Même au cours de périodes calmes, le milieu anglo-saxon qui nous entour exerce sans cesse son action et nous force à une vigilance de tous les instants.*

From that moment our people had to brave the domination of a powerful nation, a long-time enemy, inspired by strong anti-Catholic feelings, and with money-minded politics hardly favorable to a French Canadian revival. Opposing ideas, feeling, interests, were to put our survival in extreme danger. Resistance to assimilation . . . continues endlessly. Even in calm times, the Anglo-Saxon environment exercises pressure and forces us to remain ever vigilant.

Though neither text is likely to endear French and English speaking children to each other, both are accurate reflections of how each group tends to view the history of the common country created by confederation. The union was political, but emotionally two Canadas remained. It was inevitable that they would clash again.

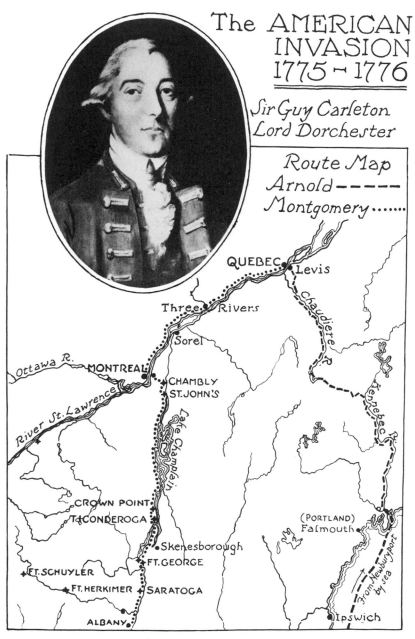

The AMERICAN INVASION 1775 – 1776

Sir Guy Carleton
Lord Dorchester

Route Map
Arnold — — — —
Montgomery ·······

QUEBEC · Levis
Chaudiere R.
Three · Rivers
Sorel
Ottawa R. · MONTREAL
CHAMBLY
ST. JOHN'S
River St. Lawrence
Lake Champlain
Kenebec R.
CROWN POINT
TICONDEROGA
(PORTLAND) Falmouth
Skenesborough
FT. GEORGE
FT. SCHUYLER
FT. HERKIMER · SARATOGA
From Newburyport by sea
ALBANY
Ipswich

COURTESY OF THE PUBLIC ARCHIVES OF CANADA.

203

Louis Joseph Papineau.
COURTESY OF THE PUBLIC ARCHIVES OF CANADA.

Passage of the Richelieu River by night, November 22, 1837. From *Lithographic views of military operations in Canada . . . during the late insurrection,* 1840.
COURTESY OF THE PUBLIC ARCHIVES OF CANADA.

Execution of the French Canadian rebels in front of the Montreal jail.
COURTESY OF THE PUBLIC ARCHIVES OF CANADA.

Conference at Quebec in October 1864 to settle the basis of a union of the
British North American Provinces.
COURTESY OF THE PUBLIC ARCHIVES OF CANADA.

Pierre Vallières. COURTESY OF LA PRESS, MONTREAL.

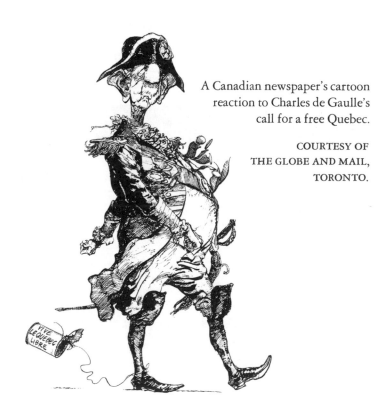

A Canadian newspaper's cartoon reaction to Charles de Gaulle's call for a free Quebec.

COURTESY OF
THE GLOBE AND MAIL,
TORONTO.

Prime Minister Elliot Trudeau. COURTESY OF
DENNIS CAMERON/CAPITOL PRESS, OTTAWA.

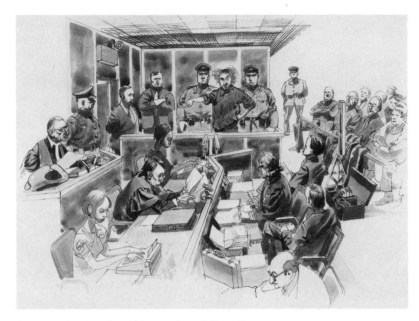

Coroners inquest into the murder of Pierre Laporte.
COURTESY OF THE PUBLIC ARCHIVES OF CANADA.

Arraignment for trial of the murderers of Pierre Laporte.
COURTESY OF THE PUBLIC ARCHIVES OF CANADA.

The Heritage

The clash was called the Quiet Revolution, but by no means was it entirely quiet. Attracting both violent and non-violent participants, activists on the one hand, theorists on the other, the struggle began in the 1950's and gathered strength through the sixties.

The activists formed the FLQ, the initials of Front de Liberation de Québec, meaning Québec's Freedom Front. Though only a few hundred strong, FLQ-ers made up in determination for what they lacked in numbers. Composed mainly of university students, with the support of some professors, journalists and labor leaders, the FLQ organization was held responsible for surging vandalism. Bombs were planted in mailboxes that were stamped with the English royal coat of arms. Government buildings were burglarized and burned. Banks were robbed. A statue of the English General Wolfe was dynamited. There were threats of political assassination. The threats were not taken seriously.

They should have been, as the Saturday morning of October 10, 1970, proved. In the crisp but sunny weather Pierre Laporte was practicing football passes on his front lawn with his thirteen-year-old son and a visiting nephew. Laporte was the labor minister for the Canadian province of Québec. His suburb of Montréal was quiet except for the voices of children playing, the rustle of leaves being raked, and now and then the whoosh of a passing car.

One of these cars stopped briefly near the Laporte home, then sped on. Three masked men, armed with machine guns, ran from the car to the Laporte yard. They forced Pierre Laporte into his green Chevrolet, parked in his driveway. They ordered him to drive where they said.

Five days earlier, James Cross, an official representing British trade interests in Québec, had also been kidnapped from his home. Two terrorists had gained entrance by posing as delivery men. Once inside, they pulled guns and made off with their man.

Shortly afterwards, one of Montréal's French language stations, CKLM, received a message stating terms on which the kidnappers would release Cross. The terms were threefold. First, $500,000 worth of gold. Secondly, postal service truck drivers who had lost their jobs in a recent strike were to get them back. Thirdly, twenty-three jailed members of the FLQ, the underground revolutionary organization to which the kidnappers belonged, were to be freed and allowed to go either to Cuba or Algeria.

CKLM relayed this message to the provincial government. The young premier of the province, Robert Bourassa, who had been only five months in office, called the seasoned Pierre Elliott Trudeau, prime minister of all Canada. Together they decided on an answer to the FLQ-ers. No.

FLQ replied with the kidnapping of Laporte. A war of nerves between kidnappers and the law was on.

The Québec Freedom Front's goal is an independent Québec. Québecois who want Québec to become a country in its own right are known as Separatists. But by no means do all Separatists share the views of the FLQ on how to accomplish this aim.

For example, the Parti Québecois, which supplies the Separatist movement with political leadership, condemns FLQ violence. The party believes in using the ballot, not force, to found a free Québec. Its own ballot count has grown from a mere 6 percent in 1966 to 31 percent in 1973, giving it the role of official opposition in the provincial legislature. The official opposition is the party receiving the second largest vote. And the P.Q., as the Parti Québecois is capsuled in the headlines, is still growing.

A second question on which the P.Q. and FLQ disagree is: what kind of government for an independent Québec? FLQ insists on a Communist government. *Without* that, they say, freedom can't exist. P.Q. says freedom can't exist *with* communism. P.Q-ers want to keep their present form of self-government, but as a nation rather than a province.

Regardless of these basic differences, the two groups spring from a common basis: their desire for independence results from the position of the French in Canada.

The six million Canadians of French descent—five million of whom live in the province of Québec—make up nearly a third of the Canadian people. They have their own language, their own religion, their own customs and culture. Even their own foods. They are numerous enough and distinctive enough to form what has been called a nation within a nation. Yet, until the 1970's they had very little political and economic power. That was almost entirely concentrated in English hands. The French were regarded as second-class citizens. They were labeled slangily as "pea soupers," a reference to the hearty split-pea soup, which stuck inexpensively to the ribs of hungry, hardworking French laborers.

French names were freely anglicized by the English. In telephone books and on official documents such as birth and death certificates, Jean became John, Pierre became Peter, Monique became Monica. Jean, Pierre and Monique were not consulted about these changes. They were made automatically. The French coined an expression to describe themselves: *nous autres*—we others. It is still often heard in Québec, an unconscious reaction to a sense of apartness.

The French language seemed to be a special irritation to the English. *"Parlez blanc"*—speak white—was a rebuke with which French-speaking Canadians became stingingly familiar.

"Do you have any objection to being called French?" a French Canadian journalist was once asked in an English section of the country. When the journalist looked bewildered, the questioner explained: "Well, when you call a nigger a nigger, he resents it."

Subsequently asked, "Do you speak white?" the journalist replied in English, "No, I don't." The questioner was mystified.[13]

The story was the same with jobs. Opportunities for most of the best ones were limited to citizens of English descent; so was the chance for advancement. In 1961 the average income of a Québec family was only half that of Canadian families as a whole. The salaries of Québec's French-speaking workers, who with their families made up 81 percent of the provincial population, was 55 percent less than the average received by their co-workers who spoke English.

Canadians of English descent ran (and still run) all five of Canada's largest banks and most of the insurance agencies and trading centers for investment of money. In other words they control a lion's share of the money flow. The French invariably account for the greater part of Canada's unemployment, which is chronic in Québec.

Until 1960 the economic bondage of the French Canadian

was advertised on a billboard that welcomed visitors to Montréal's international airport. The blurb invited the visitor to "invest in the Province of Québec, where labor is cheap and docile."

No wonder that by the 1960's many of the French had had enough. They began to assert themselves, demanding their rights through a movement they called *Le Pouvoir Québecois* —Québec Power. "Frog Power," some English Canadians called it, using a degrading word for French. "Things run well in Québec so long as the French don't get excited," the English maintained. The Québecois were advised to be "quiet" so as not to frighten foreign investors.

The Revolution was a reaction to these conditions. It had three objectives. The first was to modernize Québec's standard of living, which lagged far behind that of most English populated provinces. The second was to install a provincial government that would be the servant rather than the master of the people. Québec in the 1960's was ruled with reins of iron by Premier Maurice Duplessis. He was part of an alliance among government officials, clergy and big business, especially U.S. big business, which was out to exploit—at the expense of the Québecois—Québec's potential riches. These were her stores of raw materials such as copper, iron ore and asbestos.

The third aim, growing out of the other two, was to put the Québecois in charge of their own provincial resources— whether minerals from their mines, massive electrical energy from their rushing rivers or the minds of their young people in school. *"Maîtres chez nous"*—masters in our own house— was the rallying cry of Pouvoir Québecois.

In 1967 the then president of France, Charles de Gaulle, attempted to give Pouvoir Québecois a lift. Speaking in Montréal, during an official visit to Canada, he called for *"Québec Libre"*—a free Québec. The reaction was so indignant—not only from English Canadians and from the federal government whose guest he was, but also from Québecois—that he had to cancel the rest of his visit. Outside interference wasn't wanted, even by Separatists. "Maîtres chez nous" held for the method as well as the goal.

It was a Canadian prime minister of English descent, Lester Pearson, who gave Pouvoir Québecois its first springboard for action. In the 1960's he brought into the national government a group of French Canadians dedicated to giving Québecois equal status with other Canadians. One of them was Pierre Elliott Trudeau, who, toward the end of the decade, succeeded Pearson as Canada's prime minister.

Trudeau had received part of his education at Harvard University, the University of Paris and the London School of Economics. He and his group, similarly educated, could have remained abroad indefinitely in fine posts that were offered to them. They chose to come home.

Trudeau and five others, all in their twenties, founded a journal called *Cité Libre*—Free Citadel. It was a fighting journal. This was the 1950's; Duplessis was in power. *Cité Libre* detailed and denounced examples of conspiracies among government officials, clergy and big business to divide Québec's natural resources among themselves. It published the news of every deal reporters could uncover and document. In editorials, Québec was described as "occupied territory" and the police as the "forces of occupation." These were defiant words and Maurice Duplessis did not take kindly to defiance. Those who challenged him were likely to suffer for it.

Cité, however, survived. Its founders were not, after all, dependent on it for their livelihood. They were not easily threatened. The journal never acquired enough influence to defeat Duplessis. Death did that in 1959. The importance of *Cité* was not what it defeated, but what it accomplished. Along with other progressive publications put out by students, trade unions and political scientists, it lifted the sights of the Québecois and paved the way for the Quiet Revolution.

Some of the fighting idealists of the 1950's were already

Separatists. Trudeau was not, nor was Separatism the policy of *Cité Libre*. Nevertheless the Liberal party, to which Trudeau and Bourassa both belong and which came to power after Duplessis' death, is a staunch defender of first-class citizenship and first-class rights for the Québecois. The party's achievements, especially with respect to giving the French and English languages an equal national status, are milestones in the progress of the Quiet Revolution. Liberals believe this march can best be continued with Québec inside rather than outside the nation.

"I don't think there's any way you can keep Canada half-united," Trudeau says. To him the Cross-Laporte crisis was a test of the country's ability to accept the authority of the government chosen by a majority. When that government and the provincial government of Québec replied no to the kidnappers' demands, the FLQ sent a message to the police through station CKLM: "In the face of the arrogance of the . . . government, we have decided to move into action."

The action was the strangling of Pierre Laporte with a gold chain on which he wore a religious medal. With the message was a map that led the police to Laporte's car, parked near Montreal's Saint Hubert airport. In the car's trunk the police found Laporte's body, bloodstained at the mouth and ears from the strangling.

The government "arrogance" to which the note referred was not merely the refusal of ransom terms. Prime minister Trudeau had invoked Canada's War Measures Act. This act permits police to search, seize and arrest without the specific warrants normally required for such power in a democracy. It also permits a prisoner to be held for a week without any formal charges. At 3:00 A.M. on October 16, within an hour after the measure went into force, police cars had roared into the predawn darkness of the province of Québec. By daylight they had rounded up close to 300 people suspected of being FLQ supporters and uncovered several stores of ammunition, including 9,000 sticks of dynamite. Not without reason had Trudeau feared that Québecois evolution was on the verge of being stymied by FLQ revolution.

Just before the War Powers were applied, students at the University of Montréal and its branch in Québec City held rallies in support of the FLQ. One of the speakers was a young FLQ leader, Pierre Vallières. A newspaperman, Vallières was also editor of *Révolution Québecoise,* a journal calling for armed revolt to restore dignity and justice for Québec's French. Among those rounded up under the War Powers authority, he was jailed on grounds of having helped incite the kidnappings of Laporte and Cross.

The jail term was by no means Pierre Vallières' first. He had been a militant since 1964. During one of his prison stretches, he wrote his life story, reviewing the tortuous chain of events that had convinced him that he "could expect nothing good, nothing just from the established order." Based on this bitter conviction he decided that salvation for the French lay only in revolution. *Les Nègres Blancs d'Amérique,* he called his book. He translates this title in shock-fashion: The White Niggers of America. He knows very well that the translation is insulting. That's why he chose it. He wanted to bring home his belief that English Canadians regarded French Canadians with the same contempt that many whites on this continent have felt for blacks.

To understand how he reached his conclusions is to understand the roots of the FLQ wing of the Separatist movement, the violence of the sixties and the crisis of 1970.

In early childhood, Pierre Vallières' home was a crowded tenement in a slum neighborhood of Montréal. His father worked nights in a factory, slept during the day. Pierre saw little of him. His mother's days were spent scrimping. With his father's slim salary, his mother managed—barely—to feed and clothe the family. The oldest children of large families, both parents had had to quit school in the early grades and go to work. On their paychecks had depended the survival of *their* parents and younger brothers and sisters. Both were re-signed to their lot; indeed they were too worn out for any-thing but resignation.

Young Pierre was different. He was the family rebel. At the age of five he joined a neighborhood gang that entertained it-self by setting courtyard fires, turning in false police alarms and terrorizing girls with knives. He spent most of his first year in school shooting spitballs at the teacher or floating paper airplanes around the classroom. As he advanced, he learned how to disrupt an entire class, which usually resulted in his being sent from the room—exactly what he wanted. He was the dread of all his teachers, and school was his greatest dread.

In the meanwhile his family had moved from an urban to a suburban slum. The new neighborhood had open sewers for the scarce indoor plumbing, many outdoor privies and houses built mainly of paperboard. Here the boy Pierre met a doctor who devoted much of his career to serving the poor. The doc-tor lent him copies of newspapers and magazines that carried articles about discrimination against French Canadians. Pierre was only ten at the time, but—in spite of his behavior in school—he had learned to read well and to understand what he read. He devoured the news stories.

Further, he decided he wanted an education. On long, lonely walks through the fields that lay beyond the slum, he began asking himself: what is life all about? Why am I here? To answer his own questions, he had to know more. When he was thirteen, he found a way to get what he wanted, much against the will of his mother, who could see no gain for fam-ily finances from a son prolonging school years.

An order of Franciscan monks had opened a Church-fi-nanced secondary school not far from where he lived. At that time not many Québec public schools offered secondary edu-cation. There were Church secondary schools, but they charged tuition and Pierre had no money. But the Franciscan school was free. The monks hoped to persuade students to choose the Church as their vocation, but they demanded no commitments. Pierre enrolled. Though first in his class, he dropped out twice, returning both times after a year of underpaid work, once in a bank, once in a stockbroker's office. Half of his salary went to his parents.

During these teenage years he sought, he says, "a better acquaintance with myself, with others, with my world. . . . I wanted to give meaning to my life as a French Canadian." He showed a talent for writing and began to dream of a novel about the plight of French Canadian families like his own. He wrote one, then another and another, but was pleased with none. He destroyed them all. He knew he would never be a Gide, a Camus, a Sartre, a Proust. He was avidly reading these modern French writers, all nonconformists, often sharply critical of society's pressures on the individual.

He shifted his own work from fiction to fact and, still in school, began at nineteen writing political articles for a leading French Canadian newspaper, *Le Devoir*. He also wrote for *Cité Libre* and had met Pierre Trudeau as well as other champions of the French Canadian cause. He was still searching for a life work. Could he find it in political action? But his seeking seemed only to add to his sense of frustration, of meaninglessness. *"A quoi bon?"*—what's the use?—he kept asking himself. The question added guilt to frustration. Instead of shrugging "what's the use," shouldn't he be trying to change the order that chained his uneducated parents to a daily grindstone of drudgery?

"Your father has worked hard since he was a child and he hasn't died from it, nor have I," his mother said to him when she was urging him to quit the Franciscans and get a job.

"You aren't dead, but you live the life of a slave," he replied.

"So. You think we are a band of idiots. You look down on us. You spend your days reading. We don't read. We work. We have no time to read—and besides, we weren't taught how that well."[14]

Pierre felt guiltier than ever. Then—perhaps in hope of escaping from his feelings—he made a spur-of-the-moment decision: he would become a novice in the Franciscan order that had founded his school. What he discovered inside the order shocked him.

Election propaganda and real estate speculation in which the monks were involved brought home to him the realities of the Church-Duplessis-big business wheeler-dealing.

He left the monastery as abruptly as he had entered it. The monks let him go without regret. "Good-by, good riddance, God help you, Pierre Vallières," were their sentiments. As he had disrupted school classes in childhood, he had disrupted the discipline of his fellow novices. During lectures he was given to dancing rock and roll. He sang off-color songs in the shower and made Bronx cheers in chapel.

By the time he quit the Franciscans, Duplessis had died. The Liberal party had come to power. Vallières went to work for *Cité Libre,* of which Trudeau was then a director. The journal planned a whole issue on the subject of Separatism, for which Vallières wrote a long, thoughtful piece. It was rejected without even having been read through. The piece advocated an independent Québec. Vallières, fresh from the monastery and out of touch with political moods, had not realized that *Cité Libre* was anti-Separatist. The purpose of the special issue was to document that belief.

Vallières split with *Cité Libre* and the Liberals. He lost faith in the collective wisdom, the collective courage of his countrymen, in the entire political process. To support himself, he went to work at odd jobs, in a bookstore, on a construction project. He was disillusioned, disgusted, hopeless. He decided to leave Québec forever. He went to France.

The first exploration, then colonization and development of his country was begun more than four hundred years ago by the French. But today the differences between the Français de France, as the Québecois call the French, and the French Canadians are enormous. The French Canadian is young in history. His culture is still tinged with pioneer vigor, his nation is still building. The European French take pride in a national heritage that is three hundred centuries old. Some of them look down on French Canadians as plebeian country cousins. They, in turn, resenting this patronizing attitude, call the European French snobs.

Though both speak French, the French they speak is not the same. The accent and a good deal of the vocabulary differ sharply. For example, in Canadian French, *favori* means favorite. In French French, with an *s* added (*favoris*) it usually means whiskers. The word for well, in the sense of good, is *bien* in French, pronounced *bee-yahn.* In Canadian French it's frequently pronounced *ben,* and spelled that way. *Ben le fun,* the Québecois says when he speaks of a good time. In French the words are far more formal. *Très agréable,* very pleasant, says the Français de France.

Cultural differences were only one of the problems that rubbed Pierre Vallières the wrong way in France. He came up against attitudes that deepened his disillusion.

He chose to go to work in the vineyards and beetfields of Burgundy, a region in the eastern section of northern France. At that time, 1962, the Communist party was powerful in the area. From fellow workers who were party members he received his first introduction to the theories of Karl Marx, the German philosopher who fathered the theory of communism. He thought, at first, that he had found a system that could do away with the kind of dumb misery in which his parents had been reared; something he could live for and fight for.

But as he became more deeply involved, he saw that his fellow workers were completely controlled and sometimes exploited by Communist union bosses—for the good of the bosses who were playing footsy with the established order. But, he writes in his autobiography, "it was here that I first understood that for aware workers, revolution was not a free choice, but a responsibility." If he had not found a meaning for his life, he had found a goal.

How and where could he fulfill that responsibility? A girl-friend in Paris gave him the cue. She said, "Pierre, you won't find here the answer that you seek. You must learn to live with yourself and your country as it is, neither worse nor better than other countries. You must reconcile yourself to it. I am sure that if you succeed in doing something for your own people, in fighting for them and with them, your life will be completely transformed." Pierre Vallières returned to his Québec. He was offered and accepted the management of *Cité Libre,* aiming to make it a militant voice for Separatism. After a few issues he was told: "Soft pedal the militance or quit." He quit.

The Quiet Revolution had already begun. Vallières founded a new journal, *Révolution Québecoise.* He joined and became a leader of the just then forming FLQ. He had found at last, as he put it, his truth. He was twenty-five years old.

"My friends and I," he said at the time, "are convinced of the futility of the ballot box contest." So on with the dynamite, the burnings and the bombings. Vallières' heroes are modern revolutionaries: Fidel Castro, the premier of Cuba, Che Guevara, the Cuban guerilla killed while leading a revolt in Bolivia, and Mao Tse-tung, the founder of Communist China. The Soviet Union and its leaders he considers old-fashioned.

He is entirely satisfied to have followed the advice of his French girlfriend and to work in Québec for Québec. He says: "It is in Québec that with all my heart I hope to conquer tyranny with my comrades, or else to die with them, armed. If I were a citizen of the United States, I would fight first in the United States. Revolution is not impossible anywhere. It is necessary in every country, including today most of the countries that call themselves socialist. It doesn't matter much to which country we belong. It doesn't much matter with what difficulties we are daily confronted. Our duty as revolutionaries, wherever we are, as Guevara has so well reminded us, is to create revolution."

René Lévesque, the leader of the non-violent Separatists

who are grouped in the Parti Québecois, disagrees. He says: "The terrorists are frustrated, romantic revolutionaries who are importing tactics that have been used all over the world. They represent more of a social sickness than a political movement." His own party is made up largely of people who favor facts over feelings. By no means do they lack fire in their convictions, but their convictions are based on analysis rather than emotion. Although the party has an enthusiastic following of young people, mostly university students, the leaders are middle-aged or approaching middle age. Mainly they are economists, professors, journalists and other intellectuals. Many of them, Lévesque included, had started their political careers as members of the Liberal party and had held high government offices under it. Like the Liberals' leader, Trudeau, several won graduate degrees from French, English and American universities. They were, like Trudeau, products of the *Cité Libre* school of thought.

But by 1967 they had outdistanced that school. They had become convinced of the need for a sovereign Québec. Unable to sell their conviction to the majority of their fellow Liberals, they walked out of the party. Levesque organized a group to work for independence which, the following year, became the Parti Québecois.

The P.Q. had been a long time in the making. The FLQ was already six years old when the P.Q. came along. During those years FLQ offered the only organized opportunity for young nationalists like Vallières to feel they were working for goals that drew them. Terrorism had had no competition. But after the police roundup of FLQ-ers in 1970, little more was heard of FLQ. The organization, always underground, burrowed even deeper under. No surface traces of it remained.

Pierre Vallières went back to newspapering. The kidnappers went to Cuba. The Canadian government agreed with their request for safe conduct to that country in return for the release of Cross. Thereupon, they transferred him to the custody of the Cuban consul in Montréal. At two o'clock on the morning of December 4, 1970, he was released from custody, word having been received of the kidnappers' safe landing in Cuba. Cross had lived for two months with submachine guns pointed at his head by day, handcuffed by night and with little to eat that was nourishing, but he had not been harmed. Laporte's murderers were imprisoned for life. Two men who aided them were imprisoned for eight years each.

Violent aspects of the so-called "Quiet" Revolution lasted no longer than the scattered revolts of 1837 and 1838, but their impact forced all Canada to stop and think. Peaceful Separatists were spurred into stronger political action. The Liberal party intensified efforts to make inside the Canadian union the reforms that the Separatists maintained could only be made outside.

In 1969 Trudeau pushed through the federal legislature the Official Languages Act. Under this act the country is divided into districts, with the requirement that wherever as much as 10 percent of the people in a district are "in a linguistic minority," all federal employees must speak the languages of both minority and majority. All federal government publications must also be in both tongues. In other words, the English in a district where 10 percent or more French Canadians live must speak French to get government jobs, and a French Canadian in the reverse situation has to speak English.

A Commissioner of Official Languages was appointed to enforce this law. However, not all of its provisions took effect immediately. Time was granted to allow people to master a second language. By the end of 1974, they were supposed to have done so. But by 1973, Trudeau realized 1974 was too soon. More than half the report of the Official Languages Commissioner for the year 1971–72 had been taken up with citizens' complaints about violation of the law. A longer period was needed, not merely for learning language, but for overcoming resistance to learning.

Language had become a symbol and focus for deep-rooted hostilities. Whether French or English, it was an emotional matter, a political matter. So Trudeau asked that the deadline be postponed until 1978. The legislature agreed.

The new law bites deeply into Canadian daily life. Besides emotional and political overtones, it has economic impact. The two-language requirements for government jobs cover wide fields of employment, because the Canadian government conducts a great deal of the essential business of the nation. For example, since much transportation is government operated, the law applies to anyone supplying train and air service: stewardesses, conductors, ticket agents, mechanics. People working with the television and radio programs produced by the government are affected. So are those who are employed in liquor stores and hotel chains. Importantly, the language requirement is a means of opening up jobs for some of those most in need of them—French-speaking Canadian citizens. In 1974, 80 percent of them could speak passable English— 45 percent spoke fluently—while only 30 percent of Canada's English-speaking citizens could speak reasonable French. As the country prepares for full application of the law, bilingual citizens get first choice in jobs that open up.

In 1974, Premier Bourassa, newly and resoundingly reelected premier of Québec, moved ahead of the national government on the language question. He led his provincial legislature to proclaiming French as *the* official language of the province. At the same time he guaranteed the continuance of English schools, a bilingual police force, bilingual income tax forms and a two-language policy in other civic relationships in which the new emphasis on French could severely handicap non-French-speaking citizens. This way he appeared to keep within the federal dual-language law requirements, which would definitely apply to his province. Québec has almost double the 10 percent minority, in this case English, which makes it subject to that law. Differences with the federal government, if any, remained to be worked out within the highly elastic framework of the Confederation. However, Québec's proclamation still raises a teasing question: what if, on the same basis, the western provinces of Saskatchewan and Alberta, in both of which live a few less French than the number of English in Quebec, declared *English* the official tongue? Québec has set a precedent.

Backlash
and Headway

Obviously language will remain an issue in Canada for some time to come. Keeping it controversial is the backlash that developed after the passage of the Official Languages Act and mounted after the Québec proclamation. Listen to some of the backlash voices. An English-speaking librarian in Ottawa: "The new civil service appointees are all French who speak English. Language is all they know. They have no other qualifications for their jobs. I've been thirty years in my profession. But that doesn't count. No. To hold my job, I'm going to have to learn French. It's not fair."

An English-speaking grocer in Montréal: "See this plum jam? I import it from England. Will you tell me how I'm going to get *Confiture Aux Prunes* on that tiny label?" Québec law now requires food labels in two languages, each the same size print. American food manufacturers, for whom Canada is a big market, are not about to go to the expense of preparing two different sets of labels. Neither are Canadian producers. Therefore, coast-to-coast food labels are all bilingual. Rice is also *riz,* potato chips are also *patates frites* and ketchup is *ketchup aux tomates.* For no logical reason—feelings are often not rational—the dual labels are especially annoying to English Canadians of the far west.

Another voice, this one from a heckler in a crowd gathered in the city of Edmonton, Alberta, where in the summer of 1974 Trudeau was campaigning for reelection. He had switched into a short paragraph of French for the benefit of Alberta's 18 percent plus of French-speaking citizens. "Let's speak English, like the majority of the people do!" came the cry.

The necessity for the campaign was, in itself, partly a backlash result. Trudeau's government had fallen. That is to say, under the Canadian system, he had received too little support for measures he proposed to the federal legislature to continue in office without holding another election.

Although supposedly the lack of support had to do with the national budget and rising living costs, shrewd observers of the legislature's mood agreed that the effects of the Official Languages Act had strengthened opposition to him. Despite occasional huffy hecklers, however, Trudeau won his '74 election by a solid majority. The English Canadians saw in this product of French-English parentage and French-English education a bulwark against what they regarded as unreasonable French demands. They were joined by French Canadian businessmen who saw his progressive but not radical policies as a bulwark against Separatism, which they feared would cut into their profits.

An editorial in *Le Carabin,* a student publication of the University of Montréal, had summed up the situation earlier: "Separatism is an adventure that has a strong chance of dying stillborn. Its enemies are numerous. Their names are television, automobiles, summer homes, expensive maids and paid vacations."

Yet by no means did a mere coalition of wary English and conservative French return Trudeau to office. His mandate was far greater. With the exception of the extreme radical wing of the Separatists, it would be hard to find a French Canadian who does not take pride in his prime minister's achievements, even if he disagrees with parts of his philosophy. Separatist leaders themselves have acknowledged that the longer Trudeau can command the majority to lead the nation, the more likely Canada is to stay united. In an introduction to one of his books, Trudeau defined his philosophy of government for Canada. "This work," he wrote, "is not a hymn in honor of what my elders called 'our race' and what my juniors now call 'our nation.' But it is none the less dedicated to the progress of French Canadians." They know his dedication.

He is equally dedicated to what he calls "the wholeness of government." While maintaining that governments can't "please everybody, everywhere, all the time, about everything," he insists that they have to be "flexible." To be "accepted by most of the people . . . they must find ways in which people will want to obey them. . . . The basis of law is not the army or the machine gun. It's the acceptance by the people of the principle that the law should be obeyed." It worries him that this acceptance "has been eroded." The reason? "A lot of laws haven't kept up with the times." He speculates that had they "been changed earlier . . . they would have been obeyed."

He thinks back over the 1960's, citing events of that decade as symptoms of the need for change. "The word revolution was on everyone's lips," he points out, linking the French Canadian thrust with the demands of determined minorities in many countries. "I feared a danger of governments not being able to govern. I guess we saw that in October of 1970 in Québec." Trudeau's use of the War Measures Act at that moment was an example of his belief that the most flexible of governments must preserve "ability to act." How else, in a crisis, safeguard the "wholeness" of a people?

French Canada teeters between wholeness and Separatism. The ferment brewed by the Official Languages Act fizzes in incidents daily. These are especially obvious in school life. In one Ontario school, in a district where French Canadians are a strong majority, the students requested the right, theirs by law, to be taught in their own language. A delegation of six visited the district Council on Education, the equivalent of an American board of education, to present their request. The only action forthcoming from the Council, made up of a majority of English Canadians, was to fire a teacher who supported the students' initiative and to refuse to renew the teaching contract of another.

"That's how dictators act," commented one of the students, surprised. The principal and more teachers joined their cause. French and English newspapers picked up the story. The upshot was the resignation of the English-speaking members of the Council. Thanks to student enterprise and faculty support, the law was upheld.

English Canadians are not the only citizens to resist the law, however. French Canadians can be equally obstinate. A teacher in a Québec school was heard to introduce the English period to her students this way: *"Mes enfants, nous allons de faire pure perte de quarante minutes."* We are about to waste forty minutes. Her principal explained, with a what-can-I-do-shrug-of-the-shoulders, "she has a block against teaching the language of her economic masters."

Still another problem is the reaction of Canadians whose language is neither French nor English. Since Canada has a wide-open policy of admitting people from other nations, they make up about a quarter of the country's population. They represent a dozen different nationalities. And each one asks, "If there is to be more than one official language, what about *mine?*" The trouble is that no one group alone accounts for more than 3 percent of the population. They all have to be told no. The result usually is that they learn English. Italians are an exception; their native language is closer to French than the others.

The immigrants' choice of English over French worries the native-born French Canadian. Will the dual language law stick if the ranks of English-speaking Canadians continue to swell with foreigners? French schools are making an all-out effort to prevent this possibility by attracting the children of immigrants. They stage welcome days. They open special nursery schools where the youngest can grow into learning French. In higher grades French students and teachers are supplied with filmstrips and other dramatized materials that bring to life the culture from which foreign students have come. The purpose of such materials is to encourage warm reception of the newcomers.

Until and unless such methods begin to show results, however, the foreign-born Canadian's tendency to choose English as his language increases the edginess of French Canadians. At the same time they can congratulate themselves on rising standards for the teaching of a second language—whether French or English—whichever the minority in a given district may be.

The improvement is a product of the Quiet Revolution. It began when Québec won the long battle to have a portion of federal income taxes paid by a province earmarked for education and other community services in the province. The arrangement gives a province both more money to provide these services and more say-so in tailoring them to fit provincial needs. As a result, Québec's language program offers special inducements—paid leaves of absence, promotions and pay raises—to teachers who take advantage of intensive language-training courses. It also includes teacher-exchanges; loaning French-speaking teachers from French schools to teach French in English schools—and vice versa.

Some Québec school officials say that these efforts will bear more fruit, now that French has been declared Québec's official language. They believe the new status will be a help in removing the kind of emotional block suffered by the teacher who referred to an English lesson as a "waste of time." "One is more free to be genuinely interested in another language when one isn't worrying about one's own," explained an administrator. "But," he added, "there is some evidence that it has increased resistance to the teaching of French. Some English now feel less secure about *their* language."

Learning English is compulsory in Québec from the fifth grade on. Students whose families wish them to start earlier can begin in first grade. As Québec's minister of education and culture, François Cloutier, declared in 1973: "As participants in the North American economy [French speaking] children must learn English. Québecois with an inadequate knowledge of English are in no position to participate in commercial transactions with the other provinces. They lessen their chances of obtaining managerial positions in the [foreign] firms established in Québec."

Young Vallier LeBrun, who earns a living at odd jobs in Tadoussac, would agree. "I learned too little English in school," he says. "I am looking for how to learn more. It is necessary for good jobs." His voice has many echoes among French Canadians in their late teens. Once French-speaking children acquire English and English-speaking children acquire French, Cloutier believes they "will constitute the main channels of . . . understanding between Québec's two major . . . groups." Language is not only money; it is friendship.

Partly for this reason, the federal government of Canada is actively aiding and abetting the building of a bilingual generation. To provincial financing it adds generous grants. Five dollars per student is offered for every minute above twenty minutes of daily instruction in the minority language, English or French, as the case may be. The result in the two years between 1971 and 1973 was a better than 11 percent increase in the study of a second language.

Experimentally, some of this study takes place in a heavily

financed program called by educators "total immersion"—
that is, being ducked wholly in the language, like being
ducked over one's head in water. An "immersed" pupil doesn't
just study French or English. He studies *in* French or English.
At least half of his subjects are taught in a language other
than his own. Thus an English-speaking pupil may learn math
or history or science in French, while the French-speaking student learns these subjects in English.

Language learning, important as it is in a country where
speech has spurred hard feelings for more than two centuries,
is not, however, the only benefit the Quiet Revolution brought
to Canadian schoolchildren. Across the continent, school systems seem to have awakened to the realities of twentieth-cen-
tury life and sought out interest-holding means of exposing
students to them. Since Québec education was the most backward, and its territory was the Revolution's main battlefield,
Québec progress has been the most marked. Prior to the Revolution, a superior education was considered one which
equipped a student to become a teacher, preacher or lawyer.
Period. And this was available only to the privileged few. Men
in space, calculation by computer, nuclear power—all the
scientific growth that began mid-twentieth century—might
never have existed as far as the average Québecois student
knew. The subject nearest to technology was manual training,
in which boys learned to make birch bark canoes.

During the latter years of the Revolution, Québec organized its first modern department of education. New subjects
were introduced in new and well-equipped classrooms. Students were bused as far as fifty to sixty miles in order to learn
about electronics, computers, space modules. They learned
from brand new texts and with the help of newly developed
films and filmstrips. They learned in an environment the opposite of the one that had made Pierre Vallières rebel with
spitballs, beginning his career as a revolutionist.

Students also learned more about each other. To some extent busing pulled together under one school roof the poor

and the privileged, the English and the French Canadians, and the children of the immigrants. This was not the purpose of the arrangements, but it was one of the effects.

Not that any of these changes took place with the abracadabra of a magician. No rabbits came out of hats. Not only were the changes gradual at first—they were meant to continue that way as an evolution. And there are, of course, schools where the evolution has yet to begin.

At L'École Saint Dominique, an elementary school in Québec's capital city, evolution is in full swing. The building is old, but the teaching is new. Michel Marois, one of the teachers, has a class of twenty. They are slow learners, but their classroom behavior gives no sign of their handicap. Indeed their enthusiasm courses around the room like an electric current as they move about, which they are allowed to do at will. Some sit on their desks, which are placed at random; some perch on the window sill.

They are about to write a composition. They have a choice of subjects. They may tell about *mon chien,* my dog, or they may write a letter to *mon cousin.* Discussion about which subject to choose, and why, is lively.

Their dress is informal; jeans, shorts. So is their teacher's. He wears a turtleneck jersey and slacks. His desk is exactly like theirs. They call him Michel. They refer to him as their *"copain,"*—comrade—or sometimes, affectionately, *"le prof."*

There's no system of hand-raising. Pupils speak at will, as they would in any other conversation. If too many talk at once, Michel gives them a look. He controls the class with his eyes, which are seldom still. He is aware of what each student is doing. Very occasionally, he taps his hand lightly on the desk. Immediate quiet follows. He smiles often—and with love. His pupils smile back—and learn.

A visitor arrives. Michel quickly draws the newcomer into the class conversation. The children cluster around the stranger, asking questions. "Try your English," Michel advises them. "She speaks it." From the visitor they learn some English words about dogs. Their teacher has exploited the visitor for the benefit of the children, to the delight of both. The electricity of enthusiasm fairly crackles. Michel Marois is the new-style teacher in the post-Revolution Québec.

The revolution left almost no aspect of Québec's life-style unchanged. Another area of special importance to Québecois is management of their natural resources. Once privately owned, the tremendous energy of the province's torrential rivers now belongs to them. The energy is used to produce electric power.

The transfer of ownership called for adjustments so complicated that they defied even computers. A dozen privately owned companies were involved. So were fifty cooperatives—that is, companies to which people subscribe as members, controlling policy and sharing profits. Among the sixty-two power groups, no two were alike. There were sixty-two different pension plans for employees. Rates charged to consumers differed. So did agreements for the supply of power made with local and provincial governments and large commercial users. All these had to be reduced to one common denominator. Sixty-two had to act as one.

A further challenge was language. The prevailing language of electrical engineering had been English, because the executives had been English-speaking and so had much of the personnel on down the scale. Québec had lacked facilities for training French-speaking hydro (waterpower) people until 1950, the year Laval University opened a center for this purpose.

As students graduated from this center, they were given preference for employment in Hydro-Québec, as the newly organized provincial power system was called. At first these graduates filled middle and lower scale jobs. English Canadians remained in charge. Pressure began to rise from the bottom up to make French the language of Hydro. But nobody at the top spoke it. What to do?

Hydro commissioned a research outfit to study the question

and suggest answers. The result of their recommendations was that little by little, department by department, French started on the way to becoming the language of waterpower in Québec. After the transition to provincial ownership was completed in 1963, top jobs were opened to French Canadian engineers as vacancies occurred. Pressure to speak French, coming up from the bottom, met encouragement coming down from the top. Hydro became *Eedroh,* the French pronunciation. However, Québec-Hydro offers free courses in both French and English to all employees. And its bills to consumers are sent out in both languages.

Since the Quiet Revolution, some American-owned industries located in Québec, and some owned by English-speaking Canadians have copied Québec-Hydro's language programs. The upshot is that more English and French-speaking Canadians are working side by side, and finding a way to communicate.

These and other changes in the economic style of the province help relax tensions. One, which is purely symbolic, is especially pleasing to French Canadians in all ten provinces, though irritating to some English. The portrait of the Queen of England has disappeared from most paper currency. In her place are portraits of Canada's own prime ministers.

Still, many economic problems remain. In 1974, nearly a third of Canada's French-speaking workers, mainly concentrated in Quebec, were employed in small, outmoded industries—shoe, clothing, textile and furniture factories—or in forty-year-old pulp and paper mills, badly in need of modernization. These businesses have survived mainly because of federal aid, awarded in the hope of preventing Québec's chronic unemployment figures from zooming any higher. The actual effect, however, is to prolong the life of industries paying the lowest wages, yet in some cases turning out goods Québec can buy more cheaply than she can make.

The Separatists use this paradox as a prime example of why Québec should be independent. Jacques Parizeau, their chief economist, who served the Canadian government as economic advisor for a decade, puts it this way: "The situation can't be changed with marginal measures. It needs major shifts. You can't get economic improvement when you have no control over economic policies."

"There are two governments in Québec today," he continues, "federal and Québecois, and they spend most of their time fighting each other. There has to be one economic center. Either the Québec government has to commit suicide and let the federal government fill the economic role, or the power has to center in Québec." Oddly enough, Trudeau would agree with him. "The Québecois must be either for Federalism or Separatism," he says.

Parizeau sees a separate Québec as socialist, "but," he adds, "not like Cuba. Like Sweden." In Cuba, government owns all enterprises. In Sweden government and private ownership exist side by side. Like most Separatists, Parizeau is impatient, though not impulsive. "It is useless to wait *another* century," he says. The 1980's are his target date, a timing on which most Separatist leaders agree.

Some of the most canny American observers in Québec, veteran newspapermen and diplomatic representatives, see the timetable as no idle dream. They watch movement in that direction carefully because of U.S. industries with branches located in Québec. What would happen to the earnings that now return to the United States?

According to Parizeau, they would be split between the Québec government and the American company. According to opponents of Separatism, the companies would, under those circumstances, remove their branches from Québec, leaving it economically worse off than ever.

Parizeau is a professor at Montréal University's School of Advanced Commercial Studies. As at home in the history of Québec's past as with its present, he is able to link both with the future. He follows the first railroad tracks to the west, laid in the late nineteenth century, to trace the movement of money from French to English Canada. But first he speaks of the river, the Saint Lawrence, and the French Canadians who opened it and settled its banks. As he resurrects the past, one almost stands on the Québec rock, apprehensive. Those ships approaching—do they bring friends or foes?

Quickly he sketches the building of Montréal's big harbor. Trade is drawn to it from Québec city but still via the river. Then come the railroads into the English west. New industries grow up there. Economic decay begins in the province of Québec. English Toronto, a rail center, becomes the take-off point for the west, and the financial heart of Canada.

The climax in Parizeau's solution for Québec's plights: "The government of Québec must be Québecois."

Some Separatist philosophers speak more of "association" than independence. Among these is Claude Morin, professor both at the University of Montréal and the University of Québec's School of National Administration. Once an undersecretary in the Québec provincial government and a star in the Liberal party, he is now a star in the party of the Separatists, the Parti Québecois.

Leaning back in his chair and sucking thoughtfully on his pipe, Morin gently points out that Québec's Quiet Revolution produced benefits for all Canada—a point widely overlooked outside the province. "Québec problems were becoming explosive," he says. "The federal government had to move. Yet it could not give any one province preferential treatment. Ottawa (the seat of national government) was forced to grant Canada-wide access to the forms of financial home rule it granted Québec."

Although he considers these concessions mere stop-gaps, temporary dikes against Québec Separatism, his idea of Separatism is not a complete break with the rest of Canada. He hopes Québec and the other provinces can keep a common currency, common postal and transportation services. He wants political independence and economic association. Unlike more all-the-way Separatists, and unlike anti-Separatist Trudeau, he believes the combination is possible.

Léandre Bergeron, who teaches French at Montréal's mainly English Sir George Williams University, is an all-the-way and then-some Separatist. In his book-lined, pamphlet-cluttered, well-lived-in apartment, he lounges comfortably on a couch while expressing his opinions. His longish hair is held back by a leather band. His leather vest is fringed. He speaks a French untouched by the Canadian accent, but he writes books in *Joual,* the deep-rooted dialect of the French Canadian workingman, a dialect inherited from the habitants. His book *Pourquoi Une Revolution à Québec* (Why a Revolution in Québec) carries this note on "the mistakes in French language": "All the 'mistakes' in French in this text are intended. . . . A start must be made somewhere in writing language as the ordinary man speaks it, and quitting writing it in the manner demanded by the dominant class for the purpose of perpetuating its dominance."

By "dominant class" Bergeron means those who have the most money. He hopes for a revolution—bloodless if possible —which will make everybody everybody else's economic equal. Workers, collectively, are to become owners and bosses of the industries in which they work. *Pourquoi Une Revolution* spells out this theory in an imaginary conversation between the author and a skeptic he is trying to convince. The book is a dialogue between the two.

In the beginning the skeptic asks the author to define the term revolution. The author replies, "When at the age of twenty, you said to your father, 'Please, please, leave me alone. I'm old enough to make my own decisions,' you made a revolution. . . . You turned upside down in your mind and way of life the authority of your father. You took on your own responsibilities and your own liberties in your relationship to him. You got rid of the control he used to exercise over your life. . . . Before he was above you, on a throne. . . . You

changed the structure of your relationship. That is what a
revolution is all about . . . a change in the structure of relationships." To illustrate his point Bergeron inserts in his text one
of the line drawings he uses throughout:

Maintenant c'est:

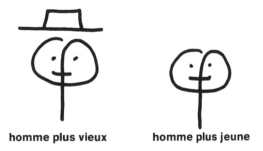

Other drawings illustrate similar changes in other relationships: between boss and workers, between male and female,
wherever in his opinion control is not equally shared by those
bound in a common venture, be it business, marriage, politics,
religion.

Québecois, he believes, are in a specially advantageous position to launch these changes because "traditional North American respect for authority has never squelched them." He recalls the early settlers' way of life: "Our ancestors . . . who put down roots along the river . . . refused to operate under bosses. . . . If French administrators tried to impose on a Canadian farmer . . . well, look here how he takes off for the woods. After some months, he comes home with his furs, sells them and returns to farming. Independent, he was, my ancestor. Against authority. . . . Against the king. Not docile. Not easily obedient. No sheep, he. Full of humor and of laughter, living the now in the now . . . defying death. Able to work like the very devil when necessary, but turned off by a command to do so. . . . He learned from the Indians to survive in the forest; they reinforced his passion for personal liberty. . . . He was part of a tribe of whites among tribes of Indians. Perfect."

"Your Québecois is much too practical to dream of turning society upside down," is the retort of young Claude Lavadour to the philosophy of revolutionaries. Claude works with the administration of the Language Act in Canada's federal government. He defines himself as a "North American of Canadian citizenship who speaks French." The moderate Separatist (along with many non-Separatist Québecois) says: "I am first Québecois, secondly Canadian and finally North American." The revolutionary Separatist states: "I am a Québecois living under English domination."

Claude doesn't think of the English as "dominating." He wouldn't agree at all with Léandre Bergeron's father-figure argument. "The problem is not the *type* of relationship between the two groups," he says. "It's the *lack* of any relationship at all." Like Cloutier, he puts his hope for relating them in language training of youth. He speaks especially of the impact of government-sponsored youth exchanges between Québecois and western Canadians. He talks of the importance of Expo '67, the World's Fair held in Montréal. "It brought thousands of westerners who had never laid eyes on a French Canadian or heard a word of French into direct contact with us." He laughs. "Would you believe that some of them expected us to look different from other Canadians? They were surprised to find us normal."

He might have added that they were also surprised to see bumper stickers on Québec cars which read: "100 Years of Injustice." When some visitors asked "What injustice?" they were introduced to the Québecois point of view on Canadian history.

Among Claude's assignments has been the task of negotiating with western provinces on behalf of the federal government. He has also represented Canada in France. Comparing the two jobs, he admits, "It is easier to come to an agreement with another nation than with our own provinces."

His personal background equips him to serve well as a bridge-builder between the two cultural Canadas. As a child, he was cared for by an English "nanny," and spent four years in western provinces. He recalls once being asked by a French teacher of English in school to take over the class. She had translated *morceau de tarte,* piece of pie, as "piece of pee." Claude corrected her pronunciation. Miffed, she told him, "All right, you get up and do the teaching if you think you're so good." He did—that time and many times thereafter. Today his speech switches effortlessly from French to English and back again.

Problems in administering two languages daily cross his desk, but he doesn't believe Separatism is the solution for any of them. He sees the sovereignty of nations, especially of small nations, on the way out in the world. He points to the European Common market, in which nine nations are unifying economic action and moving toward political unity. "Citizenship comes of age by broadening—not narrowing," he says.

In college at the University of McGill in Montréal, this was the doctrine he preached over the campus radio system, of which he was the director. The doctrine didn't win him any popularity prizes with his fellow-French Canadian students.

These were the beginning years of the Quiet Revolution and Separatism was the subject of many idealistic bull sessions. Claude was called a *"vendu,"* a sellout, and a *"mouton noir,"* a black sheep, Québecois phrases used to describe one of their own who bends over backward to please the English. Claude didn't mind then. He doesn't now. He feels at home as a North American Canadian who speaks two languages.

But a North American Canadian who speaks only one language and lives in an area where he is in a minority is far more easily ruffled than the poised and hopeful Claude Lavadour. Claude's education and experience have given him an outlook which many of his countrymen lack the resources to obtain. And despite the push toward equalizing the two languages, progress is uneven. That national 11 percent increase in language study tabbed up in 1973 could have been considerably higher if five of Canada's ten provinces hadn't shown a slight backslide. Backlash is a stubborn opponent.

Another earlier survey throws interesting light on the attitudes of the students themselves.[15] It was prepared for a commission appointed midstream in the Quiet Revolution to study Canada's double-language, double-culture problems. The young people surveyed were thirteen to twenty years old. A great majority—81 percent—believed in the goal of a bilingual Canada, *but* only 45 percent of the English-speaking youth believed they had a personal obligation to learn French. French Canadians' commitment to learn English came within 15 percent of equaling their belief in bilingualism. The older the English-speakers grew, the more their commitment declined. By the time the French-speakers were eighteen, the 15 percent gap had been almost closed.

The French Canadians felt their situation as a minority was improving. The English felt their majority position was being undermined. They were clear-cut in their conviction that enough progress had already been made in protecting French status. They wanted no more cultural laws. They were particularly vehement in expressing irritation with road signs, which, after passage of the Official Languages Act, appeared in both tongues throughout the country.

Both French and English Canadians overestimated their guesses on how much of Canada's population they represented. The English overestimate remained constant, regardless of age, but as the French teen-agers matured, they reversed themselves. They underguessed. The surveyors saw this reversal as a result of greater contact with the role of the English majority. Both groups felt they would more often agree than disagree with each other, except on one subject, Canada's future. On this they saw agreement and disagreement as fifty-fifty.

A second study, made among eighteen- to twenty-one-year-old Québecois, explored their political attitudes.[16] Asked about preferences in political parties, an overwhelming majority chose the Liberal party. At the same time, 95 percent favored socialism, which is not a Liberal party policy. When asked to choose three out of five definitions of the term "Canadian nationalism," most picked "providing more independence within the Confederation." Next most popular definition chosen was "greater respect for French Canadians, without changing the country's constitution." Only 37 percent opted for "separation of Québec from the rest of Canada"— a figure just slightly higher than Separatist representation in Québec's legislature.

At the same time, however, a little more than a quarter of the young people approved of the FLQ, the violent wing of Separatism. Wrote one student at the University of Montréal: "I admire the FLQ because they have had the courage to rise up. . . . The majority just sits, but they, the Separatists, have said, 'One must struggle for French Canada.' "

And on the subject of non-violent Separatism, another student wrote, "Myself, I am not a Separatist, but I endorse their aims because I find that these contribute to the progress French Canada."

When asked how they would describe their nationality, the

great majority replied, "French Canadian." Explaining her definition, one girl wrote, "When I look at all the history of Canada, I am not Canadian, I am uniquely French Canadian. When I speak of my nation, it is Québec and when I speak of foreign countries, I mean all the other countries of the world, including Canada."

Reviving the folklore and folkways that mirror the history that had so much meaning for this girl is a popular pursuit with today's young French Canadians. The tuque, the habitant hat resurrected by the rebels of 1837, can be seen on university campuses. Songs and dances of the early settlers are in vogue. Some French Canadian universities devote entire departments to the rediscovery and study of customs of the Canadian past. In their examination of the roots of a culture, these departments are akin to Black Studies in U.S. colleges and universities. Students enroll to find out who they are. At Laval University in Québec City, they are learning how much of their identity is antique and global. One class traced a tale about a Gaspé fisherman back to a Greek fable and then to an Egyptian taleteller in 1314 B.C. That class is now more than "uniquely French Canadian." Its heritage predates France.

For the most part, Canadian youth seems to want one country that allows for the distinctiveness of all citizens. Their ideas on how to achieve this happy state are sometimes contradictory, even within a uniform group of French or English-speaking Canadians, but, for that matter, so are those of their parents. For the cacophony of Canada—that is to say, a sound jumble—one need only listen to a French-English gathering singing "O Canada." Sung since 1880, "O Canada" became the official national anthem during the Quiet Revolution. It replaced "God Save the Queen."

Standing between a French Canadian to one's right and an English Canadian to one's left, one hears two entirely different sets of words to the same tune. They are the words each group prefers.

"O Canada! Terre de nos aieux," the French Canadian

sings. The translation is "O Canada! Land of our ancestors," but that is not what the English Canadian is singing. "O Canada! Our home and native land," is his version.

The French Canadian goes on to praise strong arms that knew how to carry the cross and the sword, victories that made Canadian history an epic. The French voices rise slightly.

To the left one hears extolled "the true North strong and free," along with the vow "from far and wide, O Canada," to "stand on guard for thee." English voices also gather strength.

By the time the English vow to "stand on guard" sounds forth, the French words are ardently recalling "bravery supported by faith," and praying that past history will "protect" their "homes and rights."

What is remarkable is that such different interpretations in two different languages can be sung to the same tune. "But we don't really sing together, you know," said Jeanne Pelletier, a Laval University student. "We sing against each other. Here in Québec, we drown out the English words. In the western provinces, the French words are drowned out. I was on an exchange program to British Columbia—far west, by the Pacific. The English-speaking family I lived with were great. Edith, their daughter, is coming to visit us next summer. But you know, she thought the English settled Canada? That before them there were only Indians and some characters from the French underworld? Yes, yes, she knew of French explorers, but nothing of the people born here, the people who gave the land life."

She paused. "That's not Edith's fault," she said. "How would she know when no one ever told her?"

Bibliography

In addition to the books listed here, there are many novels about the various exciting periods in Canada's history. Robert Chambers wrote a series of them; *The Drums of Aulone* is perhaps the most breathtaking. Willa Cather's *Shadows on the Rock* is a moving story of Quebec in the days of Frontenac and Laval. Louis Hemon's *Marie Chapdelaine* (available in French and English translation) is a sensitive story of a habitant teenager's dreams in the days of the early settlers.

Abbot, John S. C. *The Adventures of the Chevalier de La Salle and His Companions.* New York: Dodd, Mead, 1898.

An Account of the French Settlements in North America, etc. By a Gentleman. P. Charlevoix. Boston: Rogers and Fowle, 1746. Facsimile, Photostat Americana, Boston: American Antiquarian Society, 1937.

248 *Bibliography*

Achard, Eugène. *Le Corsaire de la Baie d'Hudson.* Montréal: Librarie Générale Canadienne, 1953.
Angers, Felicité. *Louis Hébert, Premier Colon du Canada.* Québec: L'Événement, 1912.
Archives des Lettres Canadiennes, vol. III, IV. Montreal: Fides, 1969–1971.
Arès, Richard S. J. *Justice et Equité, Pour la Communanté Canadienne Française.* Montréal: Edition Bellarmin, 1963.
L'Association Canadienne des Educateurs de Langue Francaise. *Facets of French Canada.* Montreal: Edition Fides, 1967.
Bédard, Hélène. *Maisons et Églises du Québec, XVII–XIC Siècles.* Québec: Musée de Québec, 1971.
Bergeron, Léandre. *Pourquoi une Révolution à Québec.* Montréal: Editions Québecoises, 1972.
Biggar, Henry P. *The Early Trading Companies of New France.* Toronto: University of Toronto Library, 1901. Reprint, Michigan: Scholarly Press, 1972.
Biggar, Henry P. "The French Hakluyt, Marc Lescarbot of Vervins." In *American Historical Review,* vol. 6, July 1901.
Bishop, Morris. *Champlain, the Life of Fortitude.* New York: Knopf, 1948.
Borer, Mary Cathcart. *Traders and Trappers.* London: Pitman and Sons, 1938.
Bourassa, Guy. *Les Relations Ethnique dans la Vie Politique Montréalaise.* Montréal: Les Presses de l'Université de Montréal, 1968.
Brebner, John Bartlet. *The Explorers of North America, 1492–1806.* London: A. & C. Black, 1933.
Brodhead, J. R., ed. *Documents Relative to the Colonial History of the State of New York.* (Contains the Journal of the Count de Frontenac's Voyage to Lake Ontario in 1673 together with Extracts of Letters from Colbert to Frontenac.) Albany: Weed, Parsons & Co., 1853–1857.
Burpee, Lawrence J. *The Discovery of Canada.* Ottawa: Graphic Publishers, 1929.
Burpee, Lawrence J. *The Search for the Western Sea.* New York: Macmillan, 1936.
Burpee, Lawrence J. *The Sieges of Quebec: The French Regime.* Toronto: Ryerson, 1925.
Campion, Pierre, ed. *Les Lettres de Père Marquette.* Montréal: Bibliothèque de la Societé Historique de Montréal, 1966.
Canada. Commissioner of Official Languages. *Deuxieme Rapport Annuel.* Ottawa: Information Canada, 1973.

Canada. Commissioner of Official Languages. *The Official Languages Act.* Ottawa: Information Canada, 1970.

Canada. Ministry of Education. *Plan de Dévelopment de l'Enseignement des Langues* by Francois Cloutier. Bul. 21. Ottawa: Information Canada, 1973.

Canada: Royal Commission on Bilingualism and Biculturalism. *Control des Moyens de Communication et Équipment Disponible dans les Mass Media au Canada* by Jacques deGuise. Ottawa: Queen's Printer, 1967.

Canada. Royal Commission on Bilingualism and Biculturalism. *Le Fédéralisme Canadien et le Principe de l'Égalité des Deux Nations* by Jacques-Yvan Morin. Ottawa: Queen's Printer, 1966.

Canada. Royal Commission on Bilingualism and Biculturalism. *Les Idées Politiques des Canadiens Français* by Charles Barber and Alfrédo Lévesque. Ottawa: Queen's Printer, 1965.

Canada. Royal Commission on Bilingualism and Biculturalism. *Preliminary Report* and vols. I–VI. Ottawa: Queen's Printer and Information Canada, 1965–1974.

Canada. Royal Commission on Bilingualism and Biculturalism. *Travel and Exchange* by Arthur Stinson. Ottawa: Queen's Printer, 1966.

Canada. Royal Commission on Bilingualism and Biculturalism. *Young People's Images of Canadian Society* by John W. C. Johnstone. Ottawa: Information Canada, 1969.

"Canada, This Very Sorry Moment." In *Time,* October 26, 1970.

Les Canadiens Français, d'un Océan à l'Autre. Ottawa: Information Canada, 1971.

Cartier, Jacques. "Les Voyages de Jacques Cartier." MS no. 5, Part. LVII. Paris: Bibliotheque Nationale.

Cartier, Jacques. "Journal." In *A General Collection of the Best and Most Interesting Voyages and Travels,* ed. by John Pinkerton. London, 1808–1814.

Casgrain, H. R. *Légendes Canadiennes, et Variétés.* Montréal: Beauchemin, 1875.

Cathelineau, Emmanuel de. "Jacques Cartier, Roberval et Quelquesuns de leur Compagnons." In *Revue des Questions Historique,* Sept. 1931.

Catherwood, Mary Hartwell. *Heroes of the Middle West: The French.* Boston: Ginn, 1898.

Cerbelaud-Salagnac, G. *Les Français au Canada, du Golfe Saint-Laurent aux Montagnes-Rocheuses.* Paris: Editions France-Empire, 1962.

Charlevoix, Pierre François Xavier de. *History and General Descrip-

tion of New France, tr. by J. G. Shea. New York: F. P. Harper, 1900.

Chesnel, Paul. *History of Cavelier de La Salle.* New York: Putnam's, 1932.

Clark, Charles Upson. *Voyageurs, Robes Noirs et Coureurs de Bois.* New York: Columbia University Press, 1934.

Colby, Charles W. *Canadian Types of the Old Regime, 1608–1698.* New York: Holt, 1908.

Colby, Charles W. *The Founder of New France: A Chronicle of Champlain.* Toronto: Glasgow, Brook and Co., 1915.

Constantin-Weyer, Maurice. *The French Adventurer: The Life and Exploits of La Salle.* New York: Macauley, 1931.

Davis, Andrew McFarland. "Canada and Louisiana." In *Narrative and Critical History of America,* ed. by Justin Winsor. Boston: Houghton-Mifflin, 1887.

Decelles, Alfred D. *The "Patriotes" of '37: A Chronicle of the Lower Canadian Rebellion.* Toronto: Glasgow, Brook and Co., 1916.

Delanglez, Jean. *Life and Voyages of Louis Jolliet, 1645–1700.* Chicago: Institute of Jesuit History, 1948.

Delanglez, Jean. *Louis Jolliet, Vie et Voyages.* Montreal: Institut de l'Histoire de l'Amerique Francais, 1950.

Desmazures, Adam Charles Gustave. *Colbert et Le Canada.* Paris: E. Belin, 1879.

Desmazures, Adam Charles Gustave. *Histoire du Chevalier d'Iberville, 1663–1706.* Montréal: J. M. Valors, 1890.

Desy, Jean. "Champlain et Frontenac." In *Revue des Questions Historique,* vol. 62, Sept.–Nov. 1934.

Le Devoir. Montréal, June 4, 7, 8, 1973.

Dionne, N. E. *La Nouvelle France de Cartier à Champlain, 1540–1603.* Québec: G. Darveau, 1891.

Doughty, Arthur G. *The Acadian Exiles: A Chronicle of the Land of Evangeline.* Toronto: Glasgow, Brook and Co., 1916.

Douglas, James. *Old France in the New World: Quebec in the Seventeenth Century.* Cleveland: Burrows Bros., 1905.

Douville, Raymond and Casanova, Jacques-Donat. *Daily Life in Early Canada: From Champlain to Montcalm.* New York: Macmillan, 1968. (*La View Quotidienne en Nouvelle-France: Le Canada de Champlain à Montcalm.* Paris: Hachette, 1964.)

Le Droit. Ottawa, May 26, 1973.

Ebersole, Harry B. "Early French Exploration in the Lake Superior Region." In *Michigan History,* vol. 18. Lansing: Michigan Historical Commission, 1934.

Eccles, William John. *Canada under Louis XIV, 1664–1701.* Toronto: McClelland & Stewart, 1964.

Eccles, William John. *Frontenac, the Courtier Governor.* Toronto: McClelland & Stewart, 1959.

Faribault, Marcel and Fowler, Robert M. *Dix Pour Un, ou le Pari Confédératif.* Montréal: Les Presses de l'Université de Montréal, 1965. (*Ten to One, the Confederation Wager.* Toronto: McClelland & Stewart, 1965.)

Gagnon, Ernest. *Louis Jolliet, Decouvreur du Mississippi, etc.* Montreal: Beauchemin, 1913.

Garraghan, Gilbert J. *Marquette.* New York: America Press, 1937.

Geary, R. W. "Early Historical Relics of Upper Canada." In *The Connoisseur,* vol. 61, London, 1922.

Glazier, Willard. *Headwaters of the Mississippi.* New York: Rand McNally, 1897.

Goldthwaite, Reuben, ed. *The Jesuit Relations.* Vol. 1, 2, 3, 4, 7, 8, 12, 13, 17, 23, 24, 29, 38, 45, 56, 58, 61, 66, 68, 70. Cleveland: Burrows Press, 1896–1901.

Un Gouvernement du Parti Quebecois S'Engage. . . . Montréal; Editions du Parti Québecois, 1973.

Graham, Gwethalyn and Chaput Rolland, Solange. *Dear Enemies.* Toronto: Macmillan, 1963.

Grant, W. L., ed. *The Voyages of Samuel de Champlain, 1604–1618.* New York: Scribners, 1907.

Groulx, Lionel Adolphe, II. *La Découverte de Canada–Jacques Cartier.* Montréal: Fides, 1966.

Groulx, Lionel. *Notre Grande Adventure: l'Empire Français en Amerique du Nord* (1535–1760). Montréal: Fides, 1958.

"The Growth of Canadian National Feeling." In *Canadian History Review,* vol. 1, 1920.

Guillet, Edwin and Mary. *The Pathfinders of North America.* Toronto: Macmillan, 1939.

Hamelin, Jean and Roby, Yves. *Histoire Économique du Québec, 1851–1896.* Montréal: Fides, 1971.

Harper, John Murdoch. *Then and Now. The Earliest Beginnings of Canada.* Toronto: Trade Publishing Co., 1908.

Hart, G. E. *The Fall of New France, 1755–1760.* Montreal: Drindale, 1888.

Hennepin, Louis. *A Description of Louisiana,* tr. by John Gilmary Shea. New York: J. G. Shea, 1880.

Hopkins, J. Castell. *French Canada and the St. Lawrence.* Philadelphia: J. C. Winston, 1913.

Hubert-Robert, Régine Marie Ghislaines. *L'Épopée de la Fourrure.* Montréal: Editions de l'Arbre, 1945.

Jacks, Leo Vincent. *La Salle.* New York: Scribner's, 1931.

Jaray, Gabriel Louis. "Les Principes de la Politique Américaine de la France, sous Henri IV, Richelieu et Colbert." In *Revue de Synthese,* vol. 13. Paris, 1937.

Jenness, Diamond. *The Indian Background of Canadian History,* bul. no. 86. Ottawa: National Museum of Canada, 1937.

Jesuits. *Letters from Missions (North America),* ed. by Edna Kenton. New York: Boni, 1925.

Johnson, Daniel. *Égalité ou Indépendence.* Montréal: Editions Renaissance, 1965.

Joutel, Henri. *Journal Historique du Dernier Voyage que feu M. de La Salle fit, etc.* Paris: Robinot, 1713.

Lanctôt, Gustave, ed. *Les Canadiens Français et Leur Voisins de Sud.* New Haven: Yale University Press, 1941.

Laroque, Robert. "Les Deux Derniers Defenseurs du Canada: Montcalm et Levis." In *Revue des Questions Historiques,* vol. 62. Sept.–Nov., 1934.

La Salle, Jean de. *Relation du Voyage Entrepris par Feu M. Robert Cavalier, Sieur de La Salle, par son Frère.* Montréal: La Press Cramoisy, 1766.

Laverdière, Charles Honoré, ed. *Ouevres de Champlain.* Publiés sous le patronage de l'Université Laval. Québec: G. E. Destats, 1870.

Leacock, Stephen. *The Mariner of St. Malo: A Chronicle of the Voyages of Jacques Cartier.* Toronto: Glasgow, Brook and Co., 1914.

Leblond de Brumath, Adrien. *Bishop Laval.* Toronto: Morang, 1906.

LeClerc, Chretien. *First Establishment of the Faith in New France.* New York: J. G. Shea, 1881.

Lejeunesse, Marcel. *L'Éducation au Québec, 19e–20e siecles.* Trois-Rivières: Boréal Express, 1971.

MacLeish, Kenneth. "Québec: French City in an Anglo-Saxon World." In *National Geographic,* March 1971.

Manning, Helen Taft. *The Revolt of French Canada, 1800–1835.* Toronto: Macmillan, 1962.

Margry, Pierre. *Découvertes et éstablissements des Français dans l'ouest et dans le sud de l'Amérique Septentrionale, 1614–1754.* Paris: Maisonveuve, 1879–88.

Margry, Pierre. *Les Normands dans les Vallées de l'Ohio et du Mississippi.* Paris, 1862.

Marquette, Jacques. *Voyage et découverte de Quelques Pays et Nations de l'Amérique Septentrionale.* Paris: Michallet, 1681.

Marquis, Thomas Guthrie. *The Jesuit Missions: A Chronicle of the Cross in the Wilderness.* Toronto: Glasgow, Brook and Co., 1916.

Monro, William Bennett. *The Seigneurs of Old Canada.* Toronto: Glasgow, Brook and Co., 1914.

Morin, Claude. *Le Combat Québécois.* Québec, Montréal: Boréal Express, 1973.

Morin, Claude. *Le Pouvoir Québécois . . . en Québécois.* Québec, Montréal: Boréal Express, 1972.

Morton, William L. *The Kingdom of Canada.* New York: Bobbs-Merrill, 1963.

New York Times. New York, Oct. 15, 17, 18, 21; Nov. 7, 15; Dec. 5, 7, 8; 1970. Oct. 1, 29, 31; Nov. 27; 1973. Feb. 10; Mar. 15; May 6, 8, 9; June 15; Jul. 1, 6, 10; 1974.

Parkman, Francis. *Francis Parkman's Works.* Boston: Little, Brown, 1902.

Québec. *Annuaire de Québec, 1973.* Québec: Provincial Printer, 1973.

Repplier, Agnes. *Père Marquette.* New York: Doubleday, Doran, 1929.

Richard, Édouard, ed. "Relation des Faits Heroiques de Mlle Marie Madgeleine de Verchère Contre Les Iroquois Agée de Quatorze Ans." *Supplement du Rapport du Docteur Brymner sur les Archives Canadiennes pour l'année, 1899.* Ottawa: S. E. Dawson, Prtr., 1901.

Rioux, Marcel. *Attitudes des Jeunes de Québec, Ages de 18–21 Ans.* Montréal: Les Presses de l'Université de Montréal, 1964.

Scanlon, Marion S. *Trails of the French Explorers.* San Antonio: Naylor, 1956.

Scott, Henri Arthur. *Bishop Laval.* London: Oxford University Press, 1926.

Shea, John Dawson Gilmary. *Discovery and Exploration of the Mississippi Valley.* New York: Redfield Press, 1852.

Skinner, Constance Lindsay. *Beaver, Kings and Cabins.* New York: Macmillan, 1933.

Steingarten, L. and Catin, L. "Éducation en Langue Minoritaire." In *Bulletin de Service, Statistique Canada,* vol. 2, no. 4, April, 1973.

"The Testing of Pierre Trudeau." In *New York Times Magazine,* Dec. 6, 1970.

Trudeau, Pierre E. *Federalism and the French Canadians.* New York: St. Martin's 1968.

Trudel, M. *Initiation à la Nouvelle France.* Toronto: Holt, Rinehart,

Winston, 1968. (*Introduction to New France: Canadian Studies.* New York: Holt, Rinehart, Winston, 1968.)

Vallières. Pierre. *Nègres Blancs d'Amerique.* Montréal: Editions Parti Pris, 1967. (*White Niggers of America: The Precocious Autobiography of a Quebec Terrorist,* tr. by Joan Pinkham. New York: Monthy Review Press, 1971.)

Wade, Mason. *The French Canadian Outlook.* New York: Viking, 1946.

Wallace, William Stewart. *Family Compact: A Chronicle of the Rebellion in Upper Canada.* Toronto: Glasgow, Brook and So., 1915.

Wood, William. *The Passing of New France: A Chronicle of Montcalm.* Toronto: Glasgow, Brook and Co., 1914.

Notes

TO THE NEW WORLD: ADVENTURE AND MISSION

1 Medical universities at the time in France.
2 This Egyptian city had a highly developed trade in drugs.

THE FOUNDING OF NEW FRANCE

3 Champlain's prophecy was fulfilled in a way he could not foresee. Revenues in 1972 from tolls on the Saint Lawrence Seaway were nearly five million dollars. The Seaway, opened in 1959, and built jointly by the United States and Canada, creates a passage from the Gulf of the Saint Lawrence to the western end of Lake Superior.
4 Crown Point.
5 Champlain is speaking of Indians.

A PEOPLE GROW

6 In old sections of Québec and Montréal, such houses still stand.

TO THE MISSISSIPPI

7   Marquette is referring to Indian territories and nations.

TO THE GULF OF MEXICO

8   In 1930, at the bottom of Lake Huron, off the western end of the island of Mackinac, the hull of a ship, corresponding to La Salle's description of the *Griffon,* was found. In a cave on the island coast were six disintegrated human skeletons. The *Griffon's* crew was six.
9   Mississippi.
10 Today's island of Haiti-Dominican Republic.

HUDSON BAY AND LOUISIANA

11 One million dollars.

PEACE AND NEW PROBLEMS

12 The Indian custom of torture has to be seen in perspective. It was not peculiar to Indians, being also employed in Europe at that time. It has been employed in Vietnam and elsewhere in our time. The United Nations has a commission to investigate its use.

THE HERITAGE

13 Dialogue excerpted from *Dear Enemies,* by Gwethalyn Graham and Solange Chaput Rolland.
14 Conversation excerpted from *Nègres Blancs d'Amérique,* by Pierre Vallières.

BACKLASH AND HEADWAY

15 Prepared by the National Opinion Research Center of the University of Chicago for the Royal Commission on Bilingualism and Biculturalism.
16 By Marcel Rioux, Department of Sociology, University of Montreal.